Forerunners of
the Reformation

HEIKO AUGUSTINUS OBERMAN

Forerunners of the Reformation

The Shape of Late Medieval Thought

Illustrated by Key Documents

FORTRESS PRESS   Philadelphia

First Fortress Press Edition 1981

Library of Congress Cataloging in Publication Data

Oberman, Heiko Augustinus.
    Forerunners of the Reformation.

    Bibliography: p. 317
    Includes index.
    1. Theology—Collected works—Middle Ages, 600–1500.
    2. Theology, Doctrinal—History—Middle Ages, 600–1500.
    I. Title.
BT10.023 1981   230'.09'02   81–66518
ISBN 0-8006-1617-0   AACR2

9027E81   Printed in the United States of America   1–1617

Contents

Preface

Whereas there was good reason to designate the later Middle Ages as terra incognita—unknown while unloved—the renewed interest of the last twenty-five years and the impressive advances made by medieval, Renaissance, and Reformation scholars have sharpened our desire to hear behind the recordings of the historians the voice of the past. These selected documents cannot be identified with the historical "record"—yet the common theme of the call for reform, ranging from hope to impatience and even despair, is not a projection of our modern sense of the times. Its raw stringency speaks to us in a strident key—which now seems even less remote than it did in 1966.

This book is unchanged, not because of its original perfection, but because of the wish expressed by many colleagues that the debate aroused by its first edition can be easily identified.

Heiko A. Oberman

Tübingen, May 1, 1981

Preface to the First Edition

The purpose of this book is to transfer the discussion of late medieval Christian thought from the private studies of the specialists to the carrels and seminars of college and university students. Although this "Late Medieval Reader" certainly does not exhaust the riches and pluriformity of the period between the high Middle Ages and the Reformation era, it introduces the reader to aspects of such major themes as conciliarism, curialism, mysticism, various types of scholasticism, the spirituality of the *Devotio Moderna,* and the impact of Renaissance humanism.

The theme of the Forerunners has grown out of the consideration that the justified rejection of a confessional reading of the past has been succeeded by an equally unhistorical disjunction of the medieval and Reformation periods. Without a grasp of the fourteenth and fifteenth centuries, the medieval history of Christian thought is not only left incomplete but, perhaps worse, Reformation and Counter Reformation seem to appear "out of the blue," or rather out of the black night of an unknown and, therefore, unbeloved period.

In the second part of the first chapter we have tried to show how this untenable axiom of discontinuity is related to the elimination of the category of Forerunner; in the first part we have drawn attention to the various roles played by the Forerunner in medieval thought, his place in medieval historiography and religious expectations.

The translations in this book have been made by Mr. Paul L. Nyhus, church historian and candidate in the Ph.D. program at Harvard University. Although I remain responsible for the final version of translation and notes, Mr. Nyhus shouldered the heavy task of bridging the distance—in language and spirituality—between late medieval Europe and the contemporary world.

Mrs. Dorothy Gillerman not only saw the book through the press, but, before it ever reached that stage, forced me time and again to use plain language rather than avail myself of the condensed but often dense veils of scholarly terminology.

Heiko A. Oberman

June 1965

Abbreviations

CIC   *Corpus iuris canonici*, ed. Emil Friedberg, 2 vols., Leipzig, 1879–1881.

CR   *Corpus Reformatorum*, Berlin, 1834– ; Leipzig, 1906– .

CSEL   *Corpus Scriptorum Ecclesiasticorum Latinorum*, Verona, 1866– .

HTR   *Harvard Theological Review*, Cambridge, Mass., 1908– .

PL   *Patrologia Latina*, ed. J. P. Migne, Paris, 1844–1890.

PG   *Patrologia Graeca*, ed. J. P. Migne, Paris, 1857–1912.

WA   *D. Martin Luther's Werke: Kritische Gesamtausgabe*, Weimar, 1883– .

WATR   *D. Martin Luther's Werke: Tischreden*, Weimar, 1912– .

Sent.   *Libri quattuor Sententiarum*

ST   *Summa Theologica*, Thomas Aquinas, *Opera omnia iussu impensaque Leonis XIII. P.M. edita*, Romae, 1882–1948.

ZTK   *Zeitschrift für Theologie und Kirche*, Tübingen, 1891– .

In quotations from the Scriptures the *Revised Standard Version* has been followed except in those cases where the context requires a literal rendering of the Vulgate or parallel Latin translations.

As noted above, most Scripture quotations are from the *Revised Standard Version of the Bible,* copyrighted 1946 and 1952 by the Division of Christian Education, National Council of Churches and used by permission.

Chapter One

The Case of the Forerunner

I. A Precarious Thesis

Four centuries of polemical and apologetical use of the term Forerunner, or "precursor," of the Reformation has left in its wake a deep-rooted sense of aversion to the whole concept. After a prolonged death the graves could finally be closed over a host of Forerunners, their memorial stones reminding the present generation of the fortunate termination of an era of transhistorical or dogmatic writing of history.

However, the Forerunners still linger on along the margins of the academic life where history continues to be regarded not as an art but as an arsenal, not as a science but as a scene on which one parades one's troops in the strongest possible formation. Just once we encounter the idea in an excellent modern history of the period, but then it turns out that the term Forerunner has been replaced by its more respectable synonym "prodrome," which in Greek may indeed mean "scout," or "runner," but in modern medical language stands for the first warnings of a hidden illness.[1]

Obviously, then, the burden of defense is on anyone who ventures to resuscitate these ghosts which had been, it was firmly believed and hoped, permanently buried. The following discussion is intended to show that there are compelling reasons for taking a fresh look at the concept of the Forerunners of the Reformation, and for re-evaluating the risks involved in a continued disregard for such a concept. We will present the case of the Forerunners by discussing the two most formidable and basic objections, namely, that (1) the idea of the Forerunner is fundamentally an ahistorical one, since it throws over any given period in intellectual thought a veil of interpretation which is alien to the period itself, rather than allowing the interpretation of the period from within and in the context of its own presuppositions; and that (2) the concept of the Forerunner is a product of a typically

3

Protestant effort to ward off the charge of innovation with its connotation of heresy. Employment of the concept of the Forerunner
displays, it is assumed, the absence of a dispassionate approach indispensable to a truly historical analysis of the antecedents of the sixteenth-century schism in Western Christianity.

As will be made clear in the following sections, it is our conviction,
to the contrary, that a careful reading of the sources not only indicates
a historical justification for the idea of the Forerunner of the Reformation, but suggests, further, that a definite and geographically extensive
continuity exists between the Middle Ages and the sixteenth-century
Reformation in the shape and context of the ongoing intellectual
quest. Only against the backdrop of this continuity can we hope to
grasp the characteristics of both Reformation and Counter Reformation.

II.   The Highway in the Wilderness

When one attempts to sum up the views of late medieval spirituality
which have been current during our century a very black picture
emerges.[2] To be sure, there are some redeeming features, but these
are usually either described as "the dawning of a new age" and, therefore, dissociated from the "real" state of affairs, or limited to stubbornly
persisting traces of the flowering high Middle Ages. By way of contrast, we may mention the truly exceptional conclusions of Johannes
Janssen in his still impressive history of the German people. In the
first of his eight large volumes, dedicated to the later Middle Ages, he
says: "In all German territories life and thought were marked by such
a vitality as never before or ever after occurred." When Ludwig von
Pastor published a new edition fourteen years later we notice that
Janssen's enthusiasm had been toned down: "Throughout Germany,
life and thought were marked by an extraordinary degree of vitality."[3]
Half a century later Joseph Lortz comes to an assessment of "Religious
Life before the Reformation," which no longer shows a trace of Janssen's optimism but emphasizes the disintegration of medieval spirituality. It should be noted, however, that Lortz is initially willing to
grant that there is not only ample evidence for secularization in public
life but there is also—and to the same extent—a well-documented

spiritual depth in private devotions. Nevertheless, in view of the great impact and astonishing echo of Luther's criticism, the conclusion is drawn that, practically seen, the exterior secularization must have been the greater force.[4]

There seems to be a basic catalog of four criticisms of the period which tend to occur over and over again in all modern studies: (1) the amorality of the laity and especially of the lower and higher clergy; (2) the frequency of absenteeism often due to multiplication of prebends; (3) the poor training of the clergy. These three criticisms are seen against the general backdrop of (4) laicizing religiosity which is at once anticlerical and superstitious.

There can be no question as to the reliability of the facts themselves. But since the interpretation of these facts is by no means obvious, we must turn now to a short discussion of each of these indictments.

(1) The richest source for our knowledge of late medieval morality is, without doubt, the collections of sermons—either sermon examples to be used by simple parish priests, or transcripts of sermons actually preached. Both kinds of sermons give us a wealth of information about aspects of life which are not elsewhere available. The transcripts are by their very nature more colorful and detailed, since they usually allow the preacher to apply his theme to a particular local situation in a way not possible in the more general prototype.

The basic understanding of the Church as guardian of morality results in an emphasis on the law, be it the Decalogue of Moses or Christ's Sermon on the Mount. In order to promote conversion, stimulate the thirst for eternal life, and thus highlight the importance of the sacraments as indispensable for salvation, there is a continuity of moral criticism throughout medieval sermon literature. It requires, therefore, a thorough knowledge of the traditional type of moral indictment to be able to use any given sermon as a source of knowledge for a particular "wickedness." Moreover, since it is the preacher's purpose to convince his listeners of the multitude and gravity of sins committed, we should realize that the dark coloration of this presentation may have more pedagogical than historical value. Thus our richest source can be tapped only for illustrating situations clearly attested elsewhere.

The increasing awareness of the great variety in political, economic, and social conditions prevailing in such geographically distant areas as southern Spain and eastern Poland has curbed the enthusiasm for general statements about late medieval conditions and encouraged studies of more restricted sections. Accordingly, since the beginning of this century, visitation records and registers of fines and dispensations have been hailed as the appropriate sources for the description of the actual situation in such natural units as episcopal dioceses.[5] But even these more technically precise and factually reliable sources do not satisfy our modern standards for statistical evidence, since frequently we do not know, when two, six, or ten clergymen are fined for living in concubinage—a term covering a variety of sexual offenses —what percentage of the total number of clergy they represent. Indeed, the situation may have been far worse than the visitation records suggest, since the visitations were not always carried out with an equal amount of thoroughness, and the timely announcement of a coming visitation may have led, in some cases, to a temporary improvement of conditions. It might also be remembered that the monastic foundations and individual dioceses were subject to great fluctuations, both spiritually and economically, so that generalization is extremely difficult.[6]

Unless one takes the term "later Middle Ages" in such a wide sense that there is hardly room left for the high Middle Ages, it is difficult to argue that these abuses add up to a *decline* of morality. The increase in complaints about the alleged immorality of the clergy might well be construed as an emergent sense of moral integrity and sanctity on the part of the community. Monastic and lay reform movements point not only to the need of reform but also to the fact that this need was widely felt, expressed, and acted upon.

(2) We can be much more concise in our comments on the other three traditional indictments against late medieval spirituality. The problem of nonresidence and pluralism in the later Middle Ages presupposes the much earlier tendency to regard office in the Church as a benefice. Thomas Aquinas did not advance a new opinion when he stated that "if one is in need, one may lawfully seek for oneself an ecclesiastical benefice without the cure of souls."[7] There is no indication that the system, as such, necessarily interfered with the diocesan machinery. Due to this understanding of benefices, students without

sufficient means could be provided with scholarships, to profit from the establishment of a growing number of universities.

The rise of the Third Estate led in the later Middle Ages to the rapid multiplication of endowments requiring the usually part-time services of a priest in saying Masses for the deceased. Thus a tremendous and unprecedented burden was laid on the clergy concerned. There is therefore reason to suggest that pluralism was not only the natural consequence but also an indication of piety on the part of the laity.[8]

(3)   In many satires of the period we encounter the figure of the parish priest, this time not so much as the incarnation of wickedness but of stupidity. The German poets exploit, naturally with great glee, the unique opportunity of their language which rhymes *Affen* (apes) with *Pfaffen* (clerics). Even the great Dutchman, Erasmus of Rotterdam, is—to say the least—less than respectful in his references to the learning of the clergy. In one often quoted story he tells how one day the great Bishop David of Utrecht (1457–1494) himself chairs the pre-ordination examinations of the candidates.[9] He poses a series of easy theological questions to the prospective subdeacons, more complex ones to the future deacons and candidates for the priesthood. Of the three hundred examined, Bishop David is willing to pass only three. When the other members of the examining board complain that it is a shame that so many are rejected, David answers that it would be a far greater shame for asses and those surpassing asses in stupidity to be admitted to these holy offices. His opponents argue that "these modern times" no longer produce a St. Paul or a St. Jerome, but David, before ultimately giving in, answers that he does not look for a Paul or a Jerome but that to ordain asses instead of human beings goes too far.

That the archives of the archbishopric of Utrecht suggest three hundred to be an unlikely number is not important. It is more relevant to bear in mind that throughout the Middle Ages "the stupid priest" had been a popular target for criticism. A careful comparison between the learning of the parish priest at the beginning of the sixteenth century and his counterpart before 1400 shows that there is good reason to believe that he is by and large considerably better trained than ever before. In that same period, however, the education of the laity shows such a sharp upward trend that the standards for the evaluation of the local priest have risen considerably. The young lawyers, physicians, and secular clerks are no longer impressed by the sheer use of Latin but insist now that its grammar and idiom be respected. The mere reading from a book of sermons as an adjunct to the reading of masses is no longer satisfactory; the new intelligentsia expect a fresh and well-prepared sermon as an integral part of the cure of souls.

Especially in the North European countries the Church seems to be aware of the new challenge of the times. Bishop David's examinations may have been a failure, but his efforts to enforce the old canonical requirements for ordination are but a part of a more general tendency to reform this aspect of the Church's life. Even the invariably critical humanist Jacobus Wimpfeling has to admit that the discovery of printing has considerably increased the number of well-trained priests.[10] The justly famous and often reprinted manual for the parish priest by John Ulrich Surgant, written late in the period under consideration, although not without precedent, is the parent of an impressive family of textbooks for practical theology.[11]

(4)   The ignorance of the clergy and the superstition of the laity are often mentioned in one breath. It cannot be our task to present here an exhaustive picture of late medieval lay religiosity. What we have said above may indicate that the results of such investigations can be valuable only in terms of particular areas. The present state of scholarship has sufficiently highlighted the multitude of contrasts within late medieval thought to make it far easier—indeed too easy—to unmask previous conclusions as untenable generalizations than it is to state positively how the resulting void is to be appropriately filled. Such phenomena as the popularity of pilgrimages replacing the earlier crusades; the multitude of new endowments, dedications of altars, chapels, and testamental Masses, which were at this time within reach of the *nouveau riche* burgher class; and, in times of economic depression, an upsurge of anticlericalism are well attested. As we have seen, anticlericalism may express itself in a sharp defamation of the public-supported, tax-exempt members of the clergy who are decried as wicked or stupid.

While there is ample evidence of a feverish religiosity that ranges from a new emphasis on private devotions to a marked preoccupation with death, standards alien to the Middle Ages are applied when these expressions are typed as superstitious. And we are even a step further removed from the sources when these phenomena are taken to reveal an unsatisfied hunger on the part of the baptized masses as a result of the secularization of the Church, which is said to be no longer able to satisfy the spiritual demands of the faithful.

III. Apocalypticism and Despair

Having questioned, at this point in our discussion, some of the most frequently formulated charges against the late medieval Church, we may well have created the impression that we are committed to defending at all costs the quality and stability of Christian thought and institutions in this period. This can be neither our task nor our purpose. It is, however, important that the more balanced and restrained interpretations, as they have been formulated in the monographic literature of the last three decades, start to find their way into the general surveys and textbooks of medieval thought. Furthermore, there are two other aspects of the foregoing which we should like to bring into the discussion, since they have a direct bearing on our theme of the Forerunners of the Reformation.

In the first place it should be clear that to endow a medieval preacher or doctor with the title of Forerunner, on the grounds that he assailed ecclesiastical abuses or called for reform, violates both the medieval *and* the Reformation understanding of the word "reformation."[12] On the one hand the call for reform, originating as personal renewal but extending thence to the community ideal of the monastic movement, and eventually given institutional status within the Church, is one of the main themes running through the whole history of medieval spirituality. The history of advocates, or carriers, of this kind of reform leads us in one continuous movement to our own times without any particular reason to terminate our survey in the sixteenth century, or to regard this century as the point where medieval reform culminates or where lines of reform converge. On the other hand, if one thinks of the Forerunners of the Reformation in the traditional sense as precursors of the Lutheran Reformation, one should realize that Luther's understanding of reformation is explicitly and consciously *not* a protest against papal or general ecclesiastical abuses. One cannot even say that abuses were, for Luther, the aftermath and concomitant result of perversions in doctrine. He was too much aware of the distinction between the militant Church on earth and the triumphant spotless Church in heaven not to realize that the Church "under the cross," hidden under the veil of sin, would always be plagued by abuses until the complete manifestation of the kingdom at the end of history.

It is because of this doctrine of the Church, intimately connected with his distinction between Law and Gospel, that Luther could criticize John Wyclif and Jan Hus, usually mentioned among the Forerunners of the Reformation: "Truth and quality of life are to be distinguished. Life is as wicked with us as with the papists. We do not criticize or condemn them for their life. This Wyclif and Hus, who attacked the life [of the papists], have not seen."[13] Luther's reformation is precisely *not* the intensification of individual or monastic reform but rather the radical criticism of this "man-made road to reformation."[14]

The second aspect of our presentation of the catalog of criticisms of late medieval spirituality is a truly important point which, due to the usual generalizations, is bound to be overlooked. Only when it is granted that the quest for reform—above all for moral reform—was part and parcel of medieval spirituality can we train our eyes on the particularities and characteristics of the quest for reform within a particular period. Thus we can mark in the transition to the fifteenth century a sharp upward curve and an exceptional radicality in the litigations and censures of public life, private devotions, and general stature of the Church.

From the moralistic commentary on the Books of Wisdom by Robert Holcot (†1349) in England, through the popular sermons by the French priest Michel Menot (†1518) and the publication of the *Ship of Fools* by the German jurist Sebastian Brant (†1521), we are presented with a vivid, at times colorful and humorous but invariably pessimistic, picture of late medieval piety. We remind ourselves of the fact that those who assume the responsibility for protecting the moral fiber of their times are seldom unbiased reporters. The history of preaching in England and on the Continent suggests that these lamentations are a timeless genre which reveal more about the moral standards of the author than about the actual situation of the period in which they originate. Once it is acknowledged that moral criticism is the normal edge of most sermons, our ears can be attuned to pick up what we consider *new* developments of the same genre.

The moralizing exegete Holcot bewails "these modern times," not restricting his comments to members of the clergy. As compared with the early Church he sees a steep decline on all levels of life. Young men no longer respect seniority as they used to; the aristocracy like sermons against wickedness only so long as they themselves are not the target; in general a decrease in works of charity is noticeable.[15] So far we are on familiar ground; when he turns to the clergy, however, one discerns a new tone of urgency:

"Some of the modern priests are angels of Satan through discord, others fallen angels through pride . . . and again others angels of the abyss through greed."

"The modern prelates do not take action against sinners when they are rich or of noble birth but only when they are poor."

"The devil has infected the priests of the Church to such an extent that *all* the branches of the Church have been poisoned."[16]

A century and a half later Menot claims of his own time that "never could less devotion be found in the Church." When somebody asks him why he does not take some kind of initiative he answers: "Friend, we do not have the man [we need]" and again: "I have no great hopes for the Church unless it be planted anew."[17] The criticism of the *Ship of Fools* touches more systematically on all aspects of life though it does not have the same prophetical edge.[18] But it is John Geiler of Keisersberg (†1510), preacher of great renown and admirer of Brant, who, in his sermons on the *Ship of Fools*, sharpens Brant's ax to such an extent that it was widely believed that Geiler had announced to Emperor Maximilian the coming of the Reformation of the sixteenth century: "Our merciful bishop Jesus Christ is about to send other more incisive reformers—they are already on their way with their divine mandate. I shall not live to see it but many of you will. At that time you will wish me back and be glad to heed my voice; but it will be too late . . ."[19] These statements do not originate in circles of heretical sects criticizing the Church from the *outside*. There is no reason to suspect the orthodoxy of Holcot, Menot, Brant, or Geiler: theirs is the cry for reform from *within* the Church.

The quotations cited above suggest a transition from a prophetic to an apocalyptic criticism of the times, new not in its despair but in the form of its hope. In its original sense, the word "apocalypse" means "revelation," or "unveiling"; in its more technical sense, "apocalypticism" is a theology of history on the basis of often secret revelation with regard to the last things, the *eschata* (hence: eschatology). The still uncharted and amazingly rich eschatological speculation in the later Middle Ages has led historians to describe the texture of late medieval thought as apocalyptic. In order to sharpen the meaning of the term as it is here used, we might contrast apocalypticism with prophecy as it is encountered in the pre-exilic period in the Old Testament. To phrase it as succinctly as possible: Prophecy judges the human condition on the basis of the acts of God; apocalypticism judges the acts of God on the basis of the human [im]moral condition. The focus of attention of prophecy is directed from God's acts in history, for example, the Exodus from Egypt, to the moral implications these acts might have for the people of the Covenant. The focus of attention of apocalypticism is directed from the moral state of the people of the Covenant, that is, the Church, to the implied future acts of God. One of the main features of the apocalyptic stance, then, is the computation of God's final acts by reading "the signs of the times." One may even go so far as to say that here prophecy has become eschatology.[20]

It would not be completely correct to say that apocalypticism is ahistorical, as is usually assumed. It *is* true that its preoccupation with history is religiously determined; it is thoroughly macabre in that it identifies the culmination of history with the regression of the powers of goodness and the increase of the powers of evil. Whereas the prophet has a positive notion of history as the God-given time for repentance, the apocalyptic herald announces that the time for repentance is past, that the superhuman powers of good and evil have taken over, and that the final showdown, the Armageddon, is at hand. The increase of evil, therefore, does not call for private and corporate *action* (reform) but for endurance and, above all, for understanding; one is called upon to realize that wickedness in all its appearances is only a prelude to the coming of God in glory.

Before we demonstrate how this nascent apocalyptic mood is related to the idea of the Forerunner, we should like to point out that the

commitment to the discovery, description, and exposure of evil should
be taken into account as an important ingredient in the thinking of
the authors on whom we have to draw for our insight in late medieval
spirituality. After this element of the peculiar and extraordinary preoccupation with evil has been noted, we should, on the other hand,
hasten to say that it would be improper to interpret the apocalyptic
tendencies as evidence of despair and sheer fatalism. There is no such
radical break in the medieval story of reform activity. But there is a
shift in the concept of reform itself. Except on the radical, sectarian
fringes of the Church, we encounter throughout the period a new
vision groping for formulation which is not simply the apocalyptic
announcement of the cosmic struggle between good and evil, beyond
the control and responsibility of men, but a real call for *re-formation*,
that is, a call for the remnant of the faithful to prepare for the coming
of God in glory. But this is not the traditional idea of reform. It is now
felt that the time for reform is past and thus the time for *restoration*
and *conservation* has run out. The call for re-formation in this context
implies not a direct but an indirect reform activity, to prepare for the
order (form) which *God* is to restore. For this purpose He is to send
His heralds or emissaries.

Since the figure of St. Francis (†1226) looms so large in late medieval
thought, it is quite appropriate to articulate the difference between
the old and the new in the documents we have referred to, by recalling
the famous words in which he received from Christ his charge to
reform: "Repair my house because it is, as you can see, in the process
of being completely destroyed." One can easily understand how the
words "completely destroyed" (*tota destruitur*) could have led to radical interpretations. But for St. Francis himself the "complete" destruction of the Church was the expression of the urgent need for reform,
and suggests the dimensions of the challenge that reached his ears.
His natural first response was to start rebuilding local dilapidated
churches; later he interpreted this charge more symbolically in what
was to become the rule of the order named after him.

When we hear at the beginning of the fourteenth century from
Holcot that "all the branches of the Church have been poisoned" by
the devil, and from Menot that "never could less devotion be found
in the Church," we are inclined to find in their warnings the con-

tinuation of the theme of "total" destruction in the sense of St. Francis. However, the new tone of urgency about which we have spoken is evident in the manifold suggestions that no immediate reform can be initiated because "we do not yet have the man" to carry out a true reform. The waiting is for God to act, to take the initiative. God is to send His agents (*ministri*), messengers (*nuntii*), heralds (*praecessores*) or forerunners (*praecursores*).[21]

IV. Reform in Suspense

In the twentieth book of his *De Civitate Dei*, St. Augustine had established the foundation for centuries of Western eschatological thinking by identifying the history of the Church with the thousand years mentioned in the Apocalypse.[22]

> I could see the souls of those who had been beheaded for the sake of God's word and their testimony to Jesus . . . these came to life again and reigned with Christ for a thousand years, though the rest of the dead did not come to life until the thousand years were over. This is the first Resurrection. Happy indeed and one of God's own people is the man who shares in his first resurrection! Upon such the second death has no claim; but they shall be priests of God and of Christ, and shall reign with him for a thousand years. When the thousand years are over Satan will be let loose from his dungeon . . .

Although for Augustine these thousand years are by no means marked by unalloyed peace, being the history of the conflict between the rule of God and the rule of the devil, nevertheless the climax of history, the millennium, had been reached by the revelation of the New Covenant, which established the Rule of Peace; the peace of the New Age is internalized, since "peace is where there is obedience to Christ."[23]

Since Cain and Abel, indeed ever since the separation of the evil and good angels, the war between the two communities (*civitates*) has raged, to last until the final victory of the Kingdom and purification of the Church. This eschatology went basically unchallenged until the time of Joachim of Flora (†1202).[24] In Joachim we encounter many new images and divisions of history, but the one which would become the most influential and indeed the one most clearly reflecting his Trinitarian thought is his tripartition of history into the period of the Father—the age of the Old Testament; the period of the Son—the age of the New Testament until about 1260; and finally the period of the Spirit—the culmination of time which transcends the second age as much as this period transcends the first. One can point to many implications of this interpretation of history.

R. G. Collingwood saw in Joachim's teaching an example of the distortions inherent in medieval historiography, since "eschatology is always an intrusive element in history."[25] Taking a more positive attitude one can, on the other hand, be deeply impressed by Joachim's "cradle theory" as a significant advance over preceding philosophies of history, and it is this theory of Joachim that especially concerns us here. According to Joachim's interpretation of history, each period has not only its own initiator but also its own precursor, while at the same time the advance from one age to the next gives rise to the appearance of one or more Antichrists. Thus the second age is initiated by the father of John the Baptist, Zechariah, but his precursor is King Uzziah, just as St. Benedict is the precursor of the Age of the Spirit. The successive periods then are not static, unrelated blocks of time, but nascent epochs intertwined in such a way that the one grows out of the other and provides the cradle for the next.

Once appropriated by the radical left wing of the Franciscan Order —the Franciscan Spirituals—Joachim's vision of a revolutionary new order of the Spirit was exported from Italy with so much enthusiasm that it is hard to distinguish between Joachim's own ideas, those of his disciples, and parallel visions with independent roots but Joachite in appearance. Recent studies, which are beginning to disentangle the fascinating complexity of assimilation and exchange, have helped us to get a perspective on such varied movements as the flagellants of Thuringia, the elusive sect of the "Free Spirits," the Taborite empire, and the theocracy of John of Leiden.[26] There is ample evidence that Joachim's double line of forerunners who announce a new birth, as in the case of Uzziah and St. Benedict, or represent the pangs that accompany their births, as in the case of the Antichrists, found deep rootage in late medieval piety.

Another highly influential document that reveals the importance

of the Forerunner theme is unrelated in origin to Joachim. We refer
to the fifteenth-century *Reformatio Sigismundi,* copied and spread all
over Western Europe. The central passage of the revelation granted
to Emperor Sigismund reads: "Sigismund, . . . prepare a road for the
coming of the divine order, because all the written law lacks righteousness. But it is not given to you to bring this [righteousness] yourself;
you will be the forerunner . . ." The revelation continues with the
prophecy of the Priest-king Frederick who will come to realize the
order of God.

This document has been given a far more revolutionary sense by its
early and modern interpreters than the original warrants.[27] Compared
to Joachite parallels, this call for reform has a down-to-earth pragmatic
and political thrust. The document was clearly intended to support
the efforts of Sigismund, Emperor and King of Bavaria (1410–1437),
to see the convocation of the Council of Basel (1431–1449) crowned
with success. The document provides Sigismund with a divine charge
to create the conditions of reform, a reform which was quite traditionally interpreted by its supporters in the Council. As the chronicler
of the Council of Basel, John of Segovia, put it: "Reform can be understood either as the extirpation of evil or as the increase of the gifts of
the Holy Spirit."

And yet the Reformation of Sigismund expresses more than the
conciliar dreams about reform in "head and members" characteristic
of the period since the Council of Pisa (1409). It suggests, rather, the
kind of indirect reform action we have encountered before, namely
reform-in-suspense, the preliminary action of preparation for the ar-
rival of the true reformer. It could still be argued that Sigismund's
task is in no respect unusual, since to prepare for the coming of the
king is the traditional way of speaking about the task of the Church
to prepare the faithful for the coming of Christ. Indeed there is here
a parallel with the usual Advent and Palm Sunday sermon which
calls upon the faithful to put the house of their soul in order and drive
out the ass, that is, sin, so that Christ can enter. But in the first place
this coming of Christ is usually presented as the coming not of the
king but of the humble servant and, in the second place, the entry into
Jerusalem is interpreted as a prelude to the ascension to heaven where,
at the right hand of the Father, Christ will exercise his kingship.

The task given to Sigismund to make preparations for reform may be conservative insofar as he has to bring to light the old order (form) of righteousness only temporarily hidden, but the real difference between his task and the charge to reform given to St. Francis appears in the role of Sigismund as a forerunner of the Priest-king Frederick.

Ever since the death of Frederick Barbarossa during the Third Crusade in 1190, prophecies began to circulate that a new Frederick would be sent to bring the thousand-year kingdom of peace. Before his death in 1250, Frederick II was widely expected to fulfill this eschatological hope. Frederick II may well have consciously accepted this role: "The sum of his speculation," his biographer Ernst Kantorowicz points out, "ultimately reduced itself to a belief that just before the end of the world everything must exactly correspond with the fullness of time of the first century."[28] Soon after his death a future Frederick was expected to bring not the end itself but a glorious and prosperous interregnum in which all wickedness would be extirpated. In the course of time, one emperor after another was to be cast in the role, including Frederick the Wise, Luther's protector.[29]

In the light of this tradition we can see how Sigismund, unlike St. Francis but like Menot and Geiler, comes down to us in the sources as the type of the Forerunner-Reformer or the Reformer-in-suspense, provided with a limited charge for an indirect, preliminary reform program. Remarkably enough, popular tradition would give Sigismund a companion Forerunner in the man who crossed his path and almost crossed his master plan for the Council of Constance (1414–1418), Jan Hus (†1415). Hus may well have regarded himself as a Forerunner and, when in prison, prophesied, very much as Geiler did in his address to Maximilian, that "after me will come a swan, which they will be . . . unable to catch." In his commemoration speech at Luther's grave in Eisleben on February 20, 1546, Justus Jonas would claim that in "our dear Father Doctor Martinus Luther" Hus's prophecy had been fulfilled.[30] In the light of the foregoing we may interpret this to mean: now the period of reform-in-suspense, of waiting for the divine initiative, has been terminated.

Jonas could base his claim on Luther's widely read answer to the imperial edict of the Diet of Augsburg (1530) in which the Reformer gives us a glimpse of his own understanding of "reformation." In the final passage he speaks about "six hundred years of distortion and corruption" disguised under the name of God and the Holy Church: "God wanted finally to terminate this and sanctify again His name, so that finally His kingdom could come and His will be done." This throws light on Luther's reference to Hus: "It shall have begun during my life and be accomplished after my death. Jan Hus has prophesied about me when he wrote from his prison in Bohemia: 'Now they roast a goose [the name Hus means goose], but in a hundred years they shall hear a swan singing, which they will not be able to do away with...' "[31]

Luther understood himself as a God-called prophet and his reformation as the execution of a God-given task. This vertical emphasis on the reformation given "from above" suggests indeed the semiapocalyptic framework of late medieval thought, which is not so thoroughly apocalyptic that it excludes the horizontal emphasis on the ongoing reformation as the restoration, preservation, and succession of truth.[32] As we shall have occasion to see, it is the dissolution of this combination of the vertical and horizontal aspects of reformation which is the demarcation line between Luther's theology and the ensuing Lutheran orthodoxy. But Luther's reference to the prophecy of Hus is not all he has to say about his Forerunners. He wrote in a letter of recommendation for the 1522 edition of Wessel's letters: "If I had read this before, it could well have left the impression with my enemies that I copied everything from Wessel—so much are our two minds at one."[33]

With reference to Wessel's discussion of indulgences and opposition to canon law, Luther could praise him as "a hidden prophet" who differs from Luther only in not being forced by "a bloody war" to become a public witness. At about the same time Luther writes in his Introduction to *Fragments of the Works of Pupper of Goch* that he now sees that a "refined but hidden theological tradition has existed and exists among Germans," first among them is John Tauler (†1361), then Wessel Gansfort (†1489)—as theologian to be ranked before his Dutch compatriot Rudolf Agricola (†1485)—and finally—"not mentioning the living"—John Pupper (†1475). These examples encouraged Luther and nourished the hope that "soon no Thomist, Albertist, Scotist, or Occamist will be left in the world, but all will be

simple children of God and true Christians."[34] Luther's concern is
not the Forerunners of the past but God's promise for the future.
These Forerunners do not provide Luther with an "argument from
tradition," as would be the case with Flacius and the *Magdeburg
Centuries*, but testify to him that the state of the Church is not beyond
repair.

In his early period, Luther was interested in establishing a genuine
national German theological tradition, contrasted with the "Roman
tyranny" of the Antichrist. He no longer shares the restraint and
despair which we encounter in the period immediately preceding. He
may not count on a complete success of his reformation, but his program is definitely not reform-in-suspense. In his last Bible commentary, the exposition of Genesis from the years 1535–1545, when the
confessional fronts have hardened, Luther draws encouragement from
individual Forerunners, but develops at length the idea of the twofold
Church, the external, hypocritical Church of Cain, and the hidden,
true Church of Abel. To understand the significance of this typology
we have to return to the medieval period.

V.   The Torchbearers for Abel: The Succession of Truth

In the foregoing section we have discussed the late medieval religious situation in the light of traditional evaluations. We were led to
the apocalyptic elements, not only in the thought of this period, but
also in the form of presentation used in the available sources. This in
turn led us to a discussion of the Forerunner theme in both Joachite
and in more conservative strains of late medieval piety.

Thus far we have largely moved in the elusive area of popular piety,
often drawing on sources that may have enjoyed wide circulation but
are nevertheless of uncertain authority as far as the teaching of the
Church is concerned. Although we found traces of semiapocalypticism
with men who cannot possibly be identified with the heretical fringe,
it would hardly be justified to assume that the Joachite and allied ideas
are representative of the major part of late medieval thought.

The Forerunner has functioned not only in the depressed areas of
medieval thought, but we also encounter the Forerunner theme in a

radically different setting—at the level of official Church teaching, in the theological workshops of a rapidly growing number of universities, and in the interpretations by the doctors of theology and canon law. In this case the setting for the Forerunner theme is not within the Joachite theology of history with its speculation about the coming third era of the Spirit, but, instead, it is within the millennium, the time of the Church, as it was characterized by St. Augustine. The war between good and evil, truth and falsehood, God and devil, does not now take place at the end of history, but it is presented as a continuous intrahistorical process. The Forerunners are not the heralds of the Antichrist to come nor the messengers of the Holy Spirit with the accompanying concept of re-formation as the establishment of the eschatological order of the New Jerusalem. In this, the prevailing medieval context, drawn from St. Augustine's *De Civitate Dei,* we encounter two different lines of Forerunners in the "two Churches" of Cain and Abel and their torchbearers. In the last stages of his writing —after the beginning of the Pelagian controversy in 412—St. Augustine had presented the two lines of succession as a variation on the theme of the two cities.[35] Here "reformation," be it individually or collectively understood, means a turning away from Cain and a return to Abel; reformation is antirevolutionary in that it is, as its synonyms "conservation" and "renovation" imply, the return to the once-and-for-all given order of God which has been constantly threatened but never lost.

The *ecclesia ab Abel* stands for the tradition of truth from the earliest times, via the patriarchs and the holy prophets and via the parallel extracurricular line of Socrates and the school of Plato to Christ, and on from Christ through the succession of the bishops and the doctors to the present time, stretching out into the future Second Coming and the establishment of the visible rule of God. The *ecclesia a Cain* stands for an equally continuous line of distortion of the truth and of an ever-renewed assault on the walls of orthodoxy by a parallel succession of heresiarchs and teachers of heresy.

When we turn first to the torchbearers in the line of Abel, one could very well make the point that whereas apocalyptic speculation is future-oriented and therefore concerned with Forerunners, the Augustinian idea of aboriginal revelation handed down through history is concerned with the past and therefore rather interested in "afterrunners." Though it is indeed important to note this difference in orientation between the conservative and radical ideas of reform, nevertheless when the question arises as to the orthodoxy of a particular doctrine or doctor, the defense invariably consists in reference to the preceding episcopal or doctoral tradition. This idea of the "Church from Abel" is indeed intended by St. Augustine and all those who follow him in this usage to show the unity of faith of the "Christians" before and after Christ. But the underlying maxim of St. Augustine—"Times change but not the faith"—is not only descriptive but also prescriptive. Thus it is the guiding standard in the constant test of the authenticity of the development of doctrine in the time of the Church after Pentecost. As the history of this idea indicates, the succession of truth from Abel onward tends to encourage the distinction between the invisible Church, which is pure and spotless, and the visible Church, in which good and evil coexist. The bond between the concept of the Church as the succession of the true believers implied in the notion of the "Church from Abel" and the objective institutional emphasis on the hierarchy and on communion with the pope in Rome was to be severely tested in the later Middle Ages.

A good case can be made for the thesis that validation by reference to the true tradition is the most crucial issue in late medieval theology, exactly because of the diversity of opinion as to the relation of the institutional Church to the "Church from Abel," of the bishop to the doctor, and of the succession of the bishops (*successio episcoporum*) to the succession of biblical truth attested by the doctors (*successio doctorum*). One can scarcely overestimate the profound impact of the "Babylonian Captivity" of the papacy at Avignon (1309–1377) and the ensuing Western Schism (1378–1417) on all levels of late medieval life and thought. So great was that impact that we can with good reason distinguish between the preschism and schism-shocked Middle Ages.[36] The various programs and ideas of reform are largely formulated in response to the confusing situation which was caused by the assertions of Boniface VIII (doctrine of the two swords, 1302) and John XXII (condemnation of the poverty ideal of the Spiritual Franciscans, 1323), and reached its climax in the conflicting claims by three rival popes after the Council of Pisa (1409).

Against this background we can understand such questions as, "Who should one rather believe, an ordained bishop or a learned doctor of theology?" "What is orthodoxy?" and behind that, "How does one establish Catholic truth?" In the beginning of our period we see that Thomas Bradwardine (†1349), at once a doctor of theology and, in the last weeks of his life, Archbishop of Canterbury, in the Preface to his *The Case of God Against Pelagius,* shows how since the days of Cain the sovereignty of God has had to be defended. Notwithstanding his belief that "our one and only doctor Jesus Christ" safeguards and protects the ship of Peter so that "the teaching authority of all Christian doctrine resides with the Roman Church," he feels forced to ask whether Peter has fallen asleep since he, Bradwardine, seems almost completely isolated in his struggle against the Neo-Pelagians.[37]

In order to assess the direction which the discussion about the relation between the authority of the hierarchy and the doctors of the theology was taking, we might mention the eloquent preacher, Ambrosius of Speyer (†1490). In a sermon published on the eve of the Reformation, he refers to Gratian, the great canon lawyer, according to whom the responsibilities between the doctors of Scripture and the pope are divided in such a way that the interpretation of Holy Scripture is said to be the task of the theologians, and the determination of legal cases that of the papacy.[38] Ambrosius observes, however, that such an answer should be taken with a grain of salt, adding with wry humor: "You may completely rely on the doctors of Scripture . . . except when the articles of faith or the sacraments are touched upon, since the power to interpret a dubious law has been granted not to the theologians but to the Pope."[39] Wessel Gansfort does not leave any doubt as to his preference, rooted in his spiritualizing ecclesiology: If the doctor of Scripture is a true doctor he knows the truth better than any untrained prelate.[40]

The disciples of William of Occam (†1349), from Peter d'Ailly (†1420) and John Brevicoxa (†1423) through Gabriel Biel (†1495), developed further a discussion they found in the *Dialogus* of Occam[41] between a teacher and his student about the foundations of Catholic truth. There it is said that there are three bases (*fundamenta*) for the truth: Holy Scripture, the apostolic doctrine handed down through the succession of generations of the faithful, and new revelation. It is intriguing that the succession mentioned in the second category is not necessarily the succession of bishops, and perhaps even more intriguing that in the third category new revelation is declared to be invalid as long as one believer opposes it: ". . . if there is one alone who does not agree, such a revelation is not to be accepted as truth, because in one person the whole faith of the Church can reside, as at the time of Christ's death the whole faith of the Church was preserved in the Blessed Virgin alone [that is when the Apostles fled, betraying their faith]. It is hardly credible that there will ever be men more in favor with God than the Apostles were before the death of Christ. If, therefore, Christ permitted his Apostles to deviate from the faith after his crucifixion and let only the Blessed Virgin firmly persevere in faith, it would be rash to assert that never again until the end of the world would God possibly allow all Christians but one to deviate from the path of orthodoxy."

Elsewhere in the *Dialogus* this argumentation, with a slightly more explicit anticlerical edge, is used against those who believe in the infallibility of the hierarchy on the basis of the last verse of the Gospel of Matthew: ". . . lo, I am with you always, to the close of the age."[42] To this the teacher answers: "They should not draw such a conclusion, since Christ directs these words to the Apostles as representatives of all those who believe or shall believe in Him. Since among these there are women as well as men one should not restrict the promise of Christ to men [that is, the clergy]."[43]

In the larger context it is clear that Occam intends to issue a warning that the majority of votes is no proof for the will of God and that, therefore, democracy is as doubtful a guarantee of orthodoxy as hierocracy. But this argument has, in the passages cited, also a sharp anti-hierarchical and anti-institutional edge. It points in the direction of a doctrine in which the Church is primarily seen as a congregation of the faithful (*congregatio fidelium*), a community which not only includes all the living but which reaches back through history to Christ and the faithful of the Old Covenant and which thus comprises the whole succession of faithful "from Abel" onward.

The way Occam uses the old tradition of the Virgin Mary as the sole representative of the Church and only link between the Church before the Passion and the earliest Christian congregation after the resurrection, suggests a remarkable parallel with ideas expressed in apocalyptically oriented thought, which can be typed as a "remnant" theology with an allusion to the faithful representing all Israelites in postexilic times. And indeed after the millennium was first identified with the history of the Church and its major mark, peace, had been internalized, the claim that with Christ the thousand-year empire had been realized is reduced to a token reality. But whereas the "remnant image" is common to both semiapocalypticism and Occam, in the latter's understanding the whole tradition of truth, and therefore the sole hope for reform, is laid in the hand of one torchbearer, the Virgin Mary.

The preservation of the remnant is not the sign and basis for a revolutionary re-formation, but rather a sign of the fidelity of God upholding His Church through all the vicissitudes of history. In line with the striking emphasis on the covenantal relationship between God and His people,[44] which prevails through late medieval theology, reform is seen as the conservation and continuation of the order of God, who has covenanted to protect and minister to the needs of His Church, by assuring the succession of the faithful torchbearers of Abel.

VI. The Torchbearers for Cain:
The Succession of Wickedness

Just as we encountered in apocalyptically inclined late medieval thought two series of Forerunners, namely the messengers of the Spirit and the heralds of the Antichrist, so we find in more respectable and authoritative circles a parallel to the succession from Abel, the succession from Cain. In the New Testament there are references to Abel as exemplifying righteousness[45] and faith,[46] whereas the name of Cain is used to invoke the dark image of evil works[47] and to indicate a particular type of heresy.[48] But it would be straining the sources to find in them mention of Cain as the archetype of all heresy.

The idea of a temporal succession and a systematic coherence of untruth and evil is not a new concept introduced by St. Augustine. We find with the Greek and Latin Fathers incipient catalogs of her-

esies which vary from short enumerations to more chronologically
and systematically arranged lists. Before St. Augustine contrasted the
successions from Abel and Cain, St. Ambrose gave this contrast a
much more limited scope in his treatise *On Cain and Abel* (375), in
which Cain becomes the type of the Synagogue and the Jews, and
Abel the type of the Church and the Christians. Actually, there is
more reason to discern behind St. Augustine the mind of Philo of
Alexandria (*c.* 50), who gave a profound and universal interpretation to the figure of Cain. In accordance with the meaning of his name,
which is given in Genesis[49] as "possession," he made Cain symbolize
the view that all things are the possession of man, in the sense of the
Protagorean doctrine that man is the measure of all things. The mind
that conceived that doctrine is characterized by Philo as being "full
of folly or rather of all impiety for instead of thinking that all things
are God's possession, it fancied that they were its own."[50]

For all those who followed in the school of Augustine—and that
embraces with varying degrees of fidelity all medieval thinkers—Cain
thus became the prototype of perversion who used (*uti*) God and enjoyed (*frui*) creation, thereby claiming possession over the world and
enjoying the sights along the road which should be used as the shortest
possible travel route to the eternal Jerusalem. It is a variation on this
theme which provides Thomas Bradwardine with the key for his
imaginative presentation of the history of heresies which, with its
hundred and forty-five large folios, has a good claim to be the most
extensive medieval catalog of the subject.[51] According to him the
earliest Forerunner of the Neo-Pelagians, Cain, called into being by
the heresiarch Lucifer, claims that justification of the sinner is man's
own domain and his possession rather than a gift of the sovereign
God. From this vantage point Bradwardine sets out to show the connections and transitions in the history of heresy. Since he feels that his
own time makes an unbelievably large contribution to this history, he
dedicates his every waking hour to doctrinal reform rather than join-
ing his contemporary, Robert Holcot, in promoting moral reform.[52]

The basic outline for high and late medieval catalogs of heresy was
provided in canon law, where we find an enumeration of the main
heresies condemned by the Church. Under the name of Innocent III

(1198–1216) a coherent structure behind the heretical multiformity was suggested by the image of the monstrous hydra, or dragon, recalling the snake of paradise: "They have indeed many heads, but their tails are joined together."[53]

The medieval method of doctrinal investigation, whether executed by a papal or academic committee or at a later date by means of the Inquisition, can be characterized as "the search for the tail," that is, the effort to reduce the particularity of any given teaching or teacher to one of the known and previously condemned types of heresy. When one reads through the *acta* of these investigations, one notices in the final reports the frequency of the accusation of Pelagianism, which suggests the centrality of the theme treated by Thomas Bradwardine, although mention is also made of other types of heresy.

It is against this background that we have to place the early investigation of the theses of Martin Luther (†1546) by the University of Paris and the publication of its findings on April 15, 1521. At the end of the Leipzig Disputation, a contract was drawn up on July 14, 1519, in which the decision of the victory in the debate between Johann Eck (†1543) and Luther was left to the universities of Paris and Erfurt. The fact that the University of Erfurt proved to be unwilling to become involved in the case of Luther increased the already mounting tension in both camps while they awaited the decision of the Sorbonne. In letters dated Worms 1521 the papal nuntius Aleander (†1542) expresses his great concern over the persistent rumors that the theological faculty of Paris would decide to support Luther. We know indeed from a letter to Zwingli by a Parisian friend, dated November 1, 1520, that at that time it was assumed to be a fact that the Parisian faculty had already decided to abstain from a judgment in Luther's case. The earlier papal bull, *Exsurge Domine* of June 15, 1520, requesting Luther to recant forty-one theses, made, the letter went on to say, a decision by the Parisian faculty redundant, "otherwise Paris would perhaps have lightly criticized some articles."[54] This assumption proved to be completely unfounded. While Luther was at the Wartburg he received the text of the Parisian *Determinatio* sometime in late June or early July. In October, Melanchthon's *Defense* came from the press, which, as we shall see, was to be an important link in the history of the concept of the Forerunner.

VII.   The Hydra With Many Heads

What we have referred to as the "search for the tail" does not start
in Paris, however, but is immediately undertaken by Luther's first
opponents. In the early summer of 1519 at Leipzig, Eck had firmly
established the connection between Hus and Luther, and while the
censure by the University of Louvain of November 7, 1519, does not
say more than that Luther's early sermons and theses contained
"many assertions that are false, scandalous, heretical, and smacking of
heresy," two months before, on August 31, the theological faculty of
Cologne had already declared that Luther's theses should be sup-
pressed, since they abounded in "errors and heresies long ago condemned."[55]

The tracing of Luther's thought to heretical Forerunners starts to
become more precise in the interesting introduction to *Exsurge Domine,* probably drawn up by Sylvester Prierias, O.P. (†1523), and
published under the seal of Pope Leo X (1513–1521). After the fourfold invocation "Rise up, Lord," "Rise up, Peter," "Rise up, Paul,"
"Rise up, all saints," Luther's antecedents are indicated: ". . . there has
reached our ears, yes what is worse, alas, we have seen and read with
our own eyes the many and various errors of which several were already condemned by councils and decrees of our predecessors, such
as the heresy of the Greeks and the Hussites."

It is in the Parisian *Determinatio,* however, that the connection between Luther and his Forerunners is explicitly pursued. Throughout
the history of the Church, it asserts, there has been the threat of the
perversion of truth through heresy which assails the body of the
Church like a cancerous growth. Some of the names in this passage
explicitly mentioned are Marcion, Sabellius, Mani, Arius, and, from
more recent times, Waldo, Wyclif, and Hus. "Alas, in our times new
members have been added to this family of vipers . . . the most important among them is a certain Martin Luther . . . who tries to re-
instate the teachings of the aforementioned heretics . . ."[56] Thus Luther
was seen as a heresiarch and a powerful reviver of old heresies.

The Parisian document concludes that with regard to the relation
of free will and grace he is Manichaean; concerning contrition, Hus-

site; Wyclifite in his doctrine of confession; a Free Spirit when dealing with the precepts of Christ; on the punishment of heretics, a Cathar; his attitude to the authority of councils is at once Waldensian and Hussite, and with regard to the observance of laws he is close to the position of the Ebionites.

The answer to the Parisian condemnation was undertaken not by Luther himself but by his young colleague, Philip Melanchthon. He put to good use the same kind of satire which had proved to be so effective in the *Letters of Obscure Men* written six years before to support the case of Philip's half uncle John Reuchlin.[57] On July 13 Luther wrote to him from the Wartburg: "I have decided to translate your *Defense* against the Parisian asses, together with their nonsense . . ."[58] Some indication of Luther's own reaction comes through to us in a letter written two days later to Georg Spalatin, his chief contact with the Elector Frederick the Wise: "I have seen the decree of the Parisian sophists, together with Philip's *Defense,* and I wholeheartedly rejoice. Christ would not have made them so blind had he not decided to use these affairs to bring about the end of their tyranny."[59]

In his *Defense,* Melanchthon pursued with great persistence the main issue in the Parisian accusation of Luther and his heretical Forerunners; no matter what direction he takes, he returns to this theme time and again. The blindness Luther referred to is, to paraphrase Melanchthon, due to the Parisian fury, which led them to call Luther a Manichaean and Montanist. Even the theologians of Cologne and Louvain knew better than to make such rash statements, which are so obviously false. The Sorbonne has indeed fallen since the time of the great Jean Gerson (†1429); take the Commentaries of John Major (†1550) on the *Sentences* of Lombard: "Good God, what a lot of empty nonsense." The accusation against Luther is not that he deviates from Scripture but that he deviates from the universities, the Fathers, and the councils. But these cannot establish articles of faith; it is possible that universities err—yes, even the Fathers and councils can err. "If you don't believe me, believe then at least your own Occam."

After he has established Scripture as the sole source of revelation, Melanchthon goes on to say that he does not mean to suggest that Luther is opposed to the Fathers or the councils. Whereas, he claims, the sophists of Paris draw on Aristotle, Scotus, Occam, and Gabriel Biel, Luther returns to the Fathers such as Augustine, Cyprian, and Chrysostom.

Melanchthon goes on to say that there are indeed aspects of Luther's teaching which one does not find easily (that is, explicitly mentioned) in the Fathers, as, for example, when the Reformer discusses the number of sacraments, confession, or the monastic vows. It must be remembered, however, that at their time Christianity was purer and fewer questions had been raised. If it was in the time of the Fathers the noontide for the Gospel, it is now, says Melanchthon, late in the evening, an era of the tyrannical laws of popes and the Paris-made articles of faith. As punishment for our sins, darkness falls so that the true tradition of the Fathers (*bona patrum pars*) is distorted and forgotten. Luther's teaching, however, agrees for a large part with the older theologians.[60] It is with them that Luther's name should be associated, Melanchthon continues, not with the names of the heretics condemned by the early councils such as Montanus, Ebion, Mani. When one recalls that Montanus relied on the inspirations of his own spirit rather than on the inspired Word of God, that the Ebionites insisted on ceremonies and laws, and that it was the Pelagians who accused St. Augustine of Manichaeism, the reader can see for himself what the impact of these heretics has been on the Sorbonne and its scholastic ideology.

After having thus placed Luther in the tradition of "a good part of the Fathers" and having traced the lineage of the great heretics right to Paris, it is interesting to note the great circumspection with which Melanchthon takes up the last part of the Parisian accusation in which Wyclif and Hus are presented as Forerunners of Luther. He returns to his point: "There have been some papal councils during this era of the reign of the Roman Antichrist against which Luther has raised his voice ..." The examples given are the Council of Vienne (1311–1312) and the Council of Constance (1414–1418) as councils which denied biblical doctrine and decreed theological positions diametrically opposed to Scripture. Melanchthon sees in this history of papal influence a clear succession of heresy and heretics. In this early treatise he does not yet mention "the Church from Cain,"[61] but for him the large number of pseudo prophets in his own time is fore-

shadowed by the many priests who bowed their knee to Baal: "Recall
the whole history of Judah and Samaria which is the prelude to the
history of the Church: how few prophets, how many idolators and—
most recently—how many Sadducees and Pharisees, or in other words,
how many priests, monks, and scholastics!"[62]

Though this is not the end of the *Defense*, enough has been said to
show how Melanchthon took up the challenge of the Parisian condemnation. We have paid much attention to this treatise because here
we find at once the *continuation* of the medieval theme of the Forerunner as "the search for the tail," and the *beginnings* of the Protestant
application of this theme. In his later works Melanchthon was to trace
the heretics further back to Cain and bring the line of witnesses to the
truth up to his own time via Bernard, Gerson, and Wessel Gansfort.
Other Reformers who pursued this theme became increasingly interested in studying the "Church from Abel" rather than the "Church
from Cain." John Calvin touches on the theme in his first edition of
the *Institutes* (1536) when he says: "And although there is often little
evidence . . . still we must hold that from the creation of the world
there was no time when the Lord did not have his Church; and until
the consummation of the age, there will be no time when he will not
have it."[63]

The most explicit and best-known treatment of the theme of Forerunners is found in the *Catalogus testium veritatis* by Flacius Illyricus,
first published in 1556. From the Preface we see that, compared with
Melanchthon, Flacius is somewhat apologetic in the emphasis on the
large rather than the small number of true witnesses. The evidence
points to the fact that "there have always been not few but many
teachers and hearers who stood with us and not on the side of our
opponents." Among the Forerunners are counted all those who opposed the power of the pope or suffered from his use of it. Wyclif and
Hus have now been firmly appropriated and integrated in the tradition of truth. While working on his *Catalog*, probably in Magdeburg,
Flacius conceived of the idea of a thirteen-volume encyclopedia for
the history of Church doctrine, each volume to be dedicated to one
century. It was published in Basel from 1559 to 1574, under the title
The Magdeburg Centuries. Less concerned with the negative criterion
of opposition to the pope than the *Catalog* and more interested in

emphasizing the positive criterion of the succession of faith, *The Magdeburg Centuries* gave the Forerunner an academic vesture of the teacher of truth which would retain its scholarly respectability until the beginning of this century.

But the Sorbonne interpretation of the Forerunners of the Reformation was accepted not only in the Protestant camp. As is to be expected in view of its medieval history we encounter this thesis of the hydra with many heads time and again in Johann Eck, Caspar Schatzgeyer, Noel Beda, St. John Fisher, and Nicolas Herborn. J. Latomus goes so far as to claim that "Luther does not teach a single original heresy; all he has are heresies long ago condemned by the councils."[64] The more or less incidental observations of this kind develop in the course of the sixteenth century into a type of book very much parallel to Flacius' *Catalog* such as A. de Castro's *Four Books Against All Heresies* published in 1534 and reprinted in 1564 and—one of the sources for the *Collectio Judiciorum* (1724) of C. du Plessis d'Argentré—Gabriel Patreolus' *On the Lives, Sects, and Teachings of All Heretics,* Cologne 1583.

Notwithstanding the profound differences and the rapidly widening gap between Reformation and Counter Reformation, there is at least a common enterprise in seeking to separate the false and true tradition, in order to distinguish between "the Church from Cain" and "the Church from Abel." The concept of the Forerunner, inherited and not invented by the sixteenth century, seemed to prosper in its new setting.

Our discussion of the two types of Forerunner—the apocalyptic herald and the Augustinian successor to Cain or Abel—would be incomplete without mention of a sermon by an unknown Carmelite preached in Paris before Francis I, probably late 1520 or early 1521. On March 13, 1521, Erasmus wrote to his young friend Alexander Schweiss (†1536): "Some Carmelite has said in a sermon preached before the French King that the Antichrist is about to come and that already four of his Forerunners have come: in Italy, some Franciscan unknown to me; in France, Stapulensis; in Germany, Reuchlin; in Brabant [the Netherlands], Erasmus." Undoubtedly the same event is referred to in Erasmus' letter of June 17 to Louis Guillard, Bishop of Tournai (†1565). This time the four Forerunners are—according to reports Erasmus received from friends in Paris—"some Franciscan in Italy, Luther in Germany, Faber in France, and Erasmus in Brabant."[65]

Here the two lines are converging and the idea of the heralds of the Antichrist prepares for the "search for the tail." It is clear that the Parisian condemnation of Luther as a heresiarch would appeal to a spirituality reaching beyond the walls of the academic community. It should be even more clear that the concept of the Forerunner is by no means alien to the period under discussion. Rather without an understanding of this key word the doors to the transitional period from Middle Ages to Reformation are not easily unlocked.

VIII. From Middle Ages to Reformation
Continuity or Discontinuity?

The last monumental effort to present the Forerunners of the Reformation as a valid category of interpretation in the history of Christian thought is the two-volume work by Karl Heinrich Ullmann published in the middle of the last century under the revealing title *Reformers Before the Reformation.*[66] The presupposition of Ullmann is that "broadly seen the Reformation is the reaction of Christianity as Gospel against Christianity as law." Medieval Christianity had increasingly denied its own genius by developing into a legalistic system. This led in turn to the reaction of a heretical, usually pantheistic, irresponsible spiritualism: "Between these two movements—the false letter and the false spirit—the Reformation came to stand in the middle . . ."

The Forerunners of the Reformation, having discovered the Pauline doctrine of free grace, undertook exactly the same war on two fronts as Luther. Some of them took the battle between Gospel and law even "more seriously and presented the issue with more insistence than did the Reformers themselves." They fought "from within and in smaller circles" for the same objective "as later the Reformers from outside and on a larger scale."[67] The final conclusion adds to this basic thesis only a romantic philosophy of history: "Everything has its time: the silent, spiritual activity of the Forerunners of the Reformation and the heroic action of the Reformers themselves. Without the first the Reformation—especially as general concern of the people—would not have been possible; without the latter the Reformation would have remained fragmentary and would not have resulted in the realization of a new and purified life of the Church."[68] Among the chief Forerunners mentioned are John Pupper of Goch, John of Wesel (†1481?), and Wessel Gansfort.

Reading Ullmann we come to understand how the conviction that the concept of the Forerunner was alien to medieval thought could have become dominant. The Forerunner idea is, in his work, so closely connected with a view of medieval theology colored by the Lutheran antithesis between Gospel and Law and by Luther's own two-front battle against Roman Catholicism and the Left-wing Reformers that no justice can be done to the teaching of the leading scholastic doctors, nor to the manifold and complex aspects of the thought of the "Reformers before the Reformation" themselves.[69]

It is not, however, for his lack of sensitivity to historical context or for his unwillingness first to describe and then evaluate medieval thought from within its own frame of reference that Ullmann was taken to task most severely. The sharpest and, it seems to us, the most decisive attack came from the pen of the German historian of theology, Albrecht Ritschl (1822–1889), who pointed to Ullmann's failure to understand Luther's doctrine of justification and the resulting inability to grasp the uniqueness of Luther's theology. According to Ritschl, the doctrine of justification of the so-called "Reformers Before the Reformation" differs sometimes in degree but never in principle from that of the realistic teachers (e.g., Thomas Aquinas) of the medieval Church, "but these teachers take the central concept of justification to mean something else than the Reformers do and have therefore a different understanding of faith which is the basis of justification." Medieval reform movements are not necessarily identical with Luther's reformation: "One should therefore expect to find Reformers before his [Luther's] Reformation, who are more unlike than like him."[70]

There can be no doubt that Albrecht Ritschl's position has had a beneficial influence on the investigation of both medieval and Reformation thought. On the one hand, the quest for the proper description of the distinctive marks of Luther's doctrine of justification could be more sharply focused and in this way continued into our own times; and on the other hand, the analyses and presentation of the medieval theological tradition could be pursued by Protestant students of the period with the necessary scholarly integrity now that the stifling harness of exterior and incompatible categories of interpretation had been cast off. Yet with these significant advances went a concomitant danger which has made itself increasingly felt over the years. The unprecedented originality in the thought of Luther and other Reformers became the main focus of all attention. The Roman Catholic view of the Reformation as *revolution*, the Protestant interest in Luther's uniqueness, and the secular historian's appropriate suspicion against working methods à la Ullmann are three very different factors which, all combined, led to an overemphasis on the discontinuity between medieval and Reformation thought.

Whereas dedication to the idea of discontinuity might *seem* an indication of a dispassionate approach to history, seen in the light of the earlier Forerunner thesis it is shown actually to be a tool for apologetics. There are few fields of historical inquiry where the impact of vested religious interests lingers on so persistently as in the area of late medieval thought. Due to a coincidence of interests, there is, however, a remarkable agreement in the over-all conclusion that this is an era of disintegration. From differing vantage points this period has been declared a no-man's-land and has been so thoroughly raked by Protestant and Roman Catholic shells that it has become almost impossible for the historian of the period to discover paths through this field. Although there are now signs of a more balanced approach, the predominance of this view of late medieval thought may well be regarded as a major factor in the interest shown by both Protestant and Roman Catholic scholars to establish a discontinuity between the medieval era and one's own particular tradition in the sixteenth century. Given this state of affairs, continuity becomes the basis of criticism as is the case—to mention only the best-known example—in the effort to show that Luther is the product of late medieval nominalism.[71]

It is understandable that in this climate the Forerunner idea cannot survive. Once a period of almost two centuries has artificially been marked off as no man's land the Forerunner stands convicted, without trial, of illegal border crossing. Ullmann's succession of Forerunners was forced to disintegrate while his interest in historical causation was pursued by those who explained the rapid spread of Reformation ideas on the grounds of political, economic, and social conditions and ideologies.[72]

Though the time seems ripe to free the question of continuity and discontinuity from its bonds of confessionalism, it is not immediately obvious what direction should be taken. Several solutions are offered to us by the impressive triumvirate of historians of Christian thought who stand out in our century: Adolf von Harnack (†1930), Friedrich Loofs (†1928), and Reinhold Seeberg (†1935). Loofs meets the question head on when he suggests that the Forerunner be defined in the following way: "Forerunner of the sixteenth-century Reformation in the strict sense of the word is only he who can be shown to have pointed beyond the Catholic understanding of Christianity."[73] In the subsequent discussion such a definition is applied to Bernard of Clairvaux "who at times formulated the Pauline doctrine of justification in a correct fashion," to an undercurrent of lay piety not determined by official dogma and to a scholastic teacher like Occam with his emphasis on the scriptural principle, as well as to those whom Ullmann had called Forerunners.

It is not our concern here to show how, in light of contemporary scholarship, each of these examples has to be re-evaluated. The basic problem is rather that whereas we can be grateful that the Forerunner is no longer negatively defined in terms of opposition to authority and protest against ecclesiastical abuses, the definition offered by Loofs suffers from the ambiguity of the words "Catholic understanding" and of "pointing beyond." Is this "Catholic understanding" to be determined by the standards of orthodoxy prevalent at the time when the given author lived, or according to the formulations of a council convened at a later date, such as the Council of Trent (1545–1563)? The difficulty with the first alternative is that many of the doctrinal issues most fervently discussed in the later Middle Ages were not officially determined until Trent; the difficulty with the second option is that it violates a sacred rule to measure a theologian's orthodoxy by standards derived from a later period. The condition of "pointing beyond" the Catholic understanding of Christianity limits the possibility of continuity with the Reformation to less typical aspects of medieval thought and precludes, therefore, the possibility that any of its main lines can be traced through to the Reformation. In short, Loofs's definition is unable to free us from the same bondage which characterized —though in a considerably less refined manner—Ullmann's thesis.

Seeberg does not object to the tradition of counting among the Forerunners men like Pupper of Goch, Wesel, and Gansfort. He feels, on the contrary, that the scope of the Forerunner should be enlarged to include not only individuals but also a large group of phenomena such as "the texture of German mysticism, the thought of Occam and the conciliarists, the Augustinian doctrine of sin and grace which have as much (as the so-called Forerunners) a positive significance in preparing for the era of the Reformation."[74] Although in general we consider Seeberg to be the most important scholar of the three as regards medieval thought, it is disturbing to sense the influence of nationalism when he attempts to indicate in one sentence *the* characteristic common to all proto-Reformation phenomena. All these currents and ideas can, according to Seeberg, be reduced to "the defense of Germanism . . . [with its religious personalism and its greater emphasis on the Church as spiritual community] against Romanism." In view of the Dutch Wessel, the Italian Gregory of Rimini, the English Occam, and the French conciliarists, this Germanism is apparently a truly international badge of honor. However, the more lasting contribution of Seeberg is that he has pointed to the breadth of issues that should be considered in connection with the idea of Forerunners, reaching beyond the single standard which Ritschl found in the "correct" doctrine of justification.

Harnack's presentation is most surprising indeed, not so much because of its content, but for the lack of attention it hitherto received. Apart from Thomas Bradwardine (†1349), who is presented as the mastermind behind the Augustinian reactions which prepared for the Reformation,[75] he is throughout very cautious, usually referring to Bradwardine's partners and partisans as the "so-called" Forerunners.[76] But when he considers the Forerunners explicitly, it becomes clear that he does not mean to argue against the "so-called Forerunners" in favor of discontinuity between medieval and Reformation thought, but on the contrary he obviously fears that such a narrowly conceived category might obscure the *many* levels of continuity between the two periods. We are here far removed from Loofs's emphasis on the atypical. Harnack raises the question whether the whole medieval Church, not just one or more of its phenomena, should not be regarded as a Forerunner. He goes on to define the medieval Church as a middle stage, a "fore-Reformation" between Christianity of the early Church and the Church of the Reformation. "None of its main movements can be omitted in this picture, including the hierarchical line, as the doctrine of the Church makes quite clear."

The opponents of the "so-called Forerunners" have expressed, albeit in a secularized and distorted way, the conviction that Christ left behind a kingdom on earth, where the risen Lord is present and where holiness is not dependent on the moral quality of its members but is rather a freely granted gift of God. Distorted as such a view might have been, it was truly an expression of Christian piety. When they thought about the pope and his power, the bishops and the Church to which the world owes subservience, "they had in mind the living and ruling Christ. Faith, in this form, was a necessary complement to the individualistic Christianity of the mystics; and the Reformation, with its thesis of the holy community and the kingdom of God with Christ as its center, has developed the Catholic ideas of Augustine and the Middle Ages in a continuous line, after it had learned from Paul and Augustine to judge spiritual things in a spiritual light."[77]

Turning now to our own effort to get the figure of the Forerunner in our sights, we can only hope that the reader has not come to share the impatience of many late medieval thinkers toward scholastic theology, expressed in the cry of dismay, *quot autores, tot opiniones:* it takes scholars to make a simple matter so complex! Guided by previous efforts, however, we will try to steer a course which avoids, on the one hand, a confessional selection of a cloud of witnesses and, on the other, an unreasonable predilection for discontinuity.

We choose as point of departure a passage of a statement of Desiderius Erasmus which not only reveals Erasmus' own position but also provides us with what we regard as the proper framework for a modern use of the concept of Forerunner of the Reformation. A year before his attack against Luther in the *Diatribe on Free Will,* Erasmus writes in September 1523 to Ulrich of Hutten:

"It does not make sense to incur death for the paradoxes of the

Lutherans and of Luther. These do not concern the Articles of Faith but rather whether the primacy of the Roman pontiff is instituted by Christ, whether bishops by their legislation can oblige one to commit mortal sin, whether free will contributes to salvation, whether the actions of man can to some degree be called good, whether the Mass can have the connotation of sacrifice. These things used to be argued to and forth by the scholastic theologians (*solent esse themata conflictationum scholasticarum*). If I were a judge I would not dare to condemn a man to death for taking a stand on any of these issues; nor would I be willing to suffer death for them myself."[78]

One may be inclined to feel that Erasmus is not taking Luther's position or the issues concerned very seriously. The important point for our discussion, however, is that Erasmus has noted that in its original form the debate between Reformation and Counter Reformation had been prepared for, not just by one or the other single theologian, but by at least two centuries of dialogue and debate on the same issues which were to dominate the first half of the sixteenth century. In this century Adolf von Harnack has come closest to this "Erasmian approach" in arguing from a different vantage point that not only Reformation and Counter Reformation have a common root but that in the search for Forerunners of the Reformation we should take into consideration not just the "so-called Forerunners" but also their opponents.[79]

On the grounds of our three findings, namely that (1) the concept of Forerunner proves to be anything but alien to the period concerned, (2) the Forerunner is *not* a product of Protestant apologetics, (3) the rejection of the Forerunner is the outcome of an ahistorical disjunction of medieval and Reformation thought, we are prepared to defend the concept of the Forerunner of the Reformation as a valid and indispensable tool for historical interpretation, provided the following clarifications and qualifications are made.

1. One of the reasons why a historian may be suspicious of the use of the term Forerunner, while operating freely and frequently with its Latin equivalent "antecedent," is its possible causative connotation. It might seem to imply a concept of history which presupposes determination by a pre-established divine plan or by its secular equivalent, immanent historical laws. We do not feel that it should be the task of

the historian of ideas to establish causal connections in the historical succession of these ideas. Rather, his goal should be, by drawing on these antecedents as illuminating parallels, to place ideas in their context and point to their particular characteristics and their changing structures. Accordingly the standard for a Forerunner cannot be that he "caused" the Reformation in one respect or another, for example by exercising direct or indirect influence on Luther; the study of the Forerunner is determined rather by the wish to give Reformation thought its proper historical context. The importance of the study of economic, political, social, and psychological factors is by no means denied by such a study. On the contrary, the shift from a causal to a contextual reading of the history of thought has the advantage of not entering into competition with any of these approaches but provides instead a perspective for measuring the changes in the configuration of questions and answers. Thus the use of the category of Forerunners does not function to establish the *nature of the cause* but to describe the *structure of the change*.

2. To take Luther's doctrine of justification as the sole standard by which to identify a Forerunner limits the Reformation to this one issue and betrays a dangerous bias of confessionalism.[80] The uniqueness of Luther's discovery is now generally admitted, but the degree of his uniqueness on this point can be measured only by a study of his context. Other aspects of his thought, such as the understanding of the relation of Scripture and Tradition, the doctrine of the Church, theology of the sacraments, and the methods of biblical exegesis, have their antecedents and thus ought to be seen in the light of the preceding discussion.

There is no valid reason to limit our point of reference to Luther's thought alone. Ulrich Zwingli (†1531) and Martin Bucer (†1551), for example, shared basic insights of Luther but made individual contributions to Reformation thought which have other antecedents. Due to his position as initiator of the Reformation and the degree of his theological originality, Luther will undoubtedly remain central in the future discussion of our theme; but there is no reason for limiting the scope of our investigation to the exclusion of other significant Reformation thinkers.

Furthermore—and here we part company with both Harnack and

Seeberg—when we use the term Forerunner, we do not understand this to be limited to the Protestant Reformation but to include what is traditionally designated as Counter Reformation. There are several considerations which force us to look in this direction.

(a) There is not only a Protestant but also a Roman Catholic tendency to claim for itself discontinuity with late medieval thought, which is motivated by the image of this period as a barren wasteland filled with many devils and little Spirit. This tendency has expressed itself above all in the inclination to view the Council of Trent primarily as a response to the challenge of the Protestant Reformers. One should not underestimate the degree to which this trend is favored by the generally accepted term Counter Reformation, which may be "merely" a name but which has subterraneously exercised a profound influence on current typologies of the Reformation era. It is not reasonable to expect that this term can be successfully eliminated, but it is important to realize that the Council of Trent gathered in the fruits of a Reformation movement which received its major impetus in the later Middle Ages. Whereas Luther claimed that this was not a reformation of doctrine and that without a preceding reformation of doctrine no moral reformation could be expected,[81] the Protestant Reformation deserves the title Counter Reformation insofar as the pre-Tridentine Reformation was rejected. Since this is not the place to marshal the available evidence, one eloquent example has to suffice.[82]

Giles of Viterbo, General of the Augustinian Order (†1532), preached the official sermon which initiated the opening on May 10, 1512, of the Fifth Lateran Council which was to last until 1517, the year that Giles received his cardinal's hat and the Augustinian monk Luther his baptism as Reformer. In this extremely interesting sermon, where such divergent elements as humanistic rhetoric, apocalyptic urgency, and conciliar curialism are brought together, Giles begins by confessing that he himself used to announce to all willing to listen that they were to see the Church stricken by strife and sword but also that they were destined to see its reform (*emendatio*). In a parallel with Luther's feeling that in him and his Reformation Hus's prophecy had been fulfilled, Giles goes on to say: "It seems appropriate that the same who said that all this would happen should also testify that it has now been fulfilled."[83]

The semiapocalypticism we noted in a man like Menot comes through in Giles's evaluation of the need for renewal. Since the time of Emperor Constantine, when luxury sapped the Church's powers, it proves to have been the case that whenever there were no councils convened the Bride (Church) fell into a winter sleep, the Bridegroom (Christ) departed, heresies flowered and amorality spread: "Since without a council faith disintegrates, we cannot be saved but by a council." Now finally the re-establishment of the Covenant is being brought about; "O, blessed are the times that witness the gathering of a council!"

It is clear that for Giles the main reason for concern is the disintegration of true piety (*religio collapsa*). This reform program is a prelude to later reform Catholicism which is primarily concerned with the resuscitation of original Christian fervor. The need of *doctrinal* reformation functions only in that the erasure of the marks of the inroads of heresy and the return to the Christian sources are the conditions for the restitution of the Church. The Church is to be brought back "to its early piety, its ancient light, its original splendor and its sources." The point of departure remains that no other period in history can be found "when there was among the people not only disregard but even disrespect for the holy things, the sacraments, the keys, and the holy commandments." In view of the central place Giles assigns to the pope as the life-giving principle of the council, it is clear that the conciliar reform program of a century before is revived in a new form.[84]

The extent to which Catholic reformers such as Albert Pighius (†1542), John Gropper (†1559), and Gasparo Contarini (†1542) are fully involved in the more doctrinal aspects of the return of the Church "to its original splendor and its sources" cannot obscure the fact that their basic reform ideology should be seen in terms of continuation of the same spiritual succession which reaches beyond Giles of Viterbo back into the Middle Ages; their reform program is not merely due to exposure to Luther or an answer to Luther's challenge. The identification of the Protestant Reformation as "Counter Reformation" is the most dramatic way of reminding us that the procession of the Forerunners of the Reformation is properly conceived of as a *two-pronged movement,* providing context and antecedents for both the Protestant and the Tridentine Reformation.

We should by all means oppose the interpretation of this two-pronged movement as two columns, one marching to Wittenberg and Geneva and the other to Trent and Rome. In that case we would not only indefensibly operate with the sixteenth-century idea of the "two Reformations" as the *necessary* outcome of a preceding medieval development, but also violate the interplay of medieval theological ideas and currents.

Forerunners of the Reformation are therefore not primarily to be regarded as individual thinkers who express particular ideas which "point beyond" themselves to a century to come, but participants in an ongoing dialogue—not necessarily friendly—that is continued in the sixteenth century. It is then not the identity of answers but the similarity of the questions which makes the categorizing of Forerunners valid and necessary. One might add at this point that this dialogue continued to an extent even after the beginnings of the Reformation in the Colloquies of Hagenau (1540), Worms (1540), and Regensburg (1541), into the middle of the sixteenth century when the developing geographic and institutional separation changed the assumption of a temporary Western Schism into the reality of two Western traditions.

We prefer not to dull the thrust of our presentation by raising the question of whether one should not speak in terms of three reformations in view of the emerging contours of a so-called Radical Reformation. The most convenient answer is that the choice of the word "radical" implies that the many scattered religious currents in the sixteenth century combined to form a variant of the Protestant Reformation.[85] Future investigation will have to establish the degree to which the religious movements thus designated could have been the inheritors of medieval radical apocalypticism, owing nothing to Luther's thought but reacting to him as to a catalyst. Insofar as the radical denial of Infant Baptism, the common platform of Reformation and Counter Reformation, does not exclude its proponents from participation in the ongoing dialogue, the history of the Forerunners of the Reformation is also a history of the antecedents of the "Radical Reformation."

In conclusion, a final observation on the principle of selection of the authors who will appear in the following pages. Once the idea of a limited number of theologians foreshadowing Luther's theological ideas is abandoned in favor of the concept of a history of the confrontation of a series of central ideas as the common point of reference for Reformation and Counter Reformation thought, any claim, desire, or semblance of completeness is out of the question.

In the selection of authors who should present alternatives or complementary views, two considerations were kept in mind. First of all, the greatest possible variety of literary types should be included. Thus we have selections from biblical commentaries, from short treatises, a papal bull, letters, sermons, and more formal presentations in the style of the medieval "Question."

Secondly, it seemed highly desirable to add to the exceedingly small number of late medieval works available in translation. The two selections from Wessel Gansfort and Jan Hus appeared in English before the modern upsurge of late medieval studies and therefore required reworking.[86] Johann von Staupitz's treatise on predestination exists in a German translation.

The fact that the following pages contain for the most part selections available only in Latin may prove to be a contribution to the appreciation of this colorful period, regardless of whether our interpretation of the Forerunners of the Reformation finds general recognition.

With the notable exception of Spain, which would come into its own in the period of the Counter Reformation, the authors chosen represent all the major European countries: England (Holcot, Bradwardine), Germany (Biel, Staupitz), France (Brevicoxa, Faber), the Czech nation (Hus), and Italy (Pius II, Cajetan, Prierias). The fact that the Netherlands are represented by twice the number of delegates (Wessel Gansfort, Hoeck, Hoen, Erasmus) of other countries may be regarded as a tribute to the contribution this country could make without the aid of a national university.

Notes

1. Émile G. Léonard, *Histoire Générale du Protestantisme*, I, *La Réformation*, Paris, 1961, p. 145.
2. The variety of views from Karl

Hagen, *Deutschlands literarische und religiöse Verhältnisse im Reformationszeitalter*, I, Erlangen, 1841, to Karl Brandi, *Deutsche Re-*

formation und Gegenreformation,
I, Leipzig, 1927, is without much
perspective presented by Paul
Wunderlich in *Die Beurteilung
der Vorreformation in der deutschen Geschichtsschreibung seit
Ranke,* Erlangen, 1930. See further
extensive references to post-1930
studies in chapters VI through
IX of "Nouveaux Milieux, Nouveaux Problèmes du XIIe au
XVIe Siècles," by F. Vandenbroucke in J. Leclercq *et al., La
Spiritualité du moyen âge,* Paris,
1961, pp. 448–664.

3. Johannes Janssen, *Geschichte des
deutschen Volkes seit dem Ausgang des Mittelalters,* I, *Die allgemeinen Zustände des deutschen
Volkes beim Ausgang des Mittelalters,* Freiburg i. Br., 1878, p. 72;
cf. 19th ed. by L. v. Pastor, Freiburg i. Br., 1892, p. 116.

4. Joseph Lortz, *Die Reformation in
Deutschland,* 2d ed., I. Freiburg i.
Br., 1941, p. 124.

5. A fine specimen of this type is
Oskar Vasella, *Reform und Reformation in der Schweiz: Zur Würdigung der Anfänge der Glaubenskrise,* Münster i. W., 1958. The
author is well aware of the limitations of this type of source (p. 19)
but can yet conclude: "Die Ver-
wilderung der Sitten im Klerus
kann auf keinen Fall bezweifelt
werden . . ." *ibid.,* p. 36. See here
for further literature.

6. See Ernest F. Jacob, *The Fifteenth
Century, 1399–1485,* Oxford, 1961,
p. 302. If Jacob's general conclusion with respect to Lincoln is
right, the situation in this diocese
compares favorably with any of
the continental dioceses hitherto
studied: "The weight of evidence
in the Lincoln visitations is not
against misdoings in the houses
so much as against the absense
of fervour and the inability to
keep intact the spirit of the rule."

7. *ST* II. ii. q 100 art. 5 ad 3.

8. Cf. Pierre Imbart de La Tour, *Les
Origines de la Réforme,* 2d ed., II,
Melun, 1944, pp. 241 f., 287 f.

9. Desiderius Erasmus, *Ecclesiastes
sive de ratione concionandi,* Basel,
1535, fol. 21 f. See the important
study by Friedrich W. Oediger,
*über die Bildung der Geistlichen
im späten Mittelalter,* Leiden,
1953, pp. 96 f.

10. Oediger, *op. cit.,* p. 136.

11. Iohannis Ulricus Surgant, *Manuale curatorum predicandi prebens
modum,* Basiliis, 1503, ". . . predi-
cationis exercitium ut precipuus
ecclesiastice potestatis actus hier-
archicus annexus cure pastorali."
Prologus.

12. See for a more detailed discussion
Gerhart B. Ladner's continuation
of his *The Idea of Reform, Its Im-
pact on Christian Thought and
Action in the Age of the Fathers,*
Cambridge, Mass., 1959, pp. 402
ff., in his article on the Gregorian
reform and the Franciscan reform,
" 'Reformatio,' " *Ecumenical Di-
alogue at Harvard,* ed. Samuel
H. Miller and G. Ernest Wright,
Cambridge, Mass., 1964, pp. 172–
190. On the same concept with
Occam and Luther, Martin A.
Schmidt, "Who Reforms the
Church?" *ibid.,* pp. 191–206. See

further the summary of the ensuing discussion by Giles Constable, "Seminar III. Reformatio," pp. 330–343, esp. p. 342. On the vocation of St. Francis and on Franciscan eschatology see the important study by Ernst Benz, *Ecclesia Spiritualis*, Stuttgart, 1964 (1st ed., 1934), pp. 58 ff., 162 ff.

13. *WATR* I, n. 624; cf. 8880. Martin Luther, *Vorlesungen über 1 Mose 35:2* (1535–1545): *WA* 44. 169, 25–35. See here especially the precious short article by Hanns Rückert, "Das Evangelische Geschichtsbewusstsein und das Mittelalter," in *Mittelalterliches Erbe—Evangelische Verantwortung*, ed. Evangelische Stift, Tübingen, 1962, pp. 13–23.

14. Note in contrast with Luther's emphasis on the priority of doctrinal reform, the programmatic unity of *doctrina* and *pietas*, of religious and moral insight, which is the very basis of the reform zeal of French and German Renaissance humanism on the eve of the Reformation. For the circle around Faber Stapulensis see Eugene F. Rice, Jr., "The Humanist Idea of Christian Antiquity: Lefèvre d'Etaples and his Circle," *Studies in the Renaissance*, IX (1962), 126–160. See further Lewis W. Spitz, *The Religious Renaissance of the German Humanists*, Cambridge, Mass., 1963, p. 274. "During the final decade before and at the outset of the Reformation the humanists took the initiative and offensive, but *their protest and reform program represented no real innovation*." (Italics mine.)

15. Robert Holcot, O.P., *Super Libros Sapientiae*, Hagenau, 1494, *Lect.* 48 F; 75 B; 4 C.

16. *Ibid.*, 182 E; 77 D; 182 C.

17. "Nunquam in ecclesia fuit minor devotio," *Sermons choisis de Michel Menot*, ed. Joseph Nève, Paris, 1924, pp. 16, 343, 374.

18. More satirical power can be found with Hans Rosenplüt (c. 1450). Cf. his "Priameln" in *Lyrik des späten Mittelalters*, ed. Hermann Maschek, Leipzig, 1939, p. 248.

19. This passage is discussed by Jane Dempsey Douglass, *Preaching Justification in the Later Middle Ages*, Leiden, 1966, ch. I.

20. Cf. Frank Moore Cross, Jr., *The Ancient Library of Qumran and Modern Biblical Studies*. Rev. ed., New York, 1961, p. 77.

21. Cf. Hans Preuss, *Die Vorstellungen vom Antichrist im späteren Mittelalter, bei Luther und in der konfessionellen Polemik*, Leipzig, 1906, p. 25. Preuss seems to regard the *praecursores* as merely forerunners of the Antichrist. However, only for dualistic sects would this imply that they did not receive their office ultimately from God.

22. Revelation 20:2–7.

23. Augustine, *De Civitate Dei*, Bk. XIX, in *PL*, vol. XLI; *CSEL*, vols. XL, XLI.

24. See the most perceptive introduction to Joachim with extensive discussion of Joachite scholarship by Morton W. Bloomfield, "Jo-

achim of Flora: A Critical Survey of his Canon, Teachings, Sources, Biography and Influence," *Traditio*, XIII (1957), 249–311. For a discussion of the systematic center of Joachim's thought see Ernst Benz, "Creator Spiritus, Die Geistlehre des Joachim von Fiore," *Eranos–Jahrbuch 1956*, XXV (1957), 285–355.

25. R. G. Collingwood, *The Idea of History*, 4th ed., New York, 1961, p. 54.

26. See the extensive bibliography of Norman Cohn, *The Pursuit of the Millennium*, Harper Torchbook, New York, 1961, pp. 436–481, and the notes of Morton W. Bloomfield, *Piers Plowman as a Fourteenth Century Apocalypse*, New Brunswick, N. J., 1961, pp. 181–232. For the continuation of this story into the sixteenth century, George H. Williams, *The Radical Reformation*, Philadelphia, 1962, and *Millennial Dreams in Action*, ed. Sylvia L. Thrupp, Comparative Studies in Society and History, Supplement II, The Hague, 1962; especially significant the discussion of chiliasm and Hussitism by Howard Kamminsky, pp. 166–186.

27. See the excellent study by Lothar Graf zu Dohna, *Reformatio Sigismundi, Beiträge zum Verständnis einer Reformschrift des fünfzehnten Jahrhunderts*, Göttingen, 1960, esp. pp. 64 ff.

28. Ernst H. Kantorowicz, *Frederick the Second, 1194–1250*, 2d ed., New York, 1957, p. 335.

29. W. E. Peuckert, *Die grosse Wende: Das apokalyptische Saeculum und Luther*, Hamburg, 1948, esp. pp. 213–243.

30. Ernst W. Zeeden, *Martin Luther und die Reformation im Urteil des deutschen Luthertums*, II, *Dokumente*, Freiburg i. Br., 1952, p. 12. See also I, *Darstellung*, Freiburg i. Br., 1950, p. 60.

31. "Glosse auf das vermeinte kaiserliche Edikt" (13 April 1531). *WA* 30. 3. 387. Cf. A. Hauffen, "Huss eine Gans—Luther ein Schwan," *Festschrift Joh. v. Kelle*, II, Prag, 1908, pp. 1–28.

32. See my "Quo Vadis? Tradition from Irenaeus to Humani Generis," *Scottish Journal of Theology*, 16 (1963), pp. 241 ff.

33. *WA* 10. 2. 236. (1522). Not long before, Luther had been more sober in his assessment when he wrote in his second commentary on the Psalms that the condition of the Church was too grave to hope for a general reformation of the Church, *WA* 5. 345. (1519–1521). Cf. John M. Headley, *Luther's View of Church History*, New Haven, 1963, pp. 61 ff. See further Jaroslav Pelikan, *Luther the Expositor*, St. Louis, 1959, pp. 95 ff.

34. *WA* 10. 2. 329 f.

35. "Illa enim incoepit a Cain; haec ab Abel." Enarratio in Psalmum LXI, n. 6. For further documentation see Yves Congar, "Ecclesia ab Abel," in *Abhandlungen über Theologie und Kirche, Festschrift für Karl Adam*, ed. Marcel Reding, Düsseldorf, 1952, pp. 79–108.

36. For this improvement upon my earlier distinction between pre-schismatic and schismatic Middle Ages I am indebted to Father D. Trapp in his "Harvest of Medieval Theology," *Augustinianum*, V (1965), 150.

37. Thomas Bradwardine, *De Causa Dei contra Pelagium*, Praefatio, fol. 4. Cf. "Simon dormis?" *ibid.*, Liber III. 53, 872 E.

38. *Corpus Iuris Canonici*, d 20 c.l.: ed. E. Friedberg, I. Leipzig, 1879, col. 65. Hereafter abbreviated as *CIC*.

39. *Liber Sermonum*, Sermo 37, Basel, 1510, fol. 265 F.

40. Wessel Gansfort, *Opera*, Groningae, 1614, fol. 758.

41. Occam, *Dialogus*, Part I, Bk. II, 26.

42. Matthew 28:20.

43. Occam, *Dialogus*, Part I, Bk. V, 32.

44. See H. A. Oberman, *The Harvest of Medieval Theology*, Cambridge, Mass., 1963, esp. pp. 172 ff. Hereafter referred to as *Harvest*.

45. Matthew 23:35.

46. Hebrews 11:4.

47. I John 3:12.

48. Jude II.

49. Genesis 4:1.

50. Harry A. Wolfson, *Philo, Foundations of Religious Philosophy in Judaism, Christianity, and Islam*, 3rd ed., I, Cambridge, Mass., 1962, p. 153.

51. Thomas Bradwardine, *De Causa Dei*, I, 1–145.

52. "Quapropter . . . ipsos disposui reformare," *op. cit.*, Praefatio, b; "Amplius autem omnes . . . per

praecedentia reformantur," *ibid.*, I, 145 A.

53. *CIC*, Cap. XIII, Decret. Greg. IX, Lib. V. VII; ed. E. Friedberg, II Leipzig, 1881, col. 787.

54. ". . . ipsa, quae quosdam articulos fortassis vellicatura erat, nunc iudicio supersedit." *Huldrich Zwingli Opera*, ed. M. Schulero et I. Schulthessio, VII, Turici, 1830, p. 151, ZW VII. 362, 10–12.

55. ". . . erroribus haeresibusque ab olim damnatis . . .," *Collectio Judiciorum de Novis Erroribus*, ed. C. du Plessis d'Argentré, I, Paris, 1724, col. 361. For *Exsurge Domine* and the *Determinationes* of Louvain, Cologne, and Paris, see col. 358–374.

56. *Collectio Judiciorum*, I, 365.

57. The original text in *Corpus Reformatorum* I, Halis Saxonum, 1834, pp. 398–416. Hereafter abbreviated: *CR*. Cf. especially p. 400, with the poem in letter viii, "Franz Gänsepreciger to Magister Ortwin Gratius," in the edition introduced by Hajo Holborn, *On the Eve of the Reformation: "Letters of Obscure Men,"* Harper Torchbook, New York, 1964, p. 19. For an English translation of Melanchthon's *Defense* see Elmer E. Flack, L. J. Satre, *Melanchthon: Selected Writings*, Minneapolis, 1962, pp. 69–87.

58. *Luther's Works*, American ed., Vol. 48, ed. G. G. Krodel, Philadelphia, 1963, pp. 257 f.

59. *Ibid.*, p. 270. For Luther's translation of Melanchthon's *Defense* see *WA* 8. 267 ff. For the place of Melanchthon's *Defense* in his

thought see Peter Fraenkel, *Testimonia Patrum; the Function of the Patristic Argument in the Theology of Philip Melanchthon,* Genève, 1961, pp. 32 ff.

60. "Vides, lector, convenire magna ex parte Luthero cum Theologis veteribus." *CR* 1, p. 405.
61. "a coetu Cain," *CR* 12. 727; quoted by Fraenkel, p. 64.
62. *Ibid.,* p. 409. On Flacius see Joachim Massner, *Kirchliche überlieferung und Autorität im Flaciuskreis,* Berlin, 1964. Further literature here, pp. 103 ff.
63. *Calvin: Institutes of the Christian Religion,* ed. John T. McNeill, transl. Ford L. Battles, Library of Christian Classics, XX, XXI, Philadelphia, 1960.
64. For documentation see Pontien Polman, *L'Élément Historique dans la controverse religieuse du XVIe siècle,* Gembloux, 1932, pp. 495 ff.
65. *Opus Epistolarum Desiderii Erasmi Roterodami,* ed. P. S. Allen, vol. IV, Oxford 1922, ep. 1192, p. 453 and ep. 1212, p. 528. Allen suggests that the unknown Italian might well be Bernadino Ochino (1564). Cf. Roland H. Bainton, *Bernadino Ochino,* Firenze, 1940.
66. Karl H. Ullmann, *Reformatoren vor der Reformation vornehmlich in Deutschland und den Niederlanden,* I, *Das Bedürfniss der Reformation in Beziehung auf den Gesammtgeist der Kirche und einzelne kirchliche Zustände,* Hamburg, 1841; II, *Die positiven Grundlagen der Reformation auf dem populären und wissenschaftlichen Gebiete,* Hamburg, 1842. See further the extensive bibliography in Friedrich Loofs, *Leitfaden zum Studium der Dogmengeschichte,* ed. Kurt Aland, 5th ed., II, Halle-Saale, 1953, pp. 525–527.
67. *Ibid.,* Preface I, pp. xiii–xvi.
68. *Ibid.,* II, p. 706.
69. For an evaluation of Ullmann's prime example of a Forerunner, namely Wessel Gansfort, see the authoritative study by Maarten van Rhijn, *Wessel Gansfort,* 's Gravenhage, 1917, pp. 16 ff., 246.
70. Albrecht Ritschl, *Die christliche Lehre von der Rechtfertigung und Versöhnung,* 4th ed., I, *Die Geschichte der Lehre,* Bonn, 1903 (first published 1870), pp. 133, 129 ff. Cf. his *Geschichte des Pietismus,* I, Bonn, 1880, pp. 7–22.
71. See *Harvest,* pp. 423 ff.
72. See the revealing selections from Wilhelm Dilthey, Ernst Troeltsch, and Hajo Holborn as part of a most useful collection edited by Lewis W. Spitz, *The Reformation, Material or Spiritual?,* Boston, 1962.
73. *Ibid.,* p. 528; cf. pp. 527, 427, 517, 546.
74. Reinhold Seeberg, *Lehrbuch der Dogmengeschichte,* III, *Die Dogmengeschichte des Mittelalters,* 5th ed., Basel, 1935 (reprint of 4th ed., 1930), p. 761.
75. A. v. Harnack, *Lehrbuch der Dogmengeschichte,* III, *Die Entwicklung des kirchlichen Dogmas,* 4th and 5th eds., Tübingen,

1932, p. 511. For the view that Bradwardine is not a Forerunner in Ullmann's sense, see my *Archbishop Thomas Bradwardine, a Fourteenth Century Augustinian; a Study of His Theology in Its Historical Context*, Utrecht, 1958, pp. 199 f., 230 f.

76. Cf. Harnack, *op. cit.*, III, pp. 12, 100 and 158.

77. *Ibid.*, p. 490.

78. Erasmus, *Spongia adversus adspergines Hutteni*, Leiden edition (LB), X, 1663, A-B, Cf. Allen, ed. *cit.*, vol. V, 309.

79. Harnack, *op. cit.*, p. 12.

80. Cf. Seeberg's aside to Ritschl in *Dogmengeschichte*, III, 5th ed., p. 761, note 1.

81. *WATR* IV, n, 4338, Tischreden 1539; *WA* 44. 169. lectures on Genesis, 1535-1545.

82. For a discussion of the continuity of late medieval and Tridentine theology see my "Duns Scotus, Nominalism, and the Council of Trent," in *John Duns Scotus, 1265-1965*, ed. John K. Ryan and Bernardine M. Bonansea, Catholic University of America, 1965, pp. 311-344.

83. *Acta Conciliorum et Epistolae Decretales*, X. A.D. 1438-1549, Parisiis 1714, cols. 1576-1581; col. 1576. The following quotations are taken—in this order—from cols. 1577, 1579, 1576, *ibid.*, 1580 and 1578.

84. See also Hubert Jedin, *Geschichte des Konzils von Trient*, I, 2d ed., Freiburg i. Br., 1957.

85. These currents have recently been gathered together in a truly magisterial effort by George Huntston Williams in *The Radical Reformation*, Philadelphia, 1962. Enno van Gelder's most interesting *The Two Reformations*, 's Gravenhage, 1962, presupposes too many as yet unproven assumptions to determine our typology.

86. In the case of Hus the new critical edition of the *Tractatus de Ecclesia*, Cambridge, 1956, by S. Harrison Thomson. could be used.

Chapter Two
Scripture and Tradition

Introduction

One of the most remarkable developments in the study of medieval thought is the attention which has been given in the last decade to the medieval discussion of the relation between Scripture and Tradition. This is an indication of the extent to which the ever-changing perspective on medieval thought is determined by the fluctuation of interest in aspects of Reformation and Counter Reformation thought, and by its relevance for contemporary theology.

The recent concern with the problem of Tradition in the field of medieval studies can be traced back to the publications of a German systematic theologian, Josef Rupert Geiselmann,[1] who suggested that the traditional interpretation of the Tridentine decree on Scripture and Tradition should be reconsidered. Whereas heretofore it had been assumed that the Council had taught that there are two complementary sources of revelation, part of the truth being derived from Scripture and part from extrascriptural Tradition, Geiselmann suggests that closer consideration of the relevant documents proves the Council to have abstained from determining whether or not all truths are contained in Holy Scripture. Notwithstanding this abstention, Geiselmann argues, in the light of the previous history of this issue, one should interpret the conciliar decree to mean that all Catholic truth is contained simultaneously in Holy Scripture and in the Holy Church. Thus interpreted, the Tridentine formulation is much closer to the central doctrine of the Reformation, and leaves the door open for further development, that the whole revelation is contained in Holy Scripture—the so-called "material sufficiency" of Holy Scripture. In the discussion that ensued concerning the validity of Geiselmann's thesis it became increasingly clear that an understanding of the medieval antecedents of the conciliar debates was essential. The result has been an ever-growing number of articles and books on this topic.

This is by no means an isolated instance of the way in which the assessment of sixteenth-century thought has influenced related medieval studies. The long-supported view that sixteenth-century polemics can be described as the clash of "Scripture alone" (*sola scriptura*), the Reformation principle, with "Scripture and Tradition," the Counter Reformation principle, has determined also the categories with which historians of medieval thought used to operate. Historians have been led to search for medieval thinkers who would represent the so-called "scriptural principle" and to contrast them with those who were willing to draw on arguments from the tradition of the Church. Occam's criticism of the canon law tradition, together with his insistence on the authority of Scripture, could result in his classification in the first category, while Wessel's willingness to respect the exegetical tradition would be sufficient proof to count him among those holding the opposite view.

Closer consideration, however, proves the impossibility of forcing medieval theologians into the strait jacket of the alternatives of Scripture or Tradition. We are, rather, confronted with the encounter of two general notions about Tradition. In the first case the sole authority of Holy Scripture is upheld as canon, or standard, of revealed truth in such a way that Scripture is not contrasted with Tradition. Scripture, it is argued, can be understood only within the Church and has been understood within the Church by the great doctors specifically committed to the task of interpretation of Scripture and especially endowed with the gift of understanding this unique source of truth. The history of obedient interpretation is the Tradition of the Church.

In the second case Tradition is a wider concept. It is argued that the Apostles did not commit everything to writing, usually on the grounds that the scriptural authors reported what Christ said and did during His lifetime but not what Christ taught His disciples in the period between the resurrection and the ascension. During these forty

days an oral Tradition originated which is to be regarded as a complement to Holy Scripture, handed down to the Church of later times
as a second source of revelation. In the first case Tradition was seen
as the instrumental vehicle of Scripture which brings the contents of
Holy Scripture to life in a constant dialogue between the doctors of
Scripture and the Church; in the second case Tradition was seen as
the authoritative vehicle of divine truth, embedded in Scripture but
overflowing in extrascriptural apostolic tradition handed down
through episcopal succession.[2]

To gain a perspective on this medieval discussion it is perhaps useful to take a look at some of its significant permutations originating
in the fourth century. In view of the present consensus that in patristic literature of both East and West the material sufficiency of Holy
Scripture was presupposed and its denial was a mark of heresy, it can
be said that a new development was prepared for in the East by Basil
the Great (c. 330–370) and was propagated half a century later in the
West by Augustine. In Basil's treatise *On the Holy Spirit* the relation
of Scripture and Tradition is discussed in connection with certain
liturgical traditions of the Church. We meet here for the first time
the idea that the Christian owes equal respect and obedience to the
written and to the unwritten ecclesiastical traditions, whether they
are contained in the canonical writings or in the secret oral tradition
handed down by the Apostles through succession.

We find this Basilean passage quoted by canonists of the early
Middle Ages. The great expert in canon law, Ivo of Chartres (†1116),
refers to it in order to insist on equal reverence for scriptural and
for extrascriptural oral traditions. Most important is that Gratian of
Bologna (†1158) copied this passage from Ivo and incorporated it
into his highly influential *Decretum*, whence it found its way to the
textbooks of both canon lawyers and theologians.

For the canon lawyer, therefore, the two-source theory has been
established: canon law stands on the two pillars of Scripture and
Tradition. This does not seem to apply, however, in the case of the
medieval doctors of theology. For them theology is the science of
Holy Scripture. Notwithstanding the constant and growing temptation to comment on the comments, Holy Scripture is understood as

the authoritative source—the standard for judging the interpretation of later commentators. The term "sacred page" for theology is indicative of this close relationship.

Nevertheless, there is in the history of medieval theology a development which corresponds with the two-source theory originating with Basil the Great. Lacking an extensive monographic literature, we are not yet in a position to draw the lines of development without some hesitation, but the medieval understanding of the famous words of Augustine on the relation of Scripture and Church presents an excellent key to the history of this relationship. While repeatedly asserting the primacy of Scripture, Augustine himself does not contrast this at all with the authority of the Catholic Church: ". . . I would not believe the Gospel, unless the authority of the Catholic Church moved me (*commovit me*)." Here the Church must be understood to have an authority to direct (*commovere*) the believer to the door which leads to the fullness of the Word itself.

Toward the end of the Middle Ages the Church came to understand Augustine's statement of the practical authority of the Church as though it implied a metaphysical priority. The moving authority of the Church becomes in late medieval versions the Church's approval or creation of Holy Scripture. Until our own time, Augustine's words have even been taken to imply that Holy Scripture is a product contingent on the life of the Church. Indeed the voice of the fourteenth-century Augustinian, Gregory of Rimini (†1358), protesting that Augustine meant merely a practical priority of the Church over Scripture, went largely unheard. For him the authority of the Church should be compared with the function of the miracles of Jesus to prompt His contemporaries to heed His words.

If it were only for the passage quoted we would not hold Augustine to be the Western counterpart of St. Basil. He himself, however, has to shoulder some of the responsibility for later misunderstandings of the passage which we discussed. Whereas Irenaeus (*c.* 200) and Tertullian (*c.* 220) had taught the sufficiency of Scripture, in Augustine we encounter an authoritative extrascriptural oral tradition. While on the one hand, the Church "moves" the faithful to discover the authority of Scripture, Scripture, on the other hand, refers the faithful back to the authority of the Church on a series of issues with which the Apostles did not deal in writing. In this case Augustine refers to the validity of baptism by heretics, Abélard later to Mariology, Bonaventura to the *filioque*, Aquinas to the form of the sacrament of confirmation and the veneration of images.

One cannot claim that a neat distinction existed between doctrinal truths and liturgical practices; here too, the life of prayer (*lex orandi*) proves to be the form of faith (*lex credendi*), and devotion proves to be the highway to doctrine and hence to dogma. The fourteenth-century theologians who believed the immaculate conception of the Virgin Mary to be among Catholic truths based one of their main arguments on the celebration of the feast of the Conception of the mother of Jesus.

One may wonder whether the *Commonitorium* of Vincent of Lerins, written in the early part of the fifth century, perhaps influenced the spread of this concept of Tradition. His thesis is that the Catholic Church must hold to that which has been believed everywhere, always, and by everyone. This seems to allow for an authoritative extrascriptural tradition. However, when we read this statement in its context, we find that Vincent did not reject the *material* sufficiency but the *formal* sufficiency of Holy Scripture. He insists on Holy Scripture's need to be interpreted by the Church, since heretics from Novatian to Nestorius have all advanced their own exegeses of biblical passages. But, he says, the sole purpose of interpretation is preservation: the faith once declared to the Apostles has to be protected against change, which represents perversion. There can be no guarantee of proper biblical exegesis in a secret oral tradition traceable to the Apostles themselves, but such a guarantee must come from the explicit consensus of the Fathers and provide a safeguard against arbitrary interpretation. Vincent echoes Tertullian in warning against rashness and lack of disciplined reason on the part of the biblical exegete.

It is important to note that Vincent does not want the interpretation of the Church, which one may call the exegetical tradition, to become a second tradition or source apart from Holy Scripture. Even the Fathers are, in principle, teachers whose utterances are probable but do not yet constitute proof. Their opinion does not represent the deposit of faith until five requirements have been met: (1) The opinion must be held by all the Fathers; (2) The formulation of the opinion must be exactly the same; (3) Their opinion should be openly and explicitly formulated and (4) repeatedly advanced; (5) Their opinion should be continuously held, written, and taught.

It has often been suggested that Vincent directs his *Commonitorium* against the sharp edges of Augustine's doctrine of grace and predestination. This may or may not have been Vincent's ulterior motive, but one does not tax the sources too heavily in concluding that Vincent directs his concept of authoritative exegetical tradition primarily against a two-source theory—a theory one can trace back not only to St. Basil but also to St. Augustine.

If, for clarity's sake, we call the single-source theory of interpreted Scripture "Tradition I," and the two-source theory, which allows for an extrabiblical oral tradition, "Tradition II," we may see that both find their medieval partisans. It is difficult to say whether the conscious elaboration of Tradition II is to be understood as a reaction against the further development of Tradition I, in the sense that the decisions of the Council of Trent are often claimed to be a mere reaction to the writings of the Reformers. One can make a good claim that the reaction worked the other way around.

In the fourteenth century, at the time of the Western Schism and the final phase of the struggle between pope and emperor, the canon lawyer was in high demand and, if we may believe the many bitter comments by doctors of theology, he not only equals but surpasses the theologian in status at both the papal curia and the royal courts. With varying degrees of enthusiasm, both curialists and conciliarists necessarily drew extensively on the decretes and decretals. And, under these circumstances, it is not surprising that the canon-law tradition starts to feed into the major theological stream and that the Basilean passage can become a truly theological argument. Gabriel Biel, "the last of the scholastics," finds in St. Basil the warrant for investing the unwritten traditions with the same apostolic authority as the Scriptures.

In the development from Augustine to Aquinas and into the later Middle Ages, theologians find an increasing number of doctrinal points on which Holy Scripture is silent. The last verse of the fourth

Gospel provided an explanation for the "silence" or material insufficiency of the Scriptures: "But there are many other things which Jesus did; were every one of them written, I suppose that the world itself could not contain the books that would be written."[3]

Whereas the canon lawyer in the Basilean line is straightforward in positing two sources requiring equal respect, it appears that the scholastic doctors of Scripture develop the oral tradition in a more subtle way. In theory the material sufficiency of Holy Scripture is upheld long after it has been given up in practice. The key term of this development is the word "implicit," and the history of this term is one of increasing loss of content. When finally the two propositions, "Holy Scripture implicitly says" and "Holy Scripture silently says," are equated, the exegetical concept of Tradition I has fully developed into what we have called Tradition II and the Basilean passage borrowed from canon law provides the rational and patristic authority.

When we turn now to the medieval development of Tradition I, it is clearly impossible to trace this concept in the early part of the Middle Ages. In this period Tradition I and Tradition II cannot be clearly separated for the simple reason that those who *de facto* hold Tradition II continue to declare themselves for the material sufficiency of Holy Scripture. But once such a man as John Brevicoxa had disentangled the confusion of terminology and arguments, the historian is in a better position to discern the contrasts. However, so long as his eyes are still blinded by the traditional contrast of Scripture versus Tradition, he is bound to err in his interpretation of the sources.

Fourteenth- and fifteenth-century theologians such as John Wyclif, Jan Hus, and Wessel Gansfort do not defend Scripture against Tradition, but they pose Tradition I against Tradition II. True to the restrictions of Vincent's five requirements for accepting as truth certain traditions, they defend along with the material sufficiency of Scripture the authority of the exegetical tradition whenever there is a common and explicit witness of the Fathers, in particular of the four great doctors of the Church, Augustine, Jerome, Ambrose, and Gregory. It should also be noted that these representatives of Tradition I do not deny the importance and validity of episcopal succession for the preservation of the truth. Indeed they regard tradition as the execution of the Church's custodial task. But in contrast to those holding to Tradition II, the emphasis falls rather on the succession of the doctors than of the bishops.

Understandably, their attack is especially directed against the canon lawyers, the most conspicuous bearers of Tradition II. But they also sharply react against the theologians' practice of building tradition into the "silent places" in Scripture. In its strongest forms this criticism may lead to the transformation of Tradition I. Here perhaps we stand by the cradle of what is usually called biblicism, which by way of certain branches of the Reformation and of seventeenth-century orthodoxy comes down to us in the form of fundamentalism.

The use of the categories Tradition I and Tradition II, as defined above, is of course no more than a working hypothesis which recommends itself because, and only so long as, it can take account of more data, facts, and factors than other hypotheses. There are indeed not two but a number of subtly differentiated late medieval solutions to the problem of the relation of Scripture and Tradition. Further investigation is bound to add to this number and sharpen our eyes for aspects and combinations of arguments hitherto overlooked. We would expect such an investigation to show, however, that these solutions can be divided into the two main categories we have indicated.

One of the most important documents in the late medieval history of the analysis of tradition in its many ramifications is the treatise by John Brevicoxa, or Courtecuisse as he is called in France, *De Fide et Ecclesia*, which, hidden in an edition of the works of his colleague Jean Gerson, has failed to attract the attention it deserves.

Notwithstanding Brevicoxa's compact style and detailed argumentation the patient reader will find the following translation most rewarding, not necessarily because of the final conclusion but because of the fair and explicit presentation of all the alternatives. Whereas in the two selections that follow Brevicoxa we can only understand the discussion between I and II by putting the letter of Hoeck and Gansfort side by side, in *De Fide et Ecclesia* we can follow two sides of the argument simultaneously; and we can see how each tradition had implications for the definition of "Catholic truth," orthodoxy, and heresy.

Little is known about Brevicoxa, and his name is absent in encyclopedias that usually include a man of his stature. We can safely say[4] only that around 1367 he entered the foremost Parisian College of Navarre where he studied grammar, philosophy, and theology. As candidate for a higher degree in theology he wrote—we may suppose around 1375—the treatise of which we excerpt a part, *A Treatise on Faith, the Church, the Roman Pontiff, and the General Council.*[5] As indicated in the title, the work is divided into three parts. The first part lays the basic foundations by determining the meaning of faith and related concepts; the second part deals with the continuity of the Church, its hierarchy and jurisdiction; and the final part raises the question, "Can the Roman Church err in matters of faith?" After having reported and discussed in his usual impartial fashion the arguments for and against this last question, Brevicoxa reaches the conclusion that the affirmative answer rests on sounder grounds and is, therefore, to be preferred (col. 888). The Gallican trend in his thought becomes even more discernible when he agrees with the "unanimous witness of all scholastics" that the Universal Church, in contrast to the Roman Church, cannot err (col. 893). Gallicanism can be conveniently described as medieval "de Gaullism" which emphasizes the independence of the French Church from the Roman Church and conceives of the two as equal partners in the Church Universal. Religiously it represents a point of view opposed to ultramontanism which looks for authority and spiritual guidance to "the other side of the mountains," that is, south of the Alps to Italy, to Rome. Politically it will not concede to either Italy or Germany the succession of the Roman Empire but presses its own political privileges and inheritance. Gallicanism is a natural breeding ground for conciliarism which emphasizes the Council as the highest authority in the Church and opposes curialism in its doctrine of papal supremacy.

Brevicoxa, however, does not feel ready to state that a general council which represents the Church Universal has a sound basis for infallibility. "I do not recall having read in all of Holy Scripture—nor has anybody shown me—a place therein from which it is clear that a general council cannot err" (col. 898). In the light of Occam's assertion of confidence in the unanimity of a council together with his warning that the faith of the Church had once been upheld by one single person, the Virgin Mary, one can well understand that Brevicoxa's greatest problem is whether an absolute consensus should be required or simply a majority and how "a sufficient majority" should be defined. At the end he has to leave the solution of this question to the canon lawyers (col. 898).

Brevicoxa's discussion, written around the beginning of the Great Western Schism, is in its whole tone and direction the opposite of Pius II's bull *Execrabilis* of less than a century later. But however vivid the contrast may be between the theses, "the Roman Church can err," (*c.* 1375), and "no appeal can be made from the pope to a future council" (1460), it should be remembered that Brevicoxa in the first part of his discussion had opted for what we have called Tradition II. He shares with curialism the basic presupposition that Catholic truths are to be found not only in Holy Scripture. When seen in terms of the attitude to Scripture and extrascriptural Tradition, Parisian conciliarism and curialism are but variations upon this same theme. Both agree on the validity of drawing upon truths that may have reached the Church by means other than Scripture, and their disagreement is not concerned with the fact nor with the channel of extrascriptural Tradition but with the means by which such a truth is acknowledged and promulgated. The Parisian sympathies with the Conciliabulum of Pisa (1510–1512) rather than with the Fifth Lateran Council convened in the same period (1512) is therefore commensurable with the support by the Sorbonne (1521) of *Exsurge Domine,* the papal condemnation of Luther's position (1520).

After having received his theological doctor's degree in 1388, Brevicoxa became a colleague of Peter d'Ailly (†1420) on the faculty of the College of Navarre and during the absence of Jean Gerson (†1429), who was involved in the Council of Constance (1414–1418), fulfilled for some time the latter's task as Chancellor of the University of Paris. He died in 1423 as Bishop of Geneva without the fame of either d'Ailly or Gerson, his fellow Navarrists, but equally concerned with the same problems. In his *De Fide et Ecclesia* he has left us a document which, free from the passionate promotion of the cause of conciliarism characteristic of those two, serves as an excellent introduction to the state of the discussion between Scripture and Tradition in the later part of the fourteenth century.

The selections taken from Jacob Hoeck (†1509) and Wessel Gansfort (†1489) give us the opportunity to see how this discussion had developed a century later. Although the exchange of letters between these two doctors of theology took place in the Netherlands the argument is as Parisian in context as in the case of Brevicoxa. In view of the fact that the Dutch were the best-represented nation at this French university this is perhaps not too surprising.[6]

Jacob Hoeck, or Jacobus Angularius, born in the first half of the fifteenth century, received in 1460 the Bachelor of Arts and in 1462 the Master of Arts degree at Paris after a preliminary schooling at Leiden. In 1466 and again in 1473 he was elected rector of the University, and in the academic years 1474–1475 and 1475–1476 he was referred to as Prior Sorbonnae. He must already have heard about Wessel while in Paris. Gansfort was there, at least from 1458 to 1460, and again after his return from Rome in 1471 until 1473 when the nominalists were for eight years expelled from the University by Louis XI's edict. The fact that Hoeck rose to great heights in the years following this edict suggests that he cannot be counted among the nominalists. His later complete disappearance from the academic scene may be explained as due to the resurgence of nominalism and its animosity toward the king's collaborators.

In 1479 we encounter Hoeck again in the Netherlands as a member of the local clergy in Wassenaar, and in 1483 as Dean of the Chapter in Naaldwijk. The death of Hoeck on November 11, 1509, was not the unnoticed or somewhat tragic departure of a man long past his prime. In the history of eucharistic theology this date was to be remembered because it sparked a series of chain reactions which would carry the fame of Wessel Gansfort into the Reformation era.

Wessel Gansfort, born in Groningen (1419–1489), was educated at Zwolle by the Brethren of the Common Life whose influence had been extended in those years through the services of Gabriel Biel into southern Germany.[7] Before leaving for the University of Cologne he came to know Thomas à Kempis, author of *The Imitation of Christ*, whom he visited repeatedly, and by whose piety he was deeply impressed. In 1450 he received the Bachelor of Arts and two years later the Master of Arts degree in Cologne. Via Louvain and Paris he returned to Germany to take a teaching position at Cologne, where at that time Pupper of Goch studied law, and Gabriel Biel, theology.

We know very little about Wessel in the period from 1460 to 1470, but it must have been then that he was converted to nominalism during a disputation at Paris. His extensive travels brought him twice to Rome, which led in 1473 to an encounter with Pope Sixtus IV (1471–1484), who made him a gift of a Hebrew and Greek Bible from the holdings of the Vatican Library. From these years also dates his friendship with the young John Reuchlin (Capnio) (1455-1522), with whom Wessel shared a great love for philology and literary style. Around 1475 Wessel returned to his native country and remained there under the protection of Bishop David of Utrecht until his death in October 1489. This protection was by no means redundant, as the following translation will indicate.

Two final observations may serve as background information and give the context of his answers to Jacob Hoeck. In the first place Wessel distinguishes between the empirical Church as the Church of the sacraments and the invisible Church of love. The pope can err and the empirical Church as a whole can err when the power of love is absent. The unity of the Church is not based on the papacy but on Christ. The authority of the Church is instrumental in character. It has the "passive" task of preserving the apostolic faith rather than the "active" task of sanctioning new truths as in the case of the indulgences.

This leads us to our second point. It has been argued that Wessel holds that the teaching of the Church relies on both Scripture and extrascriptural Tradition, in the same sense as the earlier Occam, Brevicoxa, and d'Ailly, and his contemporary Gabriel Biel. Actually, Wessel insists that no Christian ought "to subscribe to any statement of an assembly against his conscience, so long as it seems to him to assert anything contrary to Scripture."[8] "If therefore one is not bound to believe canons that have been officially published and authoritatively ratified, because they are outside of the Sacred Canon, one is not bound to believe what a pope says" (p. 780). Wessel does not deny, as can be seen in the following selection, that apostolic traditions not contained in the Canon can be part of the "rule of faith"—but only if they make explicit what is contained in the Sacred Canon. Wessel is therefore willing to say that sacramental confession falls into this category of apostolic Tradition and is part of the rule of faith, but only "since indeed it is confirmed by the general statements of John and by the more specific words of James. Therefore [!] I admit that in this rule of faith I ought to depend on the authority of the Church ..."9

It is in accordance with this principle, Wessel asserts, that a plenary indulgence is not acceptable: "Do you wish to put the authority of the pope above the Holy Scripture?"10 As a supporter of Tradition I, Wessel Gansfort did not reject the concept of Tradition, as such, but rather a use of the Tradition of the Church as a second source of equal authority to the Scriptures.

One of the principal elements in the sixteenth-century discussion and debate proves to have its antecedents in the fourteenth and fifteenth centuries. The Reformers' insistence on the authority of "Scripture alone" is not an unprecedented "deus ex machina," or supernatural breakthrough. It has to be seen, studied and understood in the context of the preceding medieval dialogue in which Brevicoxa and Wessel were key figures, the first by virtue of his cool academic analysis and fair presentation of the issues, the latter by his passionate dedication to the cause of the Church of his day.

Notes

1. For bibliography see *Christianity Divided,* ed. D. J. Callahan, H. A. Oberman, D. J. O'Hanlon, S.J., New York, 1961, p. 71. English translation of one article by Geiselmann, *ibid.,* pp. 39–70. Cf. the introduction by Father O'Hanlon, pp. 35 ff.
2. For documentation and an extended version of the following, see *Harvest,* pp. 361–412; and "Quo vadis? Tradition from Irenaeus to Humani Generis," in *Scottish Journal of Theology,* 16 (1963), pp. 225–255.
3. John 21:25.
4. Our sources are E. Du Pin in the

introduction to vol. I of the works of Gerson: *Opera Omnia,* I, Antwerpiae, 1706, pp. XL ff.; M. Hauréau, *Histoire littéraire,* III, Paris, 1871, pp. 148 ff.; P. Feret, *La Faculté de Théologie de Paris et ses Docteurs les plus célèbres,* IV, Paris, 1897, pp. 169 ff., and some interesting quotations from the archives dealing with Brevicoxa's academic maneuverings in a time of English domination in *Mémoires de la Société de l'Histoire de Paris et de l'Île de France,* IX, Paris, 1883, pp. 132 ff.
5. Text in E. L. Du Pin's edition of

Gerson, vol. I, col. 805–903. The chronicler of the history of Navarre grades it excellent, "eximius"; Feret, *op. cit.*, p. 170.

6. For data and sources on Jacobus Hoeck see Maarten van Rhijn, *Studien over Wessel Gansfort en zijn tijd*, Utrecht, 1933, pp. 112–126.

7. For data and sources regarding the life of Gansfort see Maarten van Rhijn, *Wessel Gansfort*, 's Gravenhage, 1917, pp. 23–155. Also Albert Hyma, *The Christian Renaissance: A History of the Devotio Moderna*, New York, 1925, ch. VI.

8. *Opera*, Groningen, 1614, p. 781. Cf. Oberman, *Harvest*, pp. 408 ff.

9. Gansfort, *Opera*, Groningen, 1614, p. 888.

10. *Ibid.*, pp. 892 ff.

JOHN BREVICOXA

A Treatise on Faith, the Church, the Roman Pontiff, and the General Council

Our task is to examine the content of faith. Since the content of Catholic faith is nothing other than Catholic truth, I shall raise fourteen very brief questions in order to make clear which truths are Catholic and which are not Catholic, which are heretical and which are not heretical, and to clarify certain conflicts regarding this subject. First, however, it ought to be noted that when faith is understood as "beliefs adhered to," there are four ways of defining the content of Catholic faith. One way is to think of Catholic faith as any one Catholic truth. Another way is to enumerate all truths explicitly approved by the Church. A third way is to enumerate all Catholic truths, whether or not the Church has given them explicit approval. The fourth way, which is the most comprehensive, is to enumerate, together with the truths of the third category, certain other commands, prohibitions, or counsels contained in Holy Scripture. An example of the latter would be, "You shall love the Lord your God," etc.[1]

In order, therefore, that it might be made clear which truths are Catholic and which are not, the following questions are posited:

I. What is Catholic truth?
II. What is implicit faith and what is explicit faith?
III. How many categories of Catholic truth are there that ought to be believed?
IV. Do the writings of the Fathers need approval?
V. What is heresy?
VI. Can new heresies and new truths be established?

When these questions have been answered it will be clear enough what one's position ought to be concerning this subject, that is, the content of faith.

Now I propose to treat this subject by means of these questions so that it might be made completely clear, for when one has solved even the first of the questions he can more easily attain the solution to the others.

I.   What is Catholic truth?

As to the first question, our task is to investigate Catholic truth. Provisionally, Catholic truth might be described as follows: "Catholic truth is that truth which any pilgrim,[2] of sound mind and having been sufficiently instructed in the Law of Christ, is required to believe either explicitly or implicitly as a condition for salvation." The word "pilgrim" is used to distinguish the Church militant from the Church triumphant, that is, those in heaven who perceive many truths by unmediated vision. Hence they do not need to believe in things unseen. "In sound mind" is included so as to eliminate children, of whom nothing is required, and those who are mad and demented, of whom likewise nothing is required, as long as they are in that condition. The reference to sufficient instruction in the "Law of Christ" is for the sake of those who immediately after they were baptized were reared without any contact with Christians and were never instructed in the faith (if, indeed, there be any such persons). "Explicitly or implicitly" is included because no pilgrim is required to know all Catholic truths explicitly, as no one is required to know the entire Bible explicitly even though all biblical truths are Catholic truths. "Required as a condition for salvation" is stated to rule out truths that are not Catholic, such as those of philosophy or geometry. No pilgrim is required to know these or believe these truths as a condition for salvation.

II.   What is implicit faith and what is explicit faith?

Now the second question remains: What is implicit and explicit faith? Since these terms occur in the aforesaid definition, if they were to remain obscure the whole definition might be misunderstood.

The answer to this question is that to believe implicitly means firmly to assent to a universal truth from which many things follow and not to cling stubbornly to its negation. Therefore, he who steadfastly holds that all things contained in Holy Scripture together with the teaching of the Universal Church are true and sound, and who does not stubbornly cling to any contrary assertion, holds implicitly a faith whole and uncorrupted. For anyone who believes that everything the Church asserts is true believes by implication the following statement: "Blessed Andrew was an Apostle of Christ," since this has been handed down by the Church. He believes this even though he does not know the Church makes such an assertion. And thus, if anyone assents to this statement: "Every man believes," he assents by implication to this statement, "Socrates believes," if indeed Socrates be a man. For assent to "Every man believes" is implicit assent to "Socrates believes."[3] This is what explicit assent to a general truth involves. Explicit assent to a general truth implies assent to each of its particulars. Explicit assent, on the other hand, to a proposition is direct assent to such a proposition. Therefore, if I see that Socrates believes, I assent directly and explicitly to the statement "Socrates believes," etc., etc.

III.   How many categories of Catholic truth are there that ought to be believed?

Even when this has been made clear one can reasonably ask: How many categories of Catholic truth are there that ought to be believed, and to which truths is a pilgrim required to give assent either explicitly or implicitly? Therefore, this question must be answered. It should be noted that regarding this issue there are two alternative views.

Tradition I[4]

Some say that only those truths which are asserted explicitly in the canon of the Bible or which can be deduced solely from the contents of the Bible are Catholic truths and should be believed as a condition for salvation. For example, the assertion, "Christ is true God and true man," falls directly into this category because it follows necessarily from the contents of Sacred Scripture.

One can prove this position by the following authorities and arguments:

1. By the authority of Solomon: "So do not add to his words lest he rebuke you and you be found a liar."[5]

2. It is argued by the authority of Saint Augustine, who says in a letter to Saint Jerome, "I have learned to give this regard only to those books which are called canonical so that I can firmly believe that no error crept into them as they were being written down. Even if I find something in them which appears to be contrary to the truth, or if I find a corrupt textual tradition, or if the exegesis is not faithful to the actual text or is not clear to me, I do not hesitate in my belief. But I do not have such a regard for other books or writings."[6]

3. Speaking of the writings, which are later than the Old and New Testaments, Augustine says, "The authority of this kind of writing ought to be distinguished from the authority of canonical writings. The former ought not to be read as determinative witnesses against which no conflicting theological opinions are permitted."[7]

4. No one is required as a condition for salvation to believe the truths taught by Augustine as he himself testifies.[8] And since Augustine grants this about himself, it is clear that no other writings which are not found in the Bible need be accepted as a condition for salvation. The conclusion stands because it is supported by Augustine, who is of as great authority as any of the biblical writers.

5. According to Saint Augustine, "In Divine Scripture, everything useful is found and everything harmful is condemned."[9] Therefore, no Catholic truth is found outside of Holy Scripture.

6. It is argued by the authority of Saint Jerome who, speaking of Holy Scripture, says, "An assertion not based on scriptural authority is as easily discarded as it is proved."[10]

No assertion which can be as easily discarded as proved ought to be counted among Catholic truths. Therefore, only those truths which have authority from Divine Scripture, that is, which can be plainly deduced from Scripture, ought to be counted among Catholic truths.

Tradition II

Others say that many truths not found in Sacred Scripture, nor necessarily deducible from its contents alone, ought to be assented to as a condition for salvation. This position is defended thus:

1. It is argued by the authority of Innocent III that "although the words of the sacrament of the Holy Eucharist are by no means to be found in their entirety in Scripture, nevertheless we must be firm in our belief that this formula was instituted by Christ."[11]

2. It is argued by the testimony of Pope Agathus who says, "All apostolic injunctions ought to be accepted as if they were uttered by the divine voice of Peter himself."[12] In other words, all injunctions of this kind carry an authority equal to that of the writings of Peter, which are counted among the writings of Holy Scripture. Even though many such injunctions are not contained in Divine Scripture, these and many more truths ought to be accepted as Catholic truth.

3. It is further argued thus: If this position is not accepted, the following assertions could be denied: "The Creed was drawn up by the Apostles," "The Petrine See was translated from Antioch to Rome," "The Roman popes succeed the blessed Peter." To deny such assertions would be patently false, and the premise is proved since these statements are not contained in Scripture nor can they necessarily be deduced from it. Therefore, etc.

4. It is argued thus: Catholics are required to believe the doctrinal determinations of the pope as long as they assert nothing contrary to the will of God. We know that Catholics are bound to obey these laws from canon law.[13] Therefore, we know they are also bound to believe doctrinal determinations.

5. No less reverence should be shown to the doctrines of the Apostles than to their legislation. For since both the apostolic laws recorded in

Scripture and those which were only orally commanded ought to be observed, so also *all* truths which were only orally taught and not recorded in writing ought to be firmly maintained and believed. Indeed the Apostles taught many things which are not found in any writings. For while Christ was still living in mortal flesh he taught the Apostles many things and performed acts in their presence which they later taught and preached, but which are not to be found in the Bible.

6. The writings of the pope and the Fathers which were intended to present holy dogma are of no less authority than those chronicles and histories found outside of Scripture. And since it is completely inane to say that all chronicles and histories outside the canon of the Bible could receive no approbation at all, therefore, etc., etc.

7. Finally it is argued thus. The Universal Church cannot err, since the Truth Himself testified, "I am with you always, to the close of the age,"[14] and even prayed that Peter's faith might never fail.

The Universal Church teaches many truths which are not found in Holy Scripture nor are necessarily deducible from Scripture alone. Therefore, etc.

These reasons prove that there are many truths to which one ought to assent as a necessary condition for salvation even though these truths are not contained in Holy Scripture nor can they be deduced from Scripture alone. This position appears to me to be more probable than the other.

The Categories of Truth According to Tradition II

To pursue, then, this line of argument it remains for us to examine the categories of Catholic truth which ought to be believed. To begin with it should be noted that according to this position there are five categories of Catholic truth to which Christians, that is, Catholics, ought steadfastly to assent.

The first category of Catholic truth consists of those truths found in Holy Scripture or deducible from it.

The second category consists of those which have come down to us from the Apostles by a handing down of revelation or by writings of the faithful but which are not found in Scripture nor are deducible from it.[15]

Third are truths found in chronicles and histories which in matters of faith are trustworthy and which have come down to us through narration by the faithful.

Fourth are truths which can be clearly deduced from the truths of the first or second category, or from the third category, but then only in combination with truths from the first two categories.

The fifth category, which goes beyond the truths revealed to the Apostles, consists of those truths God revealed to others or has more recently revealed or inspired. There is no question but that this revelation or inspiration has reached the Universal Church or, at least, should have reached it.

One could question the foregoing conclusion by arguing that there are *more* than five categories, since the determinations and definitions of the pope or of a general council should be steadfastly believed and counted as Catholic truth. Therefore, etc.

The response to this argument is that truths which are determined by the Church or by a general council are already subsumed under one of the five categories of Catholic truth. Furthermore it should be noted that it is not in the power of the Church, that is, the general council representing the Church, to approve or disapprove anything at all. Rather the Church approves or disapproves rightly when it bases its judgment on any of the five categories of Catholic truth.

The Foundations for Conciliar Decisions

Thus it should be noted that the pope, the general council, and also the Universal Church ought to rest its position on one of the following foundations when it condemns or rightly defines any assertion.

The first foundation is Sacred Scripture. The general council based itself primarily on this foundation when it condemned the heresies of Arius, Macedonius, Dioscuros, and many others.

The second foundation is apostolic teaching, which was not promulgated in the writings of the Apostles themselves but came down to us through the oral tradition of succeeding generations of the faithful or in writings which in matters of faith are trustworthy. Pope Nicholas based his position on this foundation when he defined as heretical the assertion that the Roman Church is not head of all churches.[16] The statement (namely that the Roman Church *is* head of all churches) is not found in Scripture although it may be deduced from it and, indeed, was taught by the Apostles. The doctrine reached us through the narration of each succeeding generation of faithful or by the writings of the Fathers. Thus this foundation relates to the second category of Catholic truth.

The third foundation is revelation or divine inspiration. If any eternal truth pertaining to salvation be revealed to the Church for the first time it should be approved as Catholic. If, however, a truth be revealed for the first time only to a few people, it is not enough to make the naked assertion that such truth has been revealed, but miracles clearly related to the revelation must confirm it. If, however, all Christians without exception firmly accept some truth as Catholic, that truth ought to be numbered among Catholic truths even though it cannot be found in Scripture or in any apostolic doctrine. For all the faithful believe steadfastly according to the promise of Christ, "I am with you always even until the end of the age," that the Universal Church never errs. However, it is obvious that no such unanimity of belief is likely to occur without the intervention of a miracle; and if a few or even just one person dissent, the truth ought not to be accepted as Catholic. For just as in the time of Christ all faith had its abode in one person, namely the Virgin Mary,[17] so now it is even more likely that this could happen, since, in the time of Christ, there were Apostles in addition to Mary.

IV.   Do the writings of the Fathers need approval?

There is another justifiable question. Should some of the writings and treatises of particular Fathers, such as Augustine, Jerome, Ambrose, and many others be accepted as Catholic and ought they to be believed as a condition for salvation? In answering I shall state two theses.

Error and Sanctity

First thesis. No assertion should be held to be consonant with Catholic truth just because a Father thinks something ought to be believed. This is proved by the authority of Augustine writing in various places, which I will not quote for the sake of brevity.[18] And I can prove the same conclusion by another argument as follows: The Holy Fathers, without detriment to their sanctity, can err against Catholic truth. Therefore, the theological position which a Father thinks the faithful ought to believe should not by itself be approved as consonant with the truth. The conclusion is obvious. The first proof comes from Augustine, who wrote many things that contradicted Catholic truth which he later retracted. Again the premise is clear, since error that is not accompanied by recalcitrance does not preclude a life of sanctity.

Second thesis. It is not necessary to adhere steadfastly to all the teachings contained in the writings of the Fathers now read throughout the Church. This thesis is proved as follows: In these well-known writings the Fathers contradict each other on issues of the faith. Therefore, all the teachings contained in these writings need not be steadfastly adhered to. The promise is proved by the differing opinions of Augustine and Jerome on Paul's teaching that "Now a bishop must be above reproach, married only once."[19] The gloss says, "Jerome perceives these things poorly but Augustine well."[20] A second example would be: Augustine reproved Saint Cyprian because he had asserted that the baptism of Christ could not be administered within heretical and schismatic churches. Therefore the thesis is established.

Error and Catholicity

Against this position it is argued thus. From these theses, especially from the second thesis, it follows that there is no authority left in the writings of the aforesaid Fathers, and that they would always be considered suspect. Augustine makes the point in speaking of Scripture: If one were to admit that error could flow from the pen of an inspired author, then Scripture would be stripped of its authority.[21] Therefore, if St. Jerome and St. Cyprian could have erred in those things which concern faith, it follows that their writings would be stripped of all authority. But their works are numbered among the approved writings of the Fathers, as is clear from the canon law.[22]

In answer to this argument it is said that the approval given to the writing of the Fathers does not extend to all the various assertions contained within them. For it is clear that there are many assertions in them which are contrary to the truth. However, all of the writings of the Fathers which were mentioned in the passage of canon law[23] are approved, except for those parts which have been corrected by the author or by others.

It is obvious, therefore, that all truths which are to be found in the writing of the Fathers ought not to be accepted as Catholic truths because the Fathers handed some down as Catholic truths, others as basic truths pertaining to the faith, and again others as only probabilities, or not basic or self-evident or determined by the Church. Anselm agrees with this in his writing.[24] And thus the answer to the fourth question is clear.

V.   What is heresy?

Now that we have seen what Catholic truth is, the next question related to this subject is: What is heresy or heretical falsehood? The answer is that heresy is false dogma, dogma contrary to the orthodox faith. Many have defined heresy in this fashion and therefore I do not want to give any other definition, as this one appears to be sufficient and good. No matter what other valid definition might be given, it would be consonant with this definition. For that heresy is false dogma is asserted by Jerome.[25]

Schism is also heretically perverted dogma, contrary to the orthodox faith. These definitions of heresy and schism make clear that errors in the fields of physics or geometry are not heretical errors. Against this definition it is argued thus: Many new heresies have arisen that have not yet begun to be false dogmas, contrary to the Catholic faith, and *this* definition would allow that there was at one time false teaching not contrary to Catholic faith but part of Catholic faith. Therefore, the given definition is not satisfactory. The premise that many new heresies arise is proved by the following evidence: "Pope Urban excommunicated Pelagius and Coelestius because they introduced a new law into the Church."[26] And Gratian said, "Every heretic either follows a heresy already damned or frames a new one."[27] Since, in fact, new heresies *are* framed, our premise holds.

VI.   Can new heresies and
new truths be established?

In order to solve this problem the following question can reasonably be asked. Is it the case that every assertion ought to be called heretical which in some way contradicts Holy Scripture, while every truth ought to be called Catholic which is consonant with Scripture or with assertions deducible from Scripture? Various opinions are held in regard to this question.

The Pope as Author of Truth

Some say that there are many assertions which contradict Scripture but which ought not to be numbered among the heresies because they have not been condemned by the pope. Not until such time as the pope condemns these assertions can they be considered heretical. In the same manner many truths consonant with Scripture ought not to be counted Catholic truths until they have been designated as such by the pope. This position is established by two arguments from tradition.

(1) The first is found in a decree from Pope Alexander where it is claimed that he asserted a new article of faith, "Christ is God and man."[28] They say further that before the time of Alexander it was permissible not to believe this.

(2) The second support is from a decree in which it is said that "from this time forward" it will be heretical to assert that the Apostles had either individual or communal possessions.[29] The inference is that up until this time the assertion was not heretical.

Once established from Tradition this position is confirmed by logical proofs.

(3) First: Many things have been asserted by theologians who were not called heretics so long as their assertion had not been condemned by the Church. However, after the assertions were condemned, the theologians were also condemned as heretical. In other words, such assertions merited the name of heresy only *after* they had been condemned. The premise is made obvious by the case of the Greeks who deny that the Holy Spirit proceeds from the Son. Before their position was condemned they were not reputed to be heretics; only after the condemnation of their position were they so labeled. Therefore our assumption holds. Likewise, those who upheld the position of Joachim, condemned by a general council, were regarded as heretics after the condemnation.[30]

(4) Secondly, it is argued thus: If we take the opposite position, that the pope cannot make the nonheretical to be heretical, it would

follow that papal definition or approval would be of no greater weight than the approval of any given doctor who makes his assertion from reason and tradition. But this conclusion is false since, assuming that the pope and the doctor have equal weight, the fact that the doctor has no authority to approve or condemn doctrine would imply that the pope likewise has no authority to approve or condemn doctrine. But obviously the pope does have this authority. Therefore the position which equates the weight of the doctor and the pope is untenable and the thesis that papal decisions establish new truths or new heresies is upheld.

The Pope as Interpreter of Truth

The opposing party holds that nothing related to our faith is dependent upon human will. Therefore, neither the pope nor even the whole Church can make a non-Catholic assertion Catholic; similarly they cannot make a false assertion true nor a nonheretical assertion heretical.

This position is proved as follows: No truth is Catholic unless it has been divinely revealed, included in Scripture, or has come to convince the Universal Church. It may be deduced from any one or several of these three, but none of these categories seems to be dependent on the approbation of the pope or of the Universal Church.

Second, this argument. If the basis for calling an assertion Catholic is that it has the approval of the pope, the approval might be of different kinds. It might be explicit and implicit, or it might be explicit only. Now if the first possibility is assumed, the popes cannot make the non-Catholic to be Catholic, since the popes have already assented to our whole faith. If the second possibility is assumed it would mean that assertions such as "Christ rose from the dead," and "Christ was God and man," and similar truths would not be reckoned as Catholic truths unless they had been approved explicitly by the pope. Now this conclusion seems inappropriate, therefore the original premise is established.

The latter position seems to be more probable, while the arguments for the former position lead to difficulties and seem to constrain the truth. But this is the time to answer these arguments and, in answering, we distinguish two ways of speaking about an article of faith.

One way of defining an article of faith is to say it is a Catholic truth quoted verbatim in an authoritative creed. We were not using this definition when we said that the pope cannot make a new article of faith. If we were to use this definition it is clear that he *can* make a new article, for it is possible to add any Catholic proposition to an authoritative creed where it does not now appear.

The second way in which an article of faith might be defined is as the sum total of all Catholic truth. It is this definition that is understood when we say that the pope cannot make a new article of faith. And, therefore, we refute the first argument from Tradition, namely the quotation from Alexander.

(1) Alexander did not make a new article of faith, but he established that no one is allowed to assert or suppose anything contrary to that which is already Catholic truth.[31] Indeed he established that such a person should be subject to excommunication.

(2) The pope, therefore, did not create any new Catholic truth, but by his approbation he defined some truths by declaring that they had always been Catholic truths, and condemned other assertions by declaring that they had always been heretical. Indeed he did not make a new article of faith, but he described in a new way the manner in which this article is now and always has been related to Catholic truth.

This should suffice to answer the two arguments from Tradition. Let us now turn to the logical proofs.

(3) First it should be noted that often heretics exist who, because they are heretics only in secret, should not be judged as heretics. And just as often a heretic may exist who voices his heresy time and again but even so it is not public knowledge that his assertion is, and always has been, heretical. Therefore, before the Church has fully discovered that his assertion is or always has been heretical, he ought not to be declared or condemned to be a heretic. When we say the Church must fully discover, we mean the general council or the pope. However, after the Church (thus defined) has fully discovered that his assertion is heretical, then if he is found to be persistent in his position, he ought to be condemned as a heretic.

The answer to the argument about the Greeks and Joachim should now be evident. Since the Church had not discovered that their assertions were heretical, there were no grounds for their condemnation as heretics. After the Church had made the discovery, there were grounds to condemn as heretics those who persisted in their position.

(4) As to the second argument in which it was inferred that the determination of the pope seemed to have no more weight than that of any doctor, the answer is that this conclusion is wrong. For although it devolves upon the pope to define authoritatively which assertions are heretical and which are Catholic, he cannot make the non-Catholic Catholic nor the nonheretical heretical. Nevertheless the definition or determination of the pope carries more weight than the determination of any doctor. The difference is that after a doctor has made a determination one is allowed to hold publicly the opposite of this determination or theological position. This is not permissible after a papal determination has been made. Thus after a papal determination, any bishop or inquisitor investigating a case of heresy is permitted to proceed according to canonical sanctions against those who oppose the determination. If, however, the latter present themselves to the pope to test the papal definition of error, the case should be put before a general council. After the determination of any doctor, this procedure is not followed. Hence it is clear that the determination of the pope does carry more weight than that of any doctor. Thus the second argument is answered and, furthermore, this completes our discussion of the sixth question.

VII.   How many categories of heresy are there?

It should be noted that opinions vary as much about heresy as they do about Catholic truth. Regarding Catholic truth some have said that only those truths are Catholic which are found explicitly or implicitly in Scripture. Others say there are many other Catholic truths beyond those found in the Canon. So also regarding heresies, there are diverse opinions.

Heresy Contra Scripture

Some say that the only propositions that are heretical are those which contradict Scripture. They distinguish three types of heresy.

1. First are those assertions which are not merely in some fashion at cross purposes with Scripture but are indeed verbal contradictions

of scriptural assertions. An example of this type would be: "The Word did not become flesh."

2. Second are those assertions which to all intelligent and enlightened people are clearly incompatible with that which is contained in Scripture. An example would be: "Christ was not born for our salvation."

3. Third are those assertions which are found to be in conflict with Scripture, but, in this case, the conflict may not be evident to everyone but only to those who are wise, steeped in Holy Scripture, and skilled in subtle considerations. An example of this type would be: "As far as His humanity is concerned Christ is not something."[32]

Heresy Contra Scripture and Tradition

Others posit five types of heresy or error, paralleling the five categories of Catholic truth.

1. The first type of heresy or error consists of those assertions which contradict things taught by Scripture only. This type includes several kinds of error, which should properly be called heresies.

2. The second type of error consists of those which in any manner contradict the teaching of the Apostles or of Scripture. This type can be divided into many kinds, just as the first.

3. The third type consists of those which in any way oppose anything revealed to or any inspiration of the Church in the post-Apostolic age.

4. The fourth type includes those which are contrary to chronicles or to the records of events or to apostolic histories.

5. The fifth type consists of those assertions which are shown to be incompatible with Holy Scripture, or with apostolic doctrine not found in Scripture, or with truths inspired by or revealed to the Church, together with other truths which one cannot rationally deny. The incompatibility need not be evident from the wording of the proposition.

An example of this type is the assertion, "The faith Augustine held was not true." Now it is granted that this assertion is not strictly and properly heresy, nevertheless it savors of manifest heresy. And from this kind of assertion, together with certain other half truths, manifest heresy clearly issues.

Thus it is clear that just as there are five categories of Catholic truth, so, according to the same pattern, there are five categories of heresy or error.

VIII.   Is every heresy condemned?

After the aforesaid, one may ask whether every heresy is condemned. The answer to this question is yes. Our first evidence comes from the General Council convoked by Innocent III, where it was said in the text dealing with excommunication, "We excommunicate and anathematize every heresy which flaunts the holy Catholic and orthodox faith."[33] Whence it follows that every heresy is condemned, just as every biblical truth is approved. Now it might be objected that in this chapter, only that heresy which flaunts the faith specifically set forth by the General Council is condemned.[34] It is answered that even if such were the case, the thesis can be established by the following argument: Since the entire Catholic faith has been approved in the aforesaid chapter,[35] every heresy has been damned and excommunicated by the General Council. The premise is proved by the following: The Council gave its express approval to the assertion that at the chosen time the Holy Trinity imparted saving doctrine to mankind through Moses and the prophets and other servants. Therefore, the doctrine which the Trinity now imparts to the faithful, whether through its servants or through itself, is saving doctrine. From this it follows that in the aforesaid chapter the whole Catholic faith is approved.[36]

Our second evidence comes from the gloss on canon law. "Every heretic has been excommunicated, however misled he may be."[37] From this it follows that every heresy has been condemned. No one is condemned, that is, excommunicated, as a heretic unless his heresy has been established first. Only learned writers sometimes make this distinction between a heresy which has been condemned and one which has not been condemned. Gratian, as earlier alleged, seemed to approve this distinction when he said, "Every heretic either follows a heresy already condemned or frames a new one."[38] In order to understand Gratian and others who made the same distinction it should be noted that some heresies are condemned explicitly and others are only condemned implicitly. Gratian and these others meant by heresies those explicitly condemned, so that what is *really* said is, "Every heretic either follows a heresy already explicitly condemned or else thinks up a new one." And by a new heresy he means one not explicitly condemned. And this is perfectly consonant with the fact that such a heresy is implicitly condemned.

IX. How many categories of
heresy are explicitly condemned?

Now the ninth question arises. What are the categories of heresy which have been explicitly condemned? The answer is that there are four categories of heresy explicitly condemned.

The first category consists of those that are condemned by a special condemnation which specifies the exact words of the heresy. The heresies of Arius, Macedonius, and many others are condemned in this way.[39]

The second category consists of those heresies which contain statements contrary to the exact words asserted and approved by all the faithful of sound mind. Such a one is: "God is not creator of all things visible and invisible."

The third category consists of those heresies which are verbatim contradictions of any volume, book, or treatise that has come to be regarded as equal in authority to canonical writing. All heresies which are verbatim contradictions of the biblical Canon ought to be counted as heresies and explicitly condemned.

The fourth category explicitly condemned consists of those assertions from which a heresy so obviously follows that it is clear even to laymen of sound mind. These are the four categories of heresy that are explicitly condemned.

Now it may be asked what heresies are implicitly condemned. To this it is answered that there exist heresies which do not fall under any of the indicated categories but which are discovered only after detailed investigation by men steeped in Holy Scripture. They can determine to what extent canonical truth is contradicted or to what extent the content of Scripture or the doctrine of the Universal Church is approved. Further they can show how less defined heresies follow from these heresies already explicitly condemned according to aforesaid categories. An example of such an implicit heresy was the questioning by the Greeks—before such a heresy was explicitly condemned by the Church—of the procession of the Holy Spirit from the Son.

X. What is a Catholic?

From the aforesaid it is evident what is Catholic truth, what indeed is heresy, and what are the categories of heresy. Nothing, however, has been said to determine what characterizes a heretic and what characterizes a Catholic. These issues should be clarified.

First, then, what characterizes a Catholic? To answer this we should note that the term "Catholic" can be defined in three ways.

One definition of a Catholic is anyone, properly baptized, who does not persist in anything contrary to the law of Christ. In this definition are included both adults, who believe in the Law of Christ, and infants, who, although baptized, no more adhere to the Law of Christ than do Mohammedans.

Another definition of a Catholic is every adult of sound mind who preserves and obeys the Catholic faith complete and uncorrupted. To preserve the Catholic faith uncorrupted means to believe without doubt all things which pertain explicitly or implicitly to the orthodox Catholic faith.

The meaning of implicit faith was clarified earlier and, as was stated before, he who holds all things contained in Scripture or taught by the Universal Church to be true and sane, and does not adhere stubbornly to anything contrary to Catholic truth, has a complete and uncorrupted faith and, according to this definition, ought to be counted as a Catholic.

When Catholic is understood in this sense, a man could be called a Catholic if he preserved the Catholic faith as previously described, even if he held the Law of Christ on rational grounds, yes, even when his very basis for adhering to the Law of Christ was suggestive arguments or indeed conclusive arguments.

The third way of defining a Catholic is one who preserves the Catholic faith as previously described and who accepts the Law of Christ, not on rational grounds but without rational proof. As we have said, the typical act of Catholic faith is an act caused by both a natural disposition and infused grace. Infused faith alone cannot cause this act without a natural disposition. Therefore, one is truly a Catholic who performs such acts as are typical of faith. And he who, on the basis of a natural disposition, together with infused faith, assents to this assertion, "the Law of Christ is true," or any equivalent assertion, and does not adhere stubbornly to anything contradictory, such a one is in the strict sense of the word a Catholic. With this distinction in mind it is clear what a Catholic is and in what ways a Catholic is defined.

XI.   What is a heretic?

There remains the task of clarifying what characterizes a heretic and whether the name heretic denotes one thing or several. To this question it is answered that the name heretic has several meanings.

The first way of understanding heretic is as one who has been excommunicated, as Pope Nicholas says.[40]

A second interpretation says that a heretic is a corrupter of sacred things. Thus one who commits simony is called a heretic in a certain gloss, where it says, "Whoever acquires ordination through money is elevated not so much to the rank of prelate as to that of heretic."[41]

The third way, much more exact, is to define heretics as those who reckon the Catholic faith to be false or contrived. Clearly, Jews and Saracens are heretics, but all doubters are also heretics, since actually they are unbelievers too.

The fourth way is to say heretics are those who now consider or have considered themselves to be Christians but who nonetheless hold stubbornly to views that are contrary to Catholic truth. "Who now consider or have considered" is included in this definition to account for those who were baptized by a rite which did not conform to the rite of the Church. They are not Christians, although they consider or have considered themselves Christians and yet continue to hold views contrary to Catholic truth. They should be punished differently from Saracens, although they are no less heretics than the Saracens.

The fifth way defines as heretics all who adhere stubbornly to any error which savors of heresy or of the perversions which accompany heresy. This way accords with the third and fourth ways because it includes as heretics Mohammedans and Jews as well as those properly baptized who err stubbornly against the faith. One might wish to consider the current definition which regards as a heretic him who has been convicted of heresy but will not recant and is, therefore, according to the usage of the Church, handed over to the secular court. When one refers in this fashion to a heretic one implies that the concept of heretic is limited to one who is baptized or conducts himself as if he has been baptized, but who stubbornly doubts or errs against the Christian faith. Jews and Mohammedans are excluded by the first part of the definition, as are those baptized in jest or baptized by a rite which does not conform to that approved by the Church. The second part of the definition includes those who imagine themselves baptized, and who live in Christian nations. The third part of the definition excludes those who, through lack of intelligence or ignorance but not through willfulness, doubt or err against the faith. It should now be clear that a heretic is one who, although informed of the truth, nevertheless persists in his doubt or error against the Catholic truth.

XII.   How can we define stubbornness?

We now go on to ask, "How can we define stubbornness?" To be stubborn is to persist in that which ought to be given up. That this definition is sound is confirmed thus: Perseverance and stubbornness are opposites: the persevering one persists in that which he ought not to give up; therefore, the stubborn one persists in an error which he ought to give up. Now if we ask when is the erring one required to give up his error, it is answered that the erring one, regardless of how long he errs against the faith, is not to be reckoned stubborn or as a heretic if he is always ready to stand corrected, and to give up his error when he has been corrected according to accepted standards. Now what is correction according to accepted standards? Only that correction satisfies the accepted standards which points out clearly to the erring one that his position obviates Catholic truth. For example, if anyone should say, out of ignorance, that there are two persons in Christ, it should be pointed out to him from the decree of the Synod of Ephesus that this has been defined as the heresy of Nestorius and has been damned by the Synod.[42] Therefore, he cannot deny that his position is contrary to Catholic truth. Such correction would be sufficient.

And thus, even though he might claim that it has not been clearly pointed out to him that his position obviates Catholic truth, if indeed it has been pointed out, he is forced to adhere to the judgment of the experts. For if the experts conclude that this had been sufficiently explained, he is, at that moment, immediately required to recant his position.

From these assertions follow certain corollaries.

First Corollary: Doctor Versus Bishop

The mere warning from a bishop or other special prelate is not sufficient to require as a condition for salvation that one immediately revoke his error. The meaning of this corollary is that one is not required, as a condition for salvation, to revoke error just because of a warning from his prelate, but only if it has been clearly pointed out to him by his prelate that the error obviates Catholic truth.

This corollary is proved thus. In the exposition of Scripture, doctors and teachers rank above prelates and those who possess jurisdictional powers. They rank above them in handing down all that pertains to the orthodox faith. Therefore, the doctors and teachers are not required by the mere warning of their prelates to recant their assertion even though they might be erroneous, unless it has been sufficiently pointed out to them that their error obviates Catholic truth. This conclusion is clear because he who has greater authority in a given field should in no wise be subject to one who has lesser authority in that field. The premise is proved by disproving its opposite: The theological experts are not required by the mere warning of a prelate to recant their positions, even though they may actually be erroneous, unless it has been sufficiently pointed out to them that their positions obviate Catholic truth. Since now the doctors are the theological experts, this very argument applies to them as it does to the untrained who rely on experts.

Secondly it is argued thus. Those who, with regard to Catholic truth, are not required to have blind faith in someone else need not recant their positions because of his mere warning. This follows because he who recants his erroneous position must hold firmly to the opposite position. Those who are subordinate are not required, as far as Catholic truth is concerned, to have blind faith in their prelates. Ergo, if it were otherwise, the faith of the subordinates would depend on human wisdom, for prelates can err just as much through their lack of information as through their stubbornness.

Thirdly it is argued by Peter, who says especially for prelates, "Sanctify Christ the Lord in your hearts and be prepared always to satisfy those who require a reason for the things that are in you,"[43] that is, for your faith. If, therefore, one is required to justify his faith to anyone who asks, those who are subordinate ought not to be required to recant their positions unless it has been pointed out to them that they obviate Catholic truth.

Second Corollary: Doctor Versus Pope

The mere warning of the pope is not sufficient to require anyone to recant his error. This is demonstrated by the fact that the pope is required to justify his faith in the same manner as other prelates, as the gloss says.[44] In all areas justification should be given if it is possible, because in questions of faith it is permissible to appeal from the pope and, furthermore, because our faith does not depend on the wisdom of the pope. Therefore, the corollary is clear.

Third Corollary: The Voice of Truth

Everyone legitimately reprimanded by his colleagues or by anyone else is required to relinquish his error immediately. It is proved thus. Our faith does not depend on the wisdom of men. If, therefore, one is required to relinquish error, once his prelate has pointed out that his position obviates orthodox faith, it follows that if anyone at all points out the error, he is required to relinquish it.

Fourth Corollary: Individual Conviction

He who finds out by himself without any warning that his error obviates Catholic truth is required to relinquish such error. This can be proved by the same argument which proved the third corollary. Moreover, it is proved by the example of Anselm who says, "I am certain that if I should say anything which contradicts Holy Scripture and which is false, I would not want to maintain it once I had discovered it."[45] Therefore the corollary is true. Its truth is further shown by the fact that there is no distinction made between reprimand given by a prelate or by one who is not a prelate with respect to relinquishing error. In either case the error ought to be relinquished if one has been properly reprimanded. In other respects, there *are* differences. The prelate can summon the erring one in order to display the truth to him; he can compel him to make public recantation, and, if he should be stubborn, he can punish him—none of which the layman can do.

XIII.   Is every doubter an unbeliever?

The text from canon law, "He who doubts the faith is an unbeliever," should be understood as follows: "He who doubts the faith," that is, who doubts the faith is true, "is an unbeliever,"[46] that is, has a weak faith. For the faithful ought to believe firmly the whole Catholic truth and, furthermore, must adhere firmly—that is, with steadfast faith—to any article in particular which is implicit. It is not required however, that everyone adhere to any particular Catholic truth explicitly. But he who doubts that the whole Christian faith is true is manifestly heretical and should be judged stubborn since he is not ready to be corrected, for no one is ready to be corrected by a doctrine which he believes to be false. That is to say, if someone doubts an axiom to an argument because he doubts one of the conclusions which he draws from the axiom, there is no reason to expect that one can ever convince him of the validity of the conclusions. But if one doubts only the conclusions, then we can expect that he can be led to accept them by reasoning from the axiom. Now, the axiom one should faithfully believe is that the Christian faith is true.

XIV.   What is the strongest reason for concluding
that one is required to know
particular articles of faith?

From all we have said above it is evident that any Catholic of sound mind is required to know certain particular articles of faith in addition to the axiom, "The Christian faith is true." Therefore, it might be asked what is the strongest reason for concluding that any believer, as for example Socrates, is required to know one particular article rather than another, for example that the Holy Spirit proceeds from the Father and the Son.

To this question it is answered that the strongest reason for this conclusion is that such an article or such a truth is held to be Catholic by all the believers and Catholics with whom Socrates lives. Furthermore, such a truth is promulgated and preached publicly and frequently by preachers of the Word of God. Finally, a truth should be believed because it can be clearly deduced by enlightened Catholics from another truth which has been promulgated as Catholic in the aforesaid manner.

Whence it follows that there are many Catholic truths which no Catholic is required to believe explicitly even though believers of straighter mind are required to give explicit assent if these truths have been sufficiently promulgated and taught among all Catholics and believers.

A possible objection to this is that it would follow that those who preach the Word of God or teach Catholic truths bind the faithful to assent explicitly to certain truths. This seems untenable because before the proclamation of such truths the faithful were not required to give explicit assent to them, while after the proclamation of these truths the faithful were required to give faithful and explicit assent to them.

To this objection it may be answered that the preachers of the Word of God and teachers of Catholic truths do not bind Christians to believe these articles explicitly. God himself binds them to believe these articles explicitly through the agency of those who proclaim and preach. The answer to this question is evident, and this completes the discussion of the content of faith.

Notes

1. Luke 10:27.
2. The word "pilgrim" is used to translate the Latin *viator*, that is, the man who has not yet completed his journey either to the new Jerusalem or to eternal damnation. Cf. *Harvest*, pp. 47, 48.
3. The Latin text as given by Du

Pin, ed. *cit.*, vol. I, is unclear at this point.

4. The subtitles introduced within the answers to the questions are not in the Latin text but are added to clarify the discussion. For the two traditions see *Harvest*, pp. 365–408.

5. Proverbs 30:6.

6. *CIC*, vol. I, col. 17.

7. *CIC*, vol. I. col. 18.

8. Brevicoxa refers to the prologue to the third book of St. Augustine's *De Trinitate*, *PL*, vol. XLII, and to quotations of Augustine in canon law, *CIC*, vol. I, col. 17, chapters beginning "Noli meis" and "Negare."

9. This quotation has not been found.

10. *Comm. in Evang. Matth.*, Bk IV, c. 24 (*PL* XXVI. 180).

11. *CIC*, vol. II, col. 637.

12. *CIC*, vol. I, col. 6.

13. Brevicoxa refers to the chapter beginning "Praeceptis," *CIC*, vol. I, col. 27.

14. Matthew 28:20.

15. The Latin text reads "revelation," but it seems probable that this represents a misreading of "relation." Gerson stating the same category of truth speaks of relation, Du Pin, ed. *cit.*, vol. I, col. 22.

16. *CIC*, vol. I, col. 17, chapter beginning "Omnes."

17. For a discussion of Mariology in this period see *Harvest*, pp. 286 ff.

18. Brevicoxa refers to the chapters of canon law beginning "Noli" and "Negare," *CIC*, vol. I, col. 17.

19. I Timothy 3:2.

20. *CIC*, vol. I, col. 95.

21. *CIC*, vol. I, col. 17.

22. *CIC*, vol. I, col. 36, 37.

23. *Ibid.*

24. Brevicoxa refers to Anselm, *Cur Deus Homo*, in *PL*, vol. CLVIII, col. 359–432, now available in the critical edition of F. S. Schmitt, O.S.B., *Sancti Anselmi Cantuariensis Archiepiscopi Opera Omnia*, Mainz, 1955, vol. II, pp. 42–133.

25. *CIC*, vol. I, Col. 997.

26. *CIC*, vol. I, col. 1000.

27. *CIC*, vol. I, col. 996.

28. *CIC*, vol. II, col. 779.

29. Brevicoxa attributes the decree to Innocent, but it comes from John XXII, *CIC*, vol. II, col. 1229, 1230.

30. *CIC*, vol. II, col. 6.

31. *CIC*, vol. II, col. 779. Cf. note 28.

32. Cf. *CIC*, vol. II, col. 779. The text in Du Pin is not clear at this point.

33. *CIC*, vol. II, col. 787.

34. Brevicoxa refers to the chapter beginning "Firmiter," *CIC*, vol. II, col. 1–6.

35. *Ibid.*

36. Brevicoxa refers to the same decree "Firmiter" (see note 30).

37. Brevicoxa refers to *CIC*, vol. I, col. 1358, c. 24, question 3, 1. Actually, the quotation comes from c. 24, question 1, 1.

38. *CIC*, vol. I, col. 966.

39. Brevicoxa refers to the following passages from canon law: chapter beginning "Canones," *CIC*, vol. I, col. 34, 35; chapter beginning "Sicut sancti," *ibid*, col. 35, 36; chapter beginning "Sancta Romana," *ibid.*, col. 36–41.

40. *CIC*, vol. I, col. 537.

41. *CIC*, vol. I, col. 358.

42. Cf. *Enchiridion Symbolorum*, 32d
ed. Ed. H. Denzinger, A. Schönmetzer, Freiburg i. Br., 1963, no.
113, 252.

43. I Peter 3:15.

44. *CIC*, vol. II, col. 18.

45. *Cur Deus Homo*, Bk. I, ch. 18,
in *PL*, vol. CLVIII, col. 308, or
in Schmitt, ed. *cit.*, p. 58.

46. Brevicoxa refers to the chapter beginning "Dubius," *CIC*, vol. II,
col. 778.

JACOB HOECK

Excerpt from a Letter of
Jacob Hoeck to Wessel Gansfort[1]

Jacob Hoeck, Dean of Naaldwijk, sends greetings to Master Wessel.

Be assured, most worthy Wessel, that for a long time I have been no less desirous to write to you than you have been to receive a letter from me. But I either had no messenger, or—as happened more often—I was so occupied with the bustle of affairs that I had neither a free moment in which to turn to your writings nor an opportunity to ponder the issues they raised. In fact, it is because of my warm heart, my inability to say no to requests, that I fall into these traps. But now, having obtained a good messenger to carry my letters, I have snatched enough time from sleep to set down my thoughts concerning you and your propositions, albeit only in a rough and disorderly fashion.

First of all, I want you to know that my high regard for you has proved to be justified, inasmuch as from personal experience with you and from your writings I have found you to be even greater than I had been led to believe from many people, some of them quite important. From your letters, however, I infer that you have one characteristic which, in my opinion, is extremely unbecoming to a great man. It is that you pride yourself on your obstinacy and want others to find in your writings some measure of distinctiveness so that in the judgment of many persons you are rightly called "The Master of Contradiction." And without doubt this distinctiveness, coming from such a learned man, offends many people. I frankly admit that I am averse to contradiction, since I am not accustomed, except for the most important reasons, to deviate from the joint witness of the earlier Fathers—I defend them rather than attack them. You remember, doubtless, that our great Buridanus held the same position, for in the Preface to his *Ethics* he says that he has been misled quite often by the bright ideas of modern doctors but never by the teachings of the early Fathers.[2]

On the subject of indulgences, I cannot but differ with you, but I do not intend to oppose you with arguments. For, I ask, what hope can I have of subduing with arguments that hard, unconquerable, undaunted head of yours, which yields neither to the hammer of common belief nor to the sword of the authority of the early Fathers. I shall merely set forth my own considered opinion in a few words.

It is true that no explicit statement concerning indulgences can be drawn from Sacred Scripture and that nothing concerning them was written by the early doctors, although it may be said, though I have not read it anywhere, that Gregory established septennial indulgences in connection with the Roman stations. Nevertheless, I dare not, and I ought not, on this account share your opinion that the prelates who practice and observe this custom err. And indeed, to be quite frank, I was so thunderstruck by this unheard-of position that I at first held back from writing you, although I never gave up hope that you had declared this view more for the sake of discussing and investigating the truth than as a positive assertion. You should not be led to base your position on the fact that nothing is to be found concerning indulgences in Sacred Scripture or in the explicit teaching of the Apostles, since you acknowledge many things which one is required under penalty of hell to believe no less than those things contained in this rule of faith. For the Evangelist says, "Jesus did many things which are not written in this book,"[3] such as the statement, to mention only one example, that Peter was at Rome.

I have no doubt that you believe that sacramental confession is necessary to salvation. Yet, I do not know whether you would really be able to establish it on grounds of the rule of faith. I know that many doctors have tried hard to do this, but whether they properly established their point so as to convince a stiff-necked man I leave to you to judge. I have seen no one that satisfied me on this point, except Scotus. Still I should not be unwilling to say (and some persons are of this opinion) that although the obligation of sacramental confession was not mentioned in the books of the Evangelists, the Apostles heard it from Christ, and that it has come down to us from the Apostles by the authority of the Church. How much one is dependent on the authority of the Church you can see for yourself. Some would like to make that same kind of statement about our indulgences. You see to what kind of argument this leads. As for myself, on this point at any rate, as the basis and foundation of our knowledge, I disagree from my heart, firmly believing and asserting that the pope can decree not only one hour, but many years of indulgences, and even plenary indulgence.

Yet you do not think me such a fool that I would agree with all those who think that whatever the pope decrees regarding indulgences would hold true even if he should be mad. What has been decreed by the pope should stand only if the key does not err and if Christ does not reject it. There comes to my mind the statement of a man of amazing restraint and great knowledge, our Master Thomas de Cursellis (whom you, I believe, knew better at Paris as the Dean of Notre Dame). To certain persons in the Council of Basel, who were unduly extending the pope's authority, he is reported to have said, "Christ declared to Peter, 'Whatever you bind on earth is bound in heaven,' but not 'Whatever you say is bound.' "[4]

Perhaps you will say that a statement does not suffice unless one adds the reason for it. Really, my dear Wessel, you ought to regard as a strong reason—nay as stronger than any reason—the authority, not only of the pope, but also of all the prelates and doctors who either grant indulgences of all kinds or write and teach that they ought to be granted. You recall the words of Augustine, "I would not believe the Gospel, if the authority of the Church had not compelled me to do so."[5] Do not many of the chapters in canon law approved by the Church also speak of indulgences? Does not the venerable Gerson seem to be of the same opinion when he says that the granting of indulgences ought not to be lightly esteemed, but rather ought to be devoutly considered in the faith, hope, and love of Christ, who gave such power to men? "For," to continue in his own words, "it is certain that, other things being equal, work that is based on such incentives is more fruitful and acceptable than any that is not. Therefore," he himself adds, "it is sound and sober wisdom for a pious man to desire to secure such indulgences, without entering into any inquisitive discussion of their precise and sure value."[6]

This same Gerson in the beginning of his treatise on indulgences, toward the end of which the aforesaid words occur, seems to be willing to base and establish pontifical authority of this sort on the Sacred Gospel. For, after citing the verse from Matthew 18:18, "Whatever you bind etc.," together with several other passages of the Sacred Gospel, he says, "Finally all power of conferring indulgences is based upon the foregoing."[7] And although this doctor of ours believes (and in my opinion rightly) that no mere man, nor even the whole Church, can establish laws that force men into mortal sin, nevertheless he opposes your position when he interprets that statement of Christ, "Whatever you bind etc.," as applying not just to sins but also to punishments. In company with these men I declare and teach the above as the truth. And so, on this subject, as the chief point of our contention you have now learned my stand, which—taking into consideration the character of my authorities—certainly has some value.

For my position in regard to indulgences is as follows: In sacramental confession, which sometimes makes the attrite person contrite, the everlasting punishment that is due for mortal sin is changed to temporal punishment. Until this temporal punishment is computed and imposed by the priest, I consider it to be before the bar of God, and not before that of the pope. But when punishment is actually imposed, and the penitent, by virtue of the keys, is obliged to it, then I consider the case to be before the bar of the Church. The Church has authority over it, not because the decision lies with the pope, so that whatever he decrees in such cases holds at the bar of God by his having so willed it, not because the pope can remit the punishment according to his will and pleasure, but because he can render satisfaction for such a person out of the treasure of the Church, and can substitute the merits of the saints and especially of Christ's suffering for such punishments. And this assertion of mine is not proved false by your propositions, which were handed to me by my teacher, Engelbert of Leiden. For in these you seem to use the words "participation in the treasure" very differently from the doctors of the Church in general, with the result that you take issue with them, not as to the fact but merely as to the words. Everyone concedes with you that the pope cannot bestow grace upon anyone, nor even decide whether he or anyone else is in grace. Much less can he command that anyone should be in grace. But that your interpretation can be drawn from these concessions, I confess I do not see. For the only inference to be made from them is that the pope can neither qualify a man for indulgences, nor can he with certitude decide that he is qualified. This again everyone affirms with you. Nevertheless, all these premises or antecedents of yours actually lead, not to the conclusion you deduce from them but to its opposite, namely, that the pope *can* confer an indulgence in the aforesaid manner to everyone who is truly contrite and has confessed and fulfilled the required conditions, or that, if the pope so decides it, he can even confer a plenary indulgence, so that such persons when they die will escape immediately to the Kingdom ...

God has not given me the leisure that he has given to Wessel. Nevertheless, I shall not postpone writing hereafter . . . Meanwhile, my dearest Master: Farewell.

Truly, your Dean, as you fully deserve.

Naaldwijk, the ninth day before the calends of August. [1489?][8]

Notes

1. The translation which follows is a partial revision of that which appears in *Wessel Gansfort,* by Jared W. Scudder and Edward W. Miller, New York, 1917, vol. I, pp. 276–283.

2. John Buridanus was teacher of the nominalist school at the University of Paris in the mid-fourteenth century. He defended the proof for the existence of God which depends on the principle of causality against attack by Occam and his school. He was also interested in physics and is considered to have made important contributions to the modern theory of mechanics.

For further information see *Die Religion in Geschichte und Gegenwart,* 3rd ed., Tübingen, I, 1529, 1530.

3. John 21:25.

4. Not located.

5. Augustine, *Contra Epistolam Manichaei,* Bk. 1, 5, in *CSEL,* vol. XXV, 197. For further discussion of this passage see *Harvest,* p. 370.

6. Gerson, "Opusculum de Indulgentiis," in *Opera Omnia,* ed. L. E. Du Pin, Antwerpiae, 1706, vol. II, col. 515, 516.

7. *Ibid.*

8. Although no conclusive proof can be given, Maarten van Rhijn is in

clined to date Wessel's answer
shortly before the latter's death.
Wessel Gansfort, *op. cit.,* p. 153.
For data on Hoeck's teacher, En-
gelbert of Leiden, see Maarten van
Rhijn, *Studiën over Wessel, op.*

cit., pp. 127–134. It is this same
Engelbert with whom Erasmus
sought to correspond and to whom
the young Erasmus dedicated some
poems and three Elegia; see Allen,
op. cit., I, 160.

WESSEL GANSFORT

From the Letter in Reply
to Hoeck by Wessel Gansfort

Chapter I

I do not deny your claim that many find my distinctiveness to be
offensive. But as early as thirty-three years ago this same issue which
I raised among Parisian doctors deeply offended me. Even then I was
by no means driven by a wish to be noticed but, I believe, out of sheer
commitment to truth. For from boyhood it seemed absurd and un-
befitting to believe that the mere appearance and intervention of a
human decree could change the value of an act good in God's eyes,
that is, to make what is worth four merits be worth eight merits.

You admit that for most important reasons you sometimes deviate
from the joint witness of the early Fathers. Now then, do you regard
as trifling and worthless those reasons that caused the Fathers before
Thomas and Albert, as they themselves testify in their writings, to
forsake the proponents of the new doctrine of indulgences? For they
label the new doctrine nothing other than a "pious fraud or an innocent guile," which served to draw the people toward piety by employing an error. Therefore, at that time not everyone believed in
indulgences nor were those who sought after the truth with genuine
concern heretical. It certainly seemed to me that for not inconsiderable
reasons they dissociated themselves from the unproven position of the
popes on the grounds of compelling loyalty to the undoubtable authority of Scripture. Let me speak more openly: as long as it seems to
me that the pope or theologians or any school assert a position con-
tradicting the truth of Scripture, my concern for scriptural truth

obliges me to give it first place, and after that I am bound to examine the evidence on both sides of the question, since it is unlikely that the majority would err. But in every case I owe more respect to canonical Scripture than to human assertions, regardless of who holds them.

It is not necessary to recall how great are the errors concerning indulgences which the Roman curia has conjured up and propagated like a plague. Today these errors would be spreading their poisons still farther were they not opposed by the wholesome strictness of a few real theologians. You yourself are a witness and attestor to this practice, which you saw in Paris and practiced and established after your return home. You know that a true piety built on a firm rock was the concern motivating your opponents. You know to what degrees we owe respect to ecclesiastical authority and to the Catholic faith. In your position you have introduced an almost totally new distinction.

Chapter II

You cite Buridanus as a witness of some weight to the truth in order to strengthen the patristic support for your position. It is not merely fit but it is even generous of you to give me the freedom, yes the incentive, to follow such a man as he who speaks favorably and rightly for the Fathers and especially for the earlier Fathers whose worth has been better tested and recommended than that of the more recent writers. For when he says that he was sometimes misled by the traditions of the Fathers, he does not thereby stigmatize Albert, Thomas, or Scotus, or anyone adhering to realist or formalist positions regarding universals, does he? He considers all these men to be recent, in fact almost contemporaries. This can easily be seen throughout his clear arguments, for whenever a problem arises he analyzes it not according to the position of realist or formalist schools but rather in accordance with the nominalists. Therefore the Fathers, who, as he said, never led him astray, must be others than those.[1]

Regarding indulgences you cannot help but differ with me, nor do you intend to oppose me with arguments because you have given up hope of penetrating my hard head, which can be softened neither by the hammer of the common belief nor by the sword of patristic au-

thority. How can you say, my good man, that you will not attack
arguments, as if my position depended not on faith but on reason?

I have already touched briefly the question of patristic authority and
will do so even more at a more opportune time. But I see that the
question of "common belief" must be discussed at somewhat greater
length. Specifically it is necessary to investigate this point with reference to your assertion regarding "the whole school," and especially
the "whole Christian religion." Now even you admit in the following
section that no individual can judge with certainty. Nor are you so
foolish as the many who consent without a doubt to anything approved by the pope in matters of faith, even if he be mad. You agree
that such assertions are firmly based only when the key does not err
and Christ does not reject it. As if the ministry of perfect love spread
abroad in the hearts of the faithful by the Holy Spirit, which Augustine calls the only key of the kingdom, could possibly err or as if the
ministry of such a key would ever be rejected by Christ.

Chapter III

You quote the venerable Gerson, who is worthy of quotation and
examination where he strongly condemns the many abuses of indulgences. First of all, he ascribes indulgences in principle more to the
power of the office than to the power of jurisdiction, which former,
he says, is "more prominent, useful, and desirable for dealing with
indulgences."[2] Now if this statement by the respected Gerson is interpreted very literally, does not the status of every indulgence and every
assertion in defense of it come into question immediately? For what
Gerson says is that the ministry of office of the simple pastor or priest
worthily administering the sacraments is "more desirable, useful, and
prominent," that is to say, comes closer to plenary remission than all
the plenitude of papal jurisdiction.

Furthermore, Gerson admits that different men teach different
things concerning indulgences. Therefore, no one unconfused doctrine
can be taught. And indeed, confused belief is not Catholic belief,
rather it is greatly sectarian because everyone follows his own light.
If you examine attentively these brief comments by Gerson you will
observe that the pope can do nothing except by papal jurisdiction itself

or by clerical order or by filial adoption[3]—these three kinds of power exist in the Church. The third is the special possession of the children of adoption and the other two are given for their sake. Those who have authority of office, be they priest or bishop, do indeed provide a ministry according to Ambrose, but they exercise no jurisdictional power.[4] If, therefore, the pope, by reason of the authority of his office, has any power, he has it through jurisdiction. And, Gerson says, the pope cannot with his power directly and principally remit any punishment except that which he is able to impose, such as excommunication, suspension, etc.[5]

Furthermore, this same doctor holds that only the highest pontiff, Christ (thereby excluding the Roman pope), together with the Father and the Holy Spirit can by full authority grant every kind of indulgence from sin and guilt. And when He confers such indulgences He at the same time grants innumerable days and infinite years of indulgences.[6] Although the last phrase appears to have been added for no special reason, when you consider seriously you find there the error of plenary remission, because Gerson speaks as if the pope had no such immense plenitude of power.

The venerable man seriously attacks the fundamental intention of indulgences when he says, and says rightly, that in the justification of the sinner grace is infused before guilt is forgiven and the sinful state is forgiven before the guilt is forgiven. Guilt cannot be forgiven before grace is infused because the privation in man can be met only by the establishment of a habit that is infused by the Holy Spirit. The sinful state is forgiven before guilt is forgiven because the law punishes only sin. Once the sin has been wiped out the punishment is terminated. When the guilt has been truly forgiven, nothing remains of the sinful state, for there is no other basis for the sinful state than guilt and sin; therefore, it stands or falls with these.[7]

Even further this same venerable Gerson expressly disapproves those indulgences given for a number of years which are found in so many of the concessions of the various popes. He calls them an enormity.[8] Therefore he censures the pope for error when he refers to the dishonesty of the indulgence treasurers and when he asserts that indulgences can only be said with some hesitance to save, since the indulgence which seeks to cover more than the penitential obligation is of no effect. And holding to the basic principle that no one can remit any punishment except that which he is able to impose, he adds, in order to complete the argument, that no minister of the Church can bind one to anything more than temporal punishment.[9]

Thus the venerable theologian concludes that the pope should limit the scope of his indulgences so that he might not detract simultaneously from divine justice and mercy.[10] If this warning is sound—and certainly it is—let it be a warning, for neither is the following of the warning impossible nor the rejection of it inevitable, such requirements not being part of a warning. The pope therefore can detract from divine justice and divine mercy by his indulgences, but this is possible only if he places himself above divine wisdom. In so doing he would, by his own stupidity and error, cause a stumbling block for the weak...

Chapter VI

You admit that neither in the Fathers nor in Scripture is there anything written about indulgences. If you mean that these sources do not justify the present expression and usage of indulgences in the Church, then I heartily agree. But I thoroughly disagree if you mean that these writings contain nothing at all either for or against indulgences. In my opinion it was not the first Pope, Peter, but the Holy Spirit through Peter who issued the one and only permanent bull of indulgence. Peter testifies that this bull is permanent because it provides ample entrance into the kingdom of God and of our Savior Jesus Christ. And Peter further testifies that the bull is the only one and adds, "Whoever lacks these things [the ten things enumerated in II Peter 1] is blind and feeling his way by hand and has forgotten that he was cleansed from his old sins." Therefore no other bull is to be received or authorized which does not include this. Every other bull is superfluous and, therefore, Scripture does speak about indulgences, because it refers to ample entrance into the kingdom. But is ample entrance into the kingdom anything else than plenary remission of punishment and guilt? Furthermore, are blindness and trembling hands anything else than exclusion from the kingdom? This now, in my opinion at least, is the one and only permanent bull of indulgence issued by the Apostle Peter. Therefore Scripture does discuss indulgences, although not in the manner customary for people today.

That "the earlier doctors wrote nothing explicit about indulgences" is because this abuse had not yet insinuated itself at the time of Augustine, Ambrose, Jerome, and Gregory. You say, "Although it may be said [while admitting that you have never read it anywhere] that Gregory the Great established septennial indulgences in connection with the Roman stations,"[11] and, on this account, say that you dare not, indeed you ought not, reject indulgences as I do. On what account? Because it is generally known? Because you have never read it anywhere? You seem to think that I have raised two issues, one as an argument which is used to support the other, the rejection of indulgences. It would, however, be highly erroneous if the supporting argument for the rejection of indulgences were accepted on account of its being generally known. Or is the reason for your unwillingness to join me in rejecting indulgences this—that you have never read it anywhere? But I do not reject this position or any other position because I have never read anywhere that Gregory the Great established septennial indulgences in connection with the Roman stations . . .

You add this assertion: "And indeed to be quite frank, I was so thunderstruck by the unheard-of position that I at first held back from writing to you." What is this truth that so great a man as yourself has never heard of? And how could it horrify you if it were true? I beg of you, if you are really not hiding anything from me, then do not hide this truth from me so that I might hear and learn the unheard-of truth from you. At all events do not stop writing me about this. For I truly declare to you that I undertake this correspondence in order that I might search for the truth. I have undertaken this venture willingly, hoping to be instructed or strengthened in the truth by you or others like you, men of good will rather than pugnacious debaters. Since boyhood I have sought this truth above all things and now more than ever I seek it because only via truth does one come to life. I shall rejoice more, or at least not less, at being defeated rather than victorious, since I desire growth for myself more than for anyone else, or so I should.

Hence it surprises me not a little when you, a man of wisdom, judge me to be one who would make unfounded, glib assertions, as, for example, when you regard my position toward indulgences to be based solely on the fact that Scripture contains nothing on the subject. I know very well that Scripture alone is not a sufficient rule of faith. I know that some things which were not written were handed down by the Apostles and that all these teachings ought to be received into the rule of faith just like Scripture. These two things, together with what can logically be deduced from them, constitute the only rule of faith and this is the only rule of faith to which I hold so strictly that I believe that no one can deviate from it without destroying his salvation. Beyond these there are many other things which on account of the piety they obviously foster ought to be believed and not rejected. The traditional position of the Church regarding sacramental confession is quite acceptable to me because it is confirmed by some general statements of John and by some more specific words of James. I agree, therefore, that regarding this rule of faith I ought to depend on the authority of the Church *with* which—not *in* which—I believe. I believe *in* the Holy Spirit who applies and preserves the rule of faith speaking through Apostles and prophets. I believe *with* the Holy Church, I believe *according* to the teachings of the Holy Church, but I do not believe *in* the Church, because believing is an act of worship, a sacrifice of theological virtue which ought to be offered to God alone.

Chapter VII

Pursuing your point you add that some of us wish to claim that indulgences are approved by the rule of faith. Who are these? Do not tell me you mean Antoninus, Bishop of Florence, who in his day was endowed with such a remarkably good reputation that many statues adorn the tomb where he rests, and who labeled heresy anything which opposed indulgences![12] Is Gerson to be labeled a heretic because he criticized the contemporary developments regarding indulgences with such serious and basic arguments? I see where the argument is leading. If what they say (that indulgences are approved by the rule of faith) were true, everyone who contradicted them would contradict the rule of faith, and, because they attack that which the Apostles handed down, would be heretics if they persisted stubbornly in their position. But where will these doctors find support for their position, or, to put it bluntly, their lie, their error? Was it handed down by the Gospel or apostolic Tradition? Is their position buttressed by the fact that the use of indulgences has been observed without interruption since apostolic times? That most industrious man, the aforementioned historian Antoninus, who has strong vested interests in favor of indulgences, admits that he has not yet discovered when they began and he assumes that some stronger evidence is needed to prove his point to the lawyers and canonists when he himself, a doctor of theology and a bishop, claims that the John who is always linked with Andrew left behind some writings about indulgences. These, he claims, were referred to by some other doctors and were first instituted by Boniface VIII on the advice of the cardinals.[13] A worthy authority, indeed, when confirmation comes from a man of such great sanctity! Boniface accomplished three feats: He persuaded Celestine to give up the apostolate, he asserted the papal lordship over all, and he established indulgences. He began like a fox, reigned like a lion, and died like a dog. Furthermore Antoninus says that Boniface claimed that plenary indulgences would continue to be valid from century to century and that he required visitation at only three churches, the Lateran, St. Peter's, and St. Mary Major.[14] This he did about the year 1300. This being the case, where and why did the apostolic teaching sleep for 1300 years if indulgences are so apostolic that they ought to belong integrally to the rule of faith in its most strictly delimited form? I do not think something determined by Boniface VIII or after him by Clement or Gregory should be said to be a part of the rule of faith. But Gerson has discussed this thoroughly. Even most revered Antoninus admits that the many bulls of Clement contain so much material divergent from the Catholic tradition that he does not believe them to have been officially authorized.[15] However, these bulls kept in the collection of privileges in Vienna, Limoges, and Poitiers today have official seals.

Furthermore you say that you disagree with me from your heart on this subject, the foundation or basis of the issue we discuss. What is so firm about this foundation or basis? Does the history of indulgences begin with the teaching of the Apostles of Christ and continue via the observation by the Fathers until the teaching finally reaches us? Since this was the immediately preceding statement I suspect that this is the foundation or basis which underlies your heartfelt opposition to me. If you have any other foundation or basis which leads you to believe steadfastly and to assert that the pope can decree plenary indulgences, point it out to me.

Chapter VIII

You steadfastly believe that you are not so foolish as to agree with the position held by many that whatever the pope determines regarding indulgences is soundly based. You believe firmly and assert that the pope can decree plenary indulgences, but the many who hold that whatever the pope determines is firmly based are, in your judgment, foolish. Both these assertions are yours. You believe in an indulgence decreed by the pope and at the same time you are not so foolish as to believe everything the pope decrees unless perhaps you refer to matters unrelated to indulgences. I do not see how such hesitating statements could be reconciled. You know our nominalist schooling forbids such sloppy and inconsistent use of words. If, therefore, you are not foolish enough to agree with all who hold that whatever the pope determines regarding indulgences is soundly based, you should not be so foolish as to think that a papal decree of plenary indulgence is soundly based.

And it seems to me that there must be some purpose in adding "even if the pope be mad" because otherwise these words would be pointless. If then, I think, you do add this purposefully, of course you agree with me that the pope can be mad when he decrees indulgences. But if he be mad with regard to such things as indulgences, then he is deviating from the rule of faith on account of ignorance, perfidy, or malevolence. And any indulgences resulting from such a worthless and untrustworthy issuance would suggest that the issuer is mad. Cautious to hedge your position with conditions and thus make it impregnable, you assert that the position established by the pope regarding indulgences is soundly based only if "the key does not err and if Christ does not reject it." Now what does this necessary condition mean "if the key does not err"? What is this key to the kingdom of heaven and what would be its error? You speak of a key that can err but at the same time can justly and effectively open the door to the kingdom, to the very kingdom of heaven. O terrible kingdom, past whose doors, bars, bolts, and keys error can steal!

The key which Augustine described is the love spread abroad in the hearts of the children of the kingdom by the Holy Spirit.[16] The Lord Jesus promised two keys to Peter before the resurrection when He said, "I will give you the keys of the kingdom of heaven," and, "whatever you bind on earth shall be bound in heaven and whatever you loose on earth shall be loosed in heaven."[17] After the resurrection He gave these keys not to one Apostle but to them all together when He breathed on them saying, "Receive the Holy Spirit. If you forgive the sins of any they are forgiven, if you retain the sins of any they are retained."[18]

According to Augustine's position it is absolutely impossible that these keys could in any fashion be rejected by Christ or subject to error. For Augustine understands the keys first of all to be the love spread abroad in the children of the kingdom, and secondly to be the Holy Spirit itself; to loose means to accept into fellowship with love, while to bind means to exclude from the fellowship apart from love. Since, therefore, the power to receive into fellowship depends more on the possession of love than on the possession of authority, no holy believer, regardless of sex or situation, is prohibited from loosing and binding, and Christ never rejects this binding since it is never subject to error.

But if you mean that the key errs when those to whom the key has been committed err, I am not about to battle over words because I adhere unwaveringly to Augustine's position, which is reliable because it has no such ambiguities. Indeed I yield completely to your position if it be admitted that the holy Pope Peter erred. From this precedent the Church of subsequent ages knew that it was not bound by the determinations of the pope but that in disagreements about the faith every believer is bound, as the example of St. Paul demonstrates, to defend the rule of faith by withstanding the pope privately or if necessary publicly. . . .

You lead on to Thomas de Cursellis, who insists that when it was said to Peter "whatever you bind" it was not said "whatever you say." Now this position is good as far as it goes, but this is not all that needs to be said. In order that Christ's word might become clear and certain it is necessary to say how and by what means Peter could loose and bind. Therefore, I shall state my understanding of this word of Christ. If a minister, following the teaching of Christ and the Gospel, administers the word of faith or the sacrament of faith, or the example of charity, his flock or his listeners should faithfully accept the fact that this minister of truth and piety does in truth loose and bind on earth what is loosed and bound in heaven. But his work is of no effect who looses or binds any other way, for nothing more was promised to Peter and his successors than a ministry of salvation. I shall continue to hold this position until you or others teach me better.

Your warning that the authority of the pope should mean more to me than reason is distasteful to me. Did the theological faculty pay more heed to the authority of Clement, where it conflicted with reason, when they criticized and rebuked him, first for his presumption in teaching the angels in heaven; second for his granting to crusaders the right to designate four to be released out of purgatory; and for his published indulgences canceling both punishment and guilt?[19] Nevertheless, officially sealed bulls containing such errors are still found today. You warn me that in these matters the authority of the pope should not merely take the place of reason but should be above it. But what is that "reason" of mine, if not Scripture? The will of the pope and the authority of Scripture have not been established on an equal footing so that the will of the pope is to be measured by the truth of Scripture and vice versa.

And, as if the authority of the pope were too weak a foundation, you add the authority of prelates and, lest still something else be lacking, you add the authority of the doctors. Your dependence on the authority of the prelates only begs the question. And not all doctors favor indulgences unless these further piety. Some who hold this position speak in understatements, since, although like you they do not regard with favor many aspects of the Church and abuse in the Church, they say that the granting of indulgences is no small issue but should be seriously considered in the light of the faith, hope, and love of Christ. Nor do I esteem them a small issue when I, devoutly in the faith, hope, and love of Christ, embrace the gifts given to the Church in the keys.

Chapter IX

Augustine's statement regarding the relation between the Church and the Gospel does not prove any more than it says: "I would not have believed the Gospel if I had not believed the Church." This statement does not compare the relative authority of Scripture with that of the Church but rather describes how faith begins. Each one who stood in the multitude listening to Peter would have said, "I would not have believed the Gospel if I had not believed Peter." Likewise I can say today, "If I, as a boy, had not believed my family and then my teachers and finally the Church, I would never have believed the Gospel today." But I believe the Gospel more than any human multitude and, what is more, I ought to believe it even if I thought everyone else disbelieved it. Even in such a case I ought to depend on the Gospel more than on men. Augustine refers in this quotation to the growing faith in a child, not to a comparison of the relative worthiness of the authority of Scripture and that of the Church.

I admit and accept as valid your statement that many chapters of canon law deal with indulgences, for I know that in the time just before John XXII indulgences were in use. And from these they got into the decretals. But I do not agree that, for that reason, I am obliged to hold them as an article of faith.

From the preceding I assume that you can, to a certain degree, gather my reaction to Gerson's restraints. Christ explicitly gave power regarding forgiveness of sins, but concerning punishments He said nothing. Regardless of how this power is understood the power to loose from sin is widely believed today. Gerson said explicitly that in the forgiveness of sins the infusion of grace is necessary prior to the remission of guilt because the remission of guilt is nothing other than the infusion of grace. "Therefore her sins, which are many, are forgiven because she loved much."[20] Gerson says further that the remission of eternal punishment precedes the turning away from sin. And in executing these three things the minister of Christ binds and looses only insofar as he co-operates with Christ, that is, only insofar as he is the executive agent following Christ in his word and ministry. But to what degree the required grace of God is present, neither he who administers nor he who receives absolution knows; nor is this at the command of the minister. And if this position of mine preserves and saves every word of the Lord, why attribute any further power to prelates?

No one doubts that a sacrament administered by an ordained minister is effective provided the recipient imposes no obstacle. But what is true for the power of the office is not true for the power of jurisdiction. And I say this because many extend this jurisdictional power to the heart of man, which is perhaps further than is appropriate.

As far as punishment is concerned, until I am better informed I simply hold that the punishment is remitted when the sin is remitted. Thus everyone once freed from sin is from that moment on no longer subject to punishment. The fact that some purgation is still required is due to a lack of fullness of grace which is explained by the presence of venial sins. But because these are not mortal sins, punishment is only temporal. If my position were based on rational arguments alone, it would influence those who emphasize the intellect as little as does this quotation from the prophet: "Blessed is the man whose transgression is forgiven, whose sin is covered . . . to whom the Lord imputes no iniquity."[21] But John gives us a much clearer witness concerning punishment: "Perfect love casts out fear for fear is fear of punishment."[22] The Holy Spirit speaking through the disciple who loved Jesus draws this conclusion: "For fear is fear of punishment and he who fears is not perfected in love." On this basis I turn the argument around to assert that those who need cleansing in purgatory live under both punishment and fear of punishment and are therefore not perfected in love.

This, I think, was the position taken by the venerable Gerson. For I know that he thought the universal authority of the apostolic See is to be tested in the light of the truth of Scripture on which it is dependent, not the other way around, that the truth of Scripture depends on the will and authority of a pope neither mad nor in error. Therefore if Gerson later, or even in this very work on indulgences, speaks more than pure theological truth would allow, I attribute it to a tacit compromise for piety's sake. For this compromise he sought to prevent the malice of certain men from making out of truth a stumbling block for the easily swayed. You know how diligent, dutiful, and pious he is, how often he defers to opposing positions allowing them to take precedence over his. However, he strays remarkably far from the proper interpretation in his letter of advice regarding the means and goals of zealous striving, where he advises that one should avoid logical precision with its multiplicity of distinctions.[23] Many of these scholastic methods are necessary, however. Who could ever attain the theological sophistication achieved by Peter d'Ailly without definitions, division, arguments, distinctions, and logical examples? These are needed for sharp-tongued theological debate, not for sermons to the people or contemplation directed toward God. How could d'Ailly have demolished the error of the fourteen conclusions of John of Montesono if he had not used distinctions and syllogistic argument to point out his deception? Therefore the theologian needs to employ logic.

And how could Gerson, himself so great a theologian, have been able to sustain his position without the aid of that most accurate logic of his teacher d'Ailly? For d'Ailly not only condemned John of Montesono, in whose condemnation Gerson participated and approved, he also expelled the Dominicans from the University of Paris for fourteen years because their younger teachers would not, because of some kind of allegiance to St. Thomas, abstain from errors which had been officially pointed out. Gerson himself says in the third part of his treatise against John of Montesono that this teaching had had no approval of sufficient strength to in any way impede the just condemnation of the doctor of Montesono.[24]

In my view Gerson was eager to promote piety and edification. He knew what extensive scandals in God's Church come from the stubborn contentiousness of the scholastics. Therefore he preferred to risk the distortion of truth rather than to cause cleavages in the way of love for the easily swayed. Thus we should interpret the more moderate statements of Gerson in light of advice to a shipwrecked man, that he throw his precious cargo overboard into the storm, as natural instincts teach him, in order to save both life and limb. Therefore, in view of this example, we do not suffer both evils but only the lesser evil and avoid thereby the greater. Hence I take myself to task today, as I did often while in Paris, for discussing this question with those who were not yet able to cope with it. I can only hope this bore no evil fruit. I often think that you and others who have a more pastoral moderation in such things are indeed blessed. I assume you have read the position Gerson took in regard to the proposition of Peter of Luna. Peter's proposition was that a generally accepted error sometimes produces right action. Gerson comments that as long as an error holds sway the wise man is legally bound to perform things which, if he had performed them spontaneously no longer bound by the presence of the error, would bring serious guilt upon himself.[25]

Therefore, I think that this prudent man, having opened the eyes of attentive readers with propositions containing unquestionable truths, does not mention the most taxing and hidden aspects of the truth in the interest of those who grasp it more slowly; and into this compromise he was forced by the contentious. How else can we reconcile the discrepancies in the positions taken by such a venerable man? For certain of his statements agree so evidently with me that I would consider basing everything I stand for on them, while, at other times, he agrees with you. In fact, where he speaks gently and quietly to the people, his position could be taken as the basis for your argument. Nor is this surprising, because I think that you, like him, have faced the threatening storm and hence you quote him with the same desire for piety that he expresses in his writings. And if you act, teach, and preach thus, I laud your intention.

Chapter X

I fully agree that in regard to the sacrament of confession the penance sometimes changes attrition into contrition. This occurs when the sinner who has come to confession puts no obstacles in the way of the sacramental covenant that he might receive the promised gift of life. Nor could he receive the gift of life without having received love in some degree, because without love he can neither live nor be in any degree contrite and humbled. This stubborn hardness of heart makes him despised by God. But if the sinner were completely contrite, he would not be bound by the Church to suffer punishment.

I am sure you recall these familiar words: "Others, however, say that God alone, not the priest, is able to forgive the debt of eternal death just as God himself gives life to the soul."[26] Just as He himself gives life to the soul so also He covers the sins of penitent sinners. For just as He retains for himself the power of baptism, so also He retains for himself the power of penance.

Furthermore, it is openly acknowledged that in the forgiveness of sins, the priest merely administers the sacrament. Thus in the sacrament of penance the Lord works in a hidden fashion through the sacrament according to the disposition of the recipient. He himself covers sins when through love He does not retain them for punishment but rather pays the debt of punishment. "Love covers a multitude of sins."[27] According to Augustine they are covered when they are blotted out by love. Regarding this, Lombard follows Augustine, saying, "When God covers sins He does not want to take note of them. And if God does not want to take note of sins He does not want to pay heed to them. And if He does not want to pay heed to them He does not want to punish them but rather wants to forgive them."[28] At the end of the chapter, Lombard concludes, "It has been clearly shown here that God himself clearly releases the penitent from his obligation to punishment. Thus He forgives when He inwardly illuminates by inspiring true contrition in the heart."[29] Further on Lombard says that "this position is more correct" than the one which states that "God forgives the guilt but the priest forgives the punishment."[30] Lombard quotes Ambrose in support of his position, "The priest certainly performs his office but he exercises no legal power."[31] Lombard goes on to quote Augustine, "No one takes away sins except the Lamb of God Who takes away the sins of the world."[32] How else does He bear sin away other than by forgiving the debt? How else does He forgive the debt other than by giving us the capacity to keep the law down to the last jot and tittle? The same One Who saves us from past sins preserves us from present sins and saves us when threatened by sin. The latter two, that is, present and future sins—in regard to both punishment and guilt—are only taken away by the Lamb of God.

Lombard logically demonstrates that Augustine's position does not contradict the words of the Lord "Whoever you bind, etc." He refers to Augustine's interpretation of Christ, that He is speaking about the love possessed by the Church which has been spread abroad in the hearts of the faithful by the Holy Spirit. This love forgives the sins of those who partake of it and of the Holy Spirit, while it retains the sins of those who do not partake of them.[33] Augustine clearly reconciles this position with the words of Christ by interpreting them thus, "Those are not bound whom you want to bind or think are bound but rather those on whom you exercise the true work of justice and mercy."[34] I do not acknowledge any other jurisdiction over sinners.

Lombard adds, "The Holy Spirit, who has been given to all the sanctified united in love, forgives sins regardless of whether the community of the sanctified knows it or not. Likewise, when someone's sins are retained, they are retained by this same community from which he has separated himself by depravity of heart, whether the sanctified know it or not."[35] According to this position, which is consonant with the previous one, the principal role in loosing and binding belongs to God alone. The Church participates only through the gift of the Spirit whose primary task is to forgive and retain sins. Augustine adds, "Sins therefore are forgiven by the Church when anyone is united to the Church of the righteous. Sins are retained by the Church when anyone is cut off from the love of the Church. The uniting to the Church or excluding from it is done by the Holy Spirit, who also gives to the Church office, ministry, and government."[36] Thus to the degree that they work together with the Spirit, to that degree they loose and bind on earth even as they are loosed and bound in heaven.

Likewise the brother of the Lord speaks with lofty words, "Whoever brings back a sinner from the error of his way will save his soul from death and will cover a multitude of sins."[37] But how might he be converted from the error of his previous ways other than by knowledge of the straight ways of God? Does this knowledge, this uprightness of walking, come primarily from the brother who brings back the sinner? And what are we supposed to call the brother, a savior? Has this brother infused love into the sinner so that the multitude of sins is covered? Then anyone at all having power neither of office nor of jurisdiction could merely by his own zeal and exercise of piety call back his brother from error. The one who is called back from his error could then possess so fervent a love that many sins and many punishments would be forgiven him. Should the forgiveness of sins and punishments be attributed more to authority than to love? Is there anyone more dedicated to God's straight path than he who calls back his brother from the error of his ways? There is no more meaningful conversion than this. I return to Lombard, who says explicitly, "The power of the priest consists in making a diagnosis in the presence of the Church, just as the priest of the Old Testament could neither heal nor take away the disease of the leper."[38] Regarding this, Lombard quotes Jerome: "Some theologians who do not understand this passage have something of the haughtiness of the Pharisee in them when they think they can condemn the innocent or absolve the guilty, whereas God is interested in the life of the accused, not in the opinion of the priests."[39] And Lombard adds, "This shows clearly that God's decision does not depend on the decision of the Church."[40]

Chapter XI

Your position on indulgences is, on the other hand, that when the attrition of the sinner is changed into contrition by the sacrament of confession, God commutes eternal punishment into temporal punishment. Before the punishment has been imposed by an ordained priest you say that the case remains in the divine court where God is judge. No increase in love therefore can decrease the punishment. But after the priest has imposed the punishment, then it becomes a case tried in the court of the Church. From that moment on God cannot extend the punishment beyond that which the priest has imposed. Any decrease in punishment still to be undergone ought not therefore to be attributed to an increase in love. For these reasons you claim the pope has jurisdiction over such a case.

However, you make this assertion with some hesitation, after saying, "The Church has authority over it," you add "not that the decision lies with the pope so that whatever he decrees in such cases holds in God's court because the pope so willed it, nor that the pope can remit such punishments according to his own will and pleasure." You seem to me to be rashly admitting the very opposite assertion. But is the following assertion any less dangerous? The Church has authority over it "because the pope can render satisfaction for such a person out of the treasury of the Church" and evidently substitute Christ's suffering for those punishments imposed by the priest and acknowledged, therefore, by the court of the Church. But now I ask you, using your own terminology, are the fruits of the Lord's passion so subject to papal will that whatever the pope decrees regarding the merits of Christ's passion will stand unchallenged in God's court? Do the sufferings of Christ avail only for him who has been decreed them by the pope? From that great store are they meted out to him only? And is all simply dependent on the will of the pope so that he can, when he desires, give of the sufferings of Christ sufficient to pay the debt for the sinner whose case, as you claim, is adjudged by the court of the Church, since the priest has already imposed the punishment?

Now if you say that the pope does not merely act willfully but with a legal basis for his action, I ask what legal basis other than mercy and justice? For it is with mercy and indeed justified mercy that God blots out the past sins of the penitent and justly accepts him by reason of the love now in him so that the penitent may share in Christ's great self-sacrifice, which is the treasure. But how can you receive from this treasure of Christ's sacrifice unless you value it as a treasure? For something is a treasure when it is regarded as precious. No one (even if he has had the power of emperor or pope) can bestow a treasure on someone who does not regard it as such. And if anyone considers that treasure to be indeed precious, he receives his share whether or not the pope gives it. Therefore, not only eternal but also temporal punishments remain solely under the jurisdiction of the court of God. Nevertheless, the pious obedience of the faithful subjects itself in humility for God's sake to the punishments imposed by the Church, knowing that such action is acceptable to God and not fruitless in his eyes.

Now I shall state my position regarding participation in the treasure of the Church. I judge that the Father, Son, and Holy Spirit, the God Three in One, the Incarnate Word, the Only-Begotten of God, the First Born of many brothers, Jesus of Nazareth, King of the Jews, Jesus Christ the Son of the living God, who through his death established the Testament—this is the treasure of the Church. Everyone knows and loves this treasure just as much as he values it. And to the degree that he knows, values, and loves this treasure he is reshaped in the image of God, and Christ takes form in him. Only through these three things, that is, by knowing, valuing, and loving God and Jesus Christ Whom He sent, and the Holy Spirit, only thus are we made participants in this treasure. I do not see how in my presentation I use the words "treasure" or "participation" in any sense other than that in which they ought to be used by the doctors of the Church. I beg of you, show me if I do. I have made my position as clear as I can. I take no little pleasure over your evaluation in which you openly assert that I am not so far wrong since I contradict the consensus of the doctors not in content but only in formulation. I regard it as most desirable to agree with all the other doctors provided of course the Scripture allows for it. All doctors agree with me, first that the pope cannot give grace to anyone, second that the pope cannot discern whether he himself or anyone else is in a state of grace, third that even less can he order that the state of grace be given to someone. It would be quite some grace if the pope could give efficaciously to any beggar treasures for the inner man. For this to happen the recipient must have already known the treasure in a profound way, valued it as glorious and magnificent, and ardently loved it.

Following this you make the seemingly significant objection which is actually inconsistent—how it is possible to reach my conclusion from these three premises—as if my position rested on these three premises alone! Have I not said that the foundation for my position is the perfect fulfillment and the necessary observance of the first and great command with unwavering perseverance until the day of the Lord? Have I not said that whatever Scripture contains regarding the function of the sacraments, the power of the ministry of the Church, or the efficacy of both, must be referred to these two commands for interpretation and limitation? Have I not said that perfect purity of heart is necessary for entrance into the kingdom? Have I not said that plenary indulgences presuppose complete participation in the heavenly Jerusalem itself and that this presupposes perfect desire and love? Have I not said that the condition for entrance to the marital chamber is the perfect preparation and adorning of the bride? Have I not said that the condition for complete freedom from punishment is complete freedom from sin? Have I not said that therefore it is impossible for the pope to decree that anyone is totally free from sin in this life? He might indeed find someone who is truly contrite and has confessed his sins, but no one is ever perfectly contrite. Not even the disciple whom Jesus loved was presumptuous enough to claim this, for he said, "If we say we have no sin we deceive ourselves and the truth is not in us."[41]

From all these assertions, together with the three you concede are commonly held, I deem it possible to deduce my conclusion. Although the consensus of the doctors regards these assertions as completely valid, nevertheless they would say that indulgences are sound. If this is their opinion I congratulate them, but I must confess my own ignorance, indeed I weep and wail over it, because I do not see how it is possible to reconcile with my ten assertions the use of indulgences as they are so loudly proclaimed and fearlessly asserted in the Church. All these conditions I have listed must be present to such a degree of perfection that human eyes would be blinded at the sight of it. The pope cannot give such perfection, but should someone achieve it, then complete immunity from punishment would follow immediately without any papal intervention.

Chapter XII

I beg of you to demonstrate to me how the conclusion which is the opposite of mine can be consistent with my assertions. After all, the mark of knowledge is the ability to convey it. You say that the pope can confer a plenary indulgence if the need arises. But when does such a need arise? Could such a need arise from outside Christendom when it becomes necessary to turn back battling infidels in war? I do not think you can say this because such wars almost by necessity lead to venial sins. Or perhaps the special need would be the rebuilding or restoration of some sacred building which had been destroyed? But I do not think you would say this. Even if some men were employing all their might in rebuilding a monastery famed for its religion, I deem this inadequate reason for giving them complete exemption from punishment.

Special attention should be paid to your phrase "if the need arises." What happens if the need arises but the pope does not issue the indulgence? Is the believer deprived of the legal action he actually deserves? Does the valid need arise then because of an interior condition? But the only requirement I admit is perfect love and whatever depends on and hinges to it. For I assert and confess that, whatever its extent and nature, I cannot really believe that the pope can give anybody plenary indulgence.

[Groningen, September 19, 1489?]

Notes

1. Cf. note 2, p. 97.
2. Gerson, "Opusculum de Indulgentiis," in *Opera Omnia,* ed. L. E. Du Pin, Antwerpiae, 1706, vol. II, col. 515.
3. Romans 8:15-17.
4. This quotation has not been found in Ambrose, but it appears in Peter Lombard, *Libri quattuor Sententiarum,* in *PL,* vol. CXCII, col. 886. Here Lombard attributes it to Ambrose.
5. Gerson, *op. cit.,* col. 515.
6. *Ibid.,* col. 515, 516.

7. *Ibid.*, col. 516.

8. *Ibid.*

9. *Ibid.*, col. 516, 517.

10. *Ibid.*

11. "Roman stations" refers to certain "station churches" in Rome at which pilgrims could receive indulgences by visiting them and participating there in festival services.

12. St. Antoninus, Bishop of Florence, an outstanding Thomist and authority on canon law, who died in 1459.

13. Antoninus of Florence, *Prima Pars totius summe maioris,* Lyon, 1516, Pars I, Titulus 10, Cap. 3, Paragraph 6.

14. *Ibid.*

15. *Ibid.*

16. Augustine, *In Joannis Evangelium,* Tractatus CXXI, 4 in *PL,* vol. XXXV, col. 1958.

17. Matthew 18:18.

18. John 20:22, 23.

19. There is as yet not sufficient evidence available to tell us more about this dispute.

20. Luke 7:47.

21. Psalm 32:1.

22. I John 4:18.

23. Gerson, *op. cit.,* vol. II, col. 102.

24. For d'Ailly's condemnation of John of Montesono see Gerson, *op. cit.,* vol. I, col. 693, 699 ff. Gerson in a letter to the students of the College of Navarre approves the condemnation. Cf. vol. I, col. 112.

25. It is not clear exactly to what

Gansfort refers. For a discussion of relations between Gerson and Peter of Luna, the later Benedict XIII, see James Connolly, *John Gerson: Reformer and Mystic,* Louvain, 1928, pp. 55–70.

26. Peter Lombard, *Sent.,* Lib. IV, Dist. XVIII, in *PL,* vol. CXCII, col. 886. Cf. Augustine, *Enarratio in Psalmum* XXXI in *PL,* vol. XXXVI, col. 264.

27. I Peter 4:8.

28. Augustine, *op. cit.,* col. 264.

29. Lombard, *op. cit.,* Lib. IV, Dist. XVIII.

30. Lombard, *ibid. PL,* vol. CXCII, col. 887.

31. *Ibid.* This quotation has not been found in Ambrose.

32. *Ibid.,* col. 886. Augustine is incorrectly quoted. Cf. *In Joannis Evangelium,* Tractatus IV, *PL,* vol. XXXV, col. 1410.

33. Lombard, *loc. cit.*

34. Ps.-Augustine, *Liber de Vera et Falsa Poenitentia,* ch. 10, *PL,* vol. XL, col. 1122.

35. Lombard, *loc. cit.*

36. *Enchiridion,* c. 45 (*PL* XL. 262–263).

37. James 5:20.

38. Gansfort paraphrases Lombard, *op. cit.,* col. 887, 888.

39. Lombard, *ibid.* Cf. Jerome, *Commentarius in Evangelium secundum Mattheam,* 16:16 in *PL,* vol. XXVI, col. 122.

40. Lombard, *ibid.*

41. I John 1:8.

Chapter Three
Justification: Man's
Eternal Predestination

Introduction

Ever since St. Augustine took his mighty pen to write against the Pelagians in 412, the relation between man and God, in justification, sanctification, and final salvation has remained a chief issue in Western theology. Augustine's stand against Pelagius and his disciples, which was to a large extent ratified by the second Council of Orange in 529, continued to alert medieval theologians to the implications of a doctrine—defined at this juncture in the most general possible way—that man can and has to earn his salvation on his own power. The central position that the discussion of the role of faith, grace, and good works holds in the sixteenth century is by no means a new development. Such a discussion was quite characteristic of medieval religious thought.

It is true that Martin Luther, especially in the course of the years 1516–1519, abandoned a whole series of technical terms and distinctions which scholastic theologians had introduced during centuries of work on this issue. His purpose was not, however, to show that the medieval preoccupation with the theology of St. Paul and with the doctrine of justification was unwarranted, nor was his presentation a mere negation of the answers of his predecessors, the medieval "Doctors of Holy Scripture." At least one aspect of Luther's thought, as well as that of other Reformers, was radical Augustinianism.

Luther singles out Gregory of Rimini (†1358), whose commentary on the Sentences of Lombard he encounters while studying for the

Leipzig Debate in 1519, and calls him the one true disciple of Augustine among the scholastic theologians:

> It is certain that the so-called "Modern Theologians," in this point of grace and free will, agree with the Scotists and Thomists except for one whom all condemn, Gregory of Rimini. . . . Also these theologians made it absolutely and convincingly clear that they are worse than the Pelagians.[1]

This is not the moment to investigate whether Luther means to include in this evaluation Thomas and Scotus themselves, or just their followers, that is, the Thomists and Scotists; nor can we concern ourselves with the question of whether this judgment can still stand in the light of modern scholarship. It was, however, in accordance with scholarship of his day, as we can see at many places in the *Theological Dictionary* which Johannes Altenstaig had published two years earlier (1517). Actually Luther owed his assessment of Gregory's uniqueness to his Leipzig opponent, Johann Eck,[2] and reports to Georg Spalatin, the court chaplain and confidant of Frederick the Wise, the Elector of Saxony:

> . . . in debating with me he [Eck] rejected Gregory of Rimini as one who alone supported my opinion against all other theologians.[3]

Acquaintance with the works of the Dominican Sylvester Prierias (†1523),[4] advisor to Pope Leo X, or with those of the influential Tridentine theologian, the Franciscan Andreas de Vega (†1560), would merely have served to confirm Luther in his position. Rather than convincing him that he should abandon his position in the light of this alleged consensus of medieval theologians, Eck only succeeded in strengthening Luther's early feeling that his was a lonely search for the recovery of the true understanding of St. Paul and St. Augustine.

As a matter of fact Gregory does not stand that alone in medieval thought. There were those before and after him who took up the Augustinian themes of God's prevenient grace, the bondage of the human will before it is set free by grace, and predestination in order to emphasize that salvation is not a human achievement but the result of God's sovereign initiative in planning and implementation.

Luther's predecessor in Wittenberg and Augustinian superior Johann von Staupitz (†1524) emphasized these three themes of prevenience of grace, the bondage of the will, and predestination, and welded them all together in a vivid mystical spirituality. Luther acknowledges his deep indebtedness to Staupitz time and again and states once, "I received everything from Dr. Staupitz."[5]

This is to be understood as an intense expression of gratitude, not of dependence. Indeed it is not our concern to deny the uniqueness of Luther in his constructive thought, but rather to see it as—initially —a particular articulation of the preceding anti-Pelagian medieval tradition in which he was to be supported by Ulrich Zwingli (†1531) and John Calvin (†1564).

Anti-Pelagianism, however, leads not only in the direction of the Lutheran Reformation, but also toward the Tridentine Reformation. In several canons appended to the sixth chapter on justification, essential elements of the Council of Orange were reiterated and Pelagianism publicly condemned. As has been said before, the term Counter Reformation is misleading insofar as it may suggest that the Tridentine Reformation is completely or largely a reaction to the Protestant Reformation. The stage of Trent was certainly set by Luther, Zwingli, and others, but the drama itself is a continuation with medieval thought and spirituality, and Trent's doctrine of justification is, just as much as Luther's, a particular articulation of the preceding medieval discussion of the relation between grace and works, divine predestination and foreknowledge.

Indeed we must go even further. There is not only continuity of discussion but also continuity in the anti-Pelagian stand. The leading theologians at the Council of Trent (1545-1563) as well as Luther, Zwingli, and Calvin—Gregory of Rimini and Johann von Staupitz, as well as Robert Holcot (†1349) and Gabriel Biel (†1495)—assume an anti-Pelagian stance. They are not exceptions. When one derives one's definition of Pelagianism from the current medieval condemnation, the first three canons of Trent's decree of justification included, one has even to come to the conclusion that no medieval doctors can be accused of Pelagianism.

Here we touch on one of the most difficult, as yet insufficiently explored, aspects of medieval thought: the flavor of the accusation

"Pelagian" and its concomitant verb "to pelagianize," shifted from author to author just as opinions varied considerably with regard to the position Pelagius actually took. The decrees of the second Council of Orange did not succeed in establishing a uniform terminology, rather Augustine's evolving anti-Pelagian thought formed a basis of evaluation that was necessarily more fluid. Probably due to the condemnation of Pelagius (†418), his numerous writings completely disappeared or have been transmitted under other names. Not until this century, when Souter discovered Pelagius' Commentaries on the Epistles of St. Paul, did we have a chance to establish the thought of Pelagius without sole dependence on his opponent Augustine.[6]

Whether historical or not, the best way to dramatize the distance between Pelagius and Pelagianism, on the one side, and Augustine's school on the other, is to report the story which Augustine records in his book *The Gift of Perseverance*. Somewhere in Rome, with his approval, a fellow bishop of Augustine met Pelagius and quoted to him a prayer from Augustine's *Confessions*: "Grant what You command, and command what You will."[7] This made Pelagius furious, Augustine reports, and we can understand why. The preceding sentence, to which Pelagius had taken exception, reads: "All my hope, O Lord, is set on Your very great mercy." To Pelagius this seemed to sanction exactly that moral indifference that he saw all around him in Rome, at a time when it had become socially "the right thing" to become a Christian. At a later stage, he and his followers would chastise Augustine for the influence of gnostic determinism (sharply opposed by earlier Fathers, especially Origen), which they detected in his doctrine of justification. And throughout history Augustinianism would be suspect for undermining the moral significance of Christianity.

St. Augustine exerted, nevertheless, a profound influence on the course of medieval theology, mitigated indeed by the ascendancy of Aristotle's authority in the thirteenth century, but even so never exterminated, as the works of Thomas Aquinas (†1274) clearly document. The fourteenth and fifteenth centuries witness a renewed search for the authentic interpretation of St. Augustine, a quest continued in the Reformation period. If one applies the standards of the Council of Trent (1545–1563), one can well argue that no medieval theologian, Pelagius himself included, was ever a "Pelagian," that is, no one taught that man can really earn his salvation without the aid of divine grace.[8]

With equal validity one can defend the thesis that all medieval theologians attempted to be as faithful as possible to St. Augustine's teaching with regard to man's justification and final salvation, and, in this sense, all were Augustinians. St. Augustine's thesis that the merits of men were the gifts of God, the rewards for His own work in and through them, has been subject to interpretation but never to elimination. In an effort to do justice to the genuine variations within this general setting, terms such as Semi-Pelagianism, Neo-Pelagianism and Semi-Augustinianism have been employed by historians of Christian thought. These or similar terms have to be invented—they are not employed by the scholastic theologians—when one wants to determine more precisely what the general anti-Pelagian, pro-Augustinian stand entailed in the case of any particular theologian.

Augustine's teaching of the prevenience and irresistibility of grace and of God's eternal predestination, election, and reprobation evoked very little enthusiasm in later centuries. It seemed to undercut Christian ethics and hamper rather than further the Church's efforts to Christianize the pagan Western world. Pure Augustinians are as hard to find as pure Pelagians.

The debate between Augustine and Pelagius has been continued through the centuries, because it was a real debate on central issues of the Christian faith. Pelagius was not the straw man of so many dialogues where the opponent of the author's hero has lost before the discussion has ever been started. Pelagius represents the Christian's concern that his faith validates itself in works of perfection, love for God and neighbor, and thus practically implements or at least approximates the high moral standards of the Sermon on the Mount (Matthew 5–7). It is Augustine's concern to show that man, impaired by the impact of the fall of Adam, acknowledges his complete poverty in both resources "of the soul," and intention "of the heart," and expects from God alone that he be called and sustained by grace in the true love for God and his fellow man; in short, God's sovereign initiative is not only acknowledged in creation but also in redemption.

Rather than the explicit and mutually exclusive positions of Augustine and Pelagius, the two related questions which underlie the opposition between them determine the shape of the debate on justification during the centuries to follow. These are: the effects of the fall of man, that is, of original sin, and the manner in which man has to be harnessed by grace to be set and kept on the way to salvation.

On the other hand, in accord once more with a more or less Pelagian position, if original sin has not really perverted man's nature so that egotistical love of one's self has replaced the love for God, it is argued that exposure to the law of God or to the example of Christ suffices to drive the sinner to contrition and to the sacrament of baptism or, after relapse in sin, to the sacrament of penance. The grace hereby transmitted enables man to set out on the way toward sanctification and salvation and to foster the hope that we will not be found wanting on the day that Christ returns "to judge the quick and the dead."

If, however, as St. Augustine emphasized, original sin has made man a rebel against God, not merely fallen but fallen in love with evil (the flesh, the devil, this transient world), grace should be more than the exterior confrontation with God; it should be an interior reshaping of the perverted will of man. An effective grace is needed to guide the sinner to contrition, to the baptismal font, and toward reinstatement by absolution.

The Augustinian position can be understood and evaluated only when it is seen that his is a *confessional theology* rather than a moral or *pastoral theology*: confessional not only in the sense that its point of departure is the confession of sins *(confessio fraudis)*, but even more in the sense that it is a thanksgiving *(confessio laudis)* for God's goodness in the gifts of creation and for God's mercy in the gifts of redemption. The basic pattern for such a theology appears in the *Confessions* where Augustine looks back in surprise and gratitude that God has brought him over a long and tortuous road into full communion with himself. Thanksgiving is so central to Augustine's theology that it is no accident that the words to which Pelagius took exception were part of a prayer. Prayer is for Augustine that form of thanksgiving where man and man's history are laid before God and seen through His eyes: looking backward man finds God present as a decisive force in the crucial junctures of life.

It was inevitable that eventually it should be asked how such a confessional theology, a theology as prayer, could speak to those at the beginning rather than the concluding stages of the road as described in the *Confessions*. How can this confessional theology function as a missionary theology? What about the task of the preacher who addresses a community of mixed membership of whom at best only a part has reached the point that Augustine regarded as the climax of his spiritual quest? Does not the condition of grace undercut man's sense of responsibility and the urgency of the need for moral self-reform in accordance with the preacher's exhortation? Missionary or pastoral theology, directed to those as yet outside the communion of grace, does not look backward in gratitude but looks forward in hope; it deals with man where he is before the reception of grace and sees God through the eyes of man.

It is in this pastoral climate that the doctrine was developed that "God does not withhold his grace from those who do their very best" (*facientibus quod in se est Deus non denegat gratiam*). In his important studies in early scholastic thought, Arthur Landgraff has shown that theology in the early Middle Ages may often seem naïvely Pelagian.[9] No one holds, however, that man's moral efforts unaided by grace are fully meritorious of God's rewards (*de condigno*) but rather that they are graciously regarded by God as half merits or merits in a metaphorical sense (*de congruo*). The relationship between God's bestowal of grace and sinful man's best effort rests on "contracted" rather than "actual" worth and is a result of God's liberality in giving "so much for so little." Man's own efforts have, in this sense, "congruity" but not "condignity." It should be noted that there are also those who are not in this sense naïvely Pelagian, who hold that no human merits whatsoever, even those that result from grace, are merits in a strict sense of the word.

In a Lombardian commentary on St. Paul, we find that interesting combination of Romans 8:18 and Hebrews 13:16 which would be taken up time and again in the succeeding period. St. Paul's statement that there is no relationship of condignity between our sufferings of the present and the glory to come is interpreted to mean that man cannot ever earn "his future glory."

The twelfth century yields further evidence of the continuing concern with the meritoriousness of man's action. We find among the errors of Peter Abelard (†1142), condemned in 1141 at the Council of Sens, the opinion that "free will as such suffices to perform something good." The complement to this conciliar decision is the condemnation by the Council of Reims in 1148 of a thesis which tends to undercut the possibility of human merit in any form: "Apart from Christ there is no meritorious human action." The course of future theologians would have to be steered between the Scylla and Charybdis of these two condemned extremes.

During the thirteenth century the question as to the possibility of human merit shifted and, apart from small pockets of resistance, it is no longer contested that the Christian in the state of grace can earn life eternal. Now the issue became whether fallen man can earn the first bestowal of grace. The influential Franciscan theologian Alexander of Hales (†1245) and Thomas Aquinas, in his early commentary on Lombard's Sentences, argue that God will give preparatory grace to all those who do their very best. The mature Thomas in his *Summa of Theology* and in his *Summa Against the Pagans*, makes quite clear, however, that the human effort is itself the result of God's preparatory grace.[10]

For Thomas the reason for an act performed in a state of grace being meritorious is to be found in the infusion of the supernatural habit of love. According to Duns Scotus (†1308), however, it is not the supernatural quality of the acts thus engendered but rather God's *acceptatio*, or willingness, to accept such an act which makes it worthy of eternal reward.[11] With Scotus we encounter again the idea that man, by doing his very best, can merit grace *de congruo*. The potential Pelagianism of this thesis is completely neutralized, however, by his emphasizing God's predestination, which, together with God's acceptance of the act, safeguards the Augustinian concept of the sovereignty of God.

The theologians in the school of William of Occam (†1349) and Gabriel Biel rejected Scotus' doctrine of predestination while retaining his understanding of the merit *de congruo*; they felt that the doctrine of acceptance sufficiently explained that God does not owe anything to man and is never his debtor. It is at the present time still a matter of discussion among students of late medieval thought as to whether the latter school, the *Via Moderna,* succeeded in maintaining their pastoral theology without yielding to the influx of Pelagian ideas.[12] There can be no doubt, however, that Occam's school sought to follow St. Augustine and regarded its own stand as explicitly anti-Pelagian.

The selections we have chosen from Robert Holcot and Gabriel Biel will help to illustrate the fallacy of the long-defended thesis that, on the eve of the Reformation, St. Augustine had been forgotten except for some isolated "Augustinian lights in a Pelagian night," such as Gregory of Rimini and Thomas Bradwardine (†1349). The Reformation period is not marked by an unprecedented ascendance of the authority of St. Augustine nor by the sudden discovery of the radical anti-Pelagianism of Augustinian theology; this era should rather be regarded as a new chapter in the history of the never-abandoned search for the authentic and catholic (that is, true) interpretation of the most influential of the Western Fathers.

Before introducing the four selected participants in the fourteenth- and fifteenth-century discussion we first give a sketch of the life of the *viator,* the Christian between predestination and acceptance, "on his pilgrimage to the eternal Jerusalem." (See diagram on page 132.)

The line from A to C represents the history of salvation of the individual Christian. The point here indicated as B can have two meanings: If the *viator* is pagan, it marks the moment when he is incorporated into the Church through the sacrament of Baptism; if the *viator* is a baptized Christian who, through mortal sin, is no longer in the state of grace, it marks the moment when he is reinstated as a communicant member through the sacrament of Penance (absolution). In either case he receives sacramental or sanctifying grace, designated by the term *gratia gratum faciens,* which makes one acceptable to God by the infusion of the habit of love in the soul. The line A–B represents the road which leads to the baptismal font or to priestly absolution. Whereas only after point B, through the habit of grace, can true meritorious (*de condigno*) acts be performed, it is generally conceded that already before that point, acts can be meritorious, *de congruo,* in a more remote sense; that is, man, by his own best efforts (*facit quod in se est*) can accomplish morally good acts which

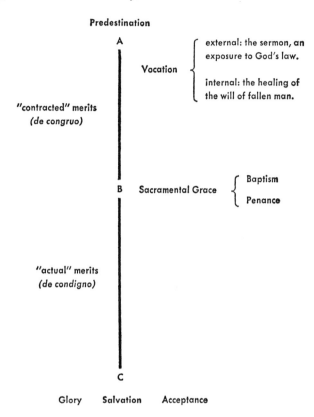

Predestination

A

Vocation

external: the sermon, an exposure to God's law.

internal: the healing of the will of fallen man.

"contracted" merits
(*de congruo*)

B   Sacramental Grace

Baptism

Penance

"actual" merits
(*de condigno*)

C

Glory   Salvation   Acceptance

have no inherent claim on God's reward but form merely an appeal to His liberality.

The crux of late medieval discussion is whether such good acts are themselves the results of a particular gift of grace (variously called *auxilium gratiae* or *gratia gratis data*). Thomas Bradwardine for one asserts this with great insistence, since the opposite opinion seems to him clearly Pelagian. The other point of view, which we encounter in the third part of the selection from Robert Holcot's writing, asserts that there exists a twofold covenant of God. According to the first covenantal commitment God will grant His grace to all who do their best, just as He has committed himself to accept works performed in a state of grace as meriting eternal life. The special gift of grace is associated with God's call (vocation) or knocking on the door of the heart of the sinner. This call can be the sermon—the word of God, an exterior confrontation with the law of God, and an exposure to the example of Christ, which sparks a feeling of remorse for one's sin and thus leads to point B. In a more strict Augustinian tradition this call, if effective, is not conceived of as a confrontation from without but as a healing from within of the sinner's will which was bent by sin on itself (*recurvata*) and is now by grace redirected toward God in remorse, humility, and love. Presupposed here is St. Augustine's conviction that fallen man without the healing power of grace cannot but sin, since even his most worthy acts are performed for the wrong reason, that is, out of love for one's self rather than out of love for God.

The late medieval discussion as regards point C, Salvation, final acceptance by God, has been indicated above insofar as it concerns the difference of opinion between followers of Aquinas and followers of Scotus. In the first and second parts of the Holcot selection this difference is touched upon, and the thesis condemned by the Council of Reims in 1148 is newly refuted. It may well be that Holcot saw a revival of this condemned position in the thought of Thomas Bradwardine. It is certainly clear that this position informed the thought of John Wyclif (†1384) on this point, whence it can be traced to Jan Hus (†1415).

By thus drawing upon Robert Holcot's *Commentary on the Wisdom of Solomon* to clarify the foregoing sketch, we have already introduced his main themes in the selection which follows.

Robert Holcot is a fascinating theologian. A Dominican friar, he is nevertheless an enthusiastic though not servile student of William of Occam. A moralizing preacher, he has been acclaimed as a man of unparalleled wit. A protohumanist in his interest in classical studies, he has none of the later humanist's optimism about the birth of a new age. In page after page he bewails "these modern times," his esteem for antiquity always serving to show how low his own age had sunk. Acutely aware of the great divide between assembled knowledge (*scientia*) and true wisdom (*sapientia*), he has a high regard for scholarship and culture. Given to short adages he can express this by saying, "An illiterate king is a crowned ass" (*Rex illiteratus est asinus coronatus*).

It should not surprise us that a man of so many paradoxes has been interpreted in many different ways. He has been generally recognized, however, as an opponent of Thomas Bradwardine, rejecting the latter's radical Augustinianism. Holcot and a host of later interpreters found Bradwardine's defense of the "case of God" was at the expense of the dignity of man. First student and later lecturer at Oxford from 1326 until 1334, Holcot probably taught another eight years at Cambridge. Strangely enough—perhaps due to his theological convictions —he then leaves the academic community, and we find him in the last years of his life (†1349) mentioned in the records as licensed to hear confessions in the Northampton archdeaconry.[13] His *Commentary on the Wisdom of Solomon*, from which our selections have been taken, became exceedingly popular, as the wide distribution of copies all over Europe indicates.

In our second fourteenth-century theologian, Thomas Bradwardine, we encounter a spokesman for the prevenience of grace. God's eternal predestination selects the elect, not on grounds of their foreseen merits but on grounds of His own will to elect those who, through the gift of prevenient grace, are to be freed from the bondage of sin. This grace is not merely offered to the sinner; in that case God would be as a merchant trying to sell his wares. For God "to give implies not only the offer of grace but also the acceptance of this offer," Bradwardine states in his great work, *The Case of God Against Pelagius*.[14] Without the aid of grace, man is unable to release the bolt on the doors of his heart; God himself must open the heart of man for the grace offered.[15]

Although not responsible for the evil intention of an evil action, and therefore not responsible for sin, God is the senior partner in every act of man. This position has often been interpreted as determinism; Bradwardine reflects here, however, the general medieval notion of divine co-operation and especially Aquinas' insistence on the activity of God as creator and "first mover." God joins as coagent in producing any act; a special act of grace (that which scholastic theologians call *gratia gratis data*) makes the act good; the infusion of the *habit* of grace (*gratia gratum faciens*) provides for a *meritorious* act. The doctrine of predestination serves to correlate this threefold emphasis on the prevenience of God. In the selection we have chosen, the central question of *The Case of God* comes to the fore: How is this doctrine of predestination and justification related to or reconciled with the responsibility of man as a moral agent?

Thomas Bradwardine was a contemporary and, for a time, even a companion of Robert Holcot. Both were born sometime between 1290 and 1295; both died in the same year, 1349, when a whole generation of leading English theologians was exterminated by the Black Death. Again, like Holcot, an Oxford man, Bradwardine was a student and lecturer at Merton College. In the late twenties he had a conversion experience which he describes in the following fashion: "Idle and a fool in God's wisdom, I was misled by an unorthodox error at a time when I was still pursuing philosophical studies. Sometimes I went to listen to the theologians discussing this matter [of grace and free will], and the school of Pelagius seemed to me nearest the truth. . . . In the philosophical faculty I seldom heard a reference to grace, except for some ambiguous remarks. What I heard day in and day out was that we are masters of our own free acts, that ours is the choice to act well or badly, to have virtues or sins and much more along this line." Bradwardine goes on to relate how he was so profoundly influenced by this view that "every time I listened to the Epistle reading in church and heard how Paul magnified grace and belittled free will—as is the case in Romans 9, 'It is obviously not a question of human will and effort, but of divine mercy,' and its many parallels—grace displeased me, ungrateful as I was."[16]

This problem continued to haunt him, and before he became a theological student a decisive event occurred which would make Romans 9:16 the basic point of departure for all his future theological writing. "However, even before I transferred to the faculty of theology, the text mentioned came to me as a beam of grace and, captured by a vision of the truth, it seemed I saw from afar how the grace of God precedes all good works with a temporal priority [God as Savior through predestination] and natural precedence [God continues to provide for His creation as 'first mover']. . . . That is why I express my gratitude to Him who has given me this grace as a free gift."[17]

As a lecturer at Merton College, Oxford, Bradwardine started to write his chief work, *The Case of God Against Pelagius,* which was probably completed in 1344 in London, where he had been Chancellor of St. Paul's since 1337. In 1335 he had left Oxford to join the Bishop of Durham, Richard de Bury. Here Bradwardine found not only one of the richest libraries of medieval England but also a very stimulating and learned circle of theologians—among them the future Archbishop of Armagh, Richard FitzRalph (†1360), and Bradwardine's opponent Robert Holcot. After serving the Crown and the Church in several positions, he was consecrated Archbishop of Canterbury in Avignon, but succumbed thirty-eight days later, on August 26, 1349, to the pestilence.

Bradwardine's insistence on the "potter and the pot" simile (Romans 9:21) as indicative of the relation between God and man may explain why his position has often been characterized as deterministic. It is exactly with reference to this image that the difference between Bradwardine and Holcot becomes most obvious. In the last section of our selection from Holcot, Bradwardine's beloved simile is politely but firmly rejected. Whereas Bradwardine had regarded man as the *instrument* of God who was the first to move (in creation) and the first to choose (in redemption), Holcot saw man as the *partner* of God, in a covenantal relationship to which God had freely committed himself. Within this covenantal relationship, immutable because of God's fidelity and inner consistency, man had to determine the course of his own life and shoulder the responsibility for his eternal lot; God would support his serious efforts. Holcot's image of man as *partner* of God did not leave room for St. Augustine's notion of God's prevenience in predestination and justification. Bradwardine was certainly fully committed to repossess this part of St. Augustine's heritage, but so concerned was he to present man as the *instrument* of God that he established the *dependence of man on God* rather than the *rebellion of man against God,* which had been a central point of departure for St. Augustine.

In the centuries to come Covenant theology would continue to provide a structure for the understanding of revelation. Elaborated in many different directions, it became an even more basic and explicit theme in the theology of Ulrich Zwingli, John Calvin, and Johannes Cocceius (†1699), and was carried from the Dutch to the English shores. It finally came into full bloom in New England Puritan theology.

Gabriel Biel and Johann von Staupitz, whom we have chosen to represent the discussion on justification at the eve of the Reformation, appear frequently on the pages of Reformation studies because both played a significant role. Gabriel Biel, "the last of the scholastics," was an obedient disciple of Occam and a dedicated participant in the movement of the Brethren of the Common Life—the *Devotio Moderna*. He was well known and widely read by Luther, a true arsenal for Luther's first opponents, and quoted as a Catholic authority at the Council of Trent.

The sermon, "On the Circumcision of the Lord,"[18] was probably preached in the Cathedral at Mainz around 1460. It is one of Biel's best sermons; crisp and compact, it presents in a nutshell one of the main themes of his theology, the doctrine of justification, while still managing to retain the character of a sermon. The final parable is at once quite delightful and most revealing of Biel's thought on the matter.

In comparing Biel with Staupitz it strikes one with new force how momentous is the difference between a "pastoral" and a "confessional" theology. Biel, like Holcot before him, regards religion and revelation as a means by which man is morally stimulated, elevated, and finally perfected—ready for heaven. Staupitz stands in the Augustinian tradition, which emphasizes that the basis of theology is praise and thanksgiving, and points out that the purpose of religion and revelation is for man to return thanks to God, even if this should mean abandoning his hope for heaven and salvation. Though not mutually exclusive, these two emphases produce different vantage points.

As is suggested in this sermon, as throughout his writings, Biel stresses the idea which we noted in Holcot, that God has made a covenant with man which establishes man as His partner. As the parable puts it, the King graciously delegates power to His former opponents and grants them magnificent rewards for their services to Him. God's mercy underlies the making of the Covenant; God's justice obliges man to live according to the laws of the Covenant.

Through the Covenant "mercy and truth encounter each other, justice and peace kiss each other" (Psalm 85:11). In the Incarnation this word of the Psalm had come true, as Bernard of Clairvaux had so eloquently argued in his first sermon for the Day of Annunciation.[19] Through Christ justice and mercy are reconciled; in Christ the wrath of God's justice is refashioned into peace for the soul.

In the sermon that follows Biel makes the same point referring to John 1:17, "Grace and truth came through Jesus Christ," as support for the doctrine that God has committed himself to grant His grace to all those who make their best effort.

Truth, or its medieval equivalent justice, requires that man use his native capacities to fulfill as much as possible the law of God. God will grant him His aid of grace, and when man perseveres to the end in imitation of Christ, God will graciously accept man's work as worthy of eternal reward.

In Staupitz's rich treatise on predestination we move into a completely different world of thought. To begin with, man is here not primarily the *partner* but rather the *instrument* of God, used by God and upheld by Him above the abyss of nothingness to which he would return when left to himself. Whereas this suggests a clear parallel with the theology of Thomas Bradwardine, the different character of Staupitz's thought appears in the words of the Preface: "By preaching *Christ* I have tried to clarify the doctrine of predestination." In Bradwardine's defense of the case of God, there was little space given to a discussion of the role of Christ. In his bitter attack on the "modern Pelagians," Bradwardine was more concerned to void the proud claim of man by reference to God's sovereignty and power than to show the mercy of God in the Incarnation and the inhabitation of Christ in the soul. Furthermore, Bradwardine was convinced that he could rely on philosophy to stem the rising tide of Pelagianism; Staupitz, on the other hand, felt that apart from the existence of one being, the beginning and goal of everything, "the outcome of all philosophical studies is but to know our own ignorance."[20] With Bradwardine he can stress the anti-Pelagian thesis: Our salvation is outside ourselves (*extra nos*); but, unlike Bradwardine, he goes on to say: Outside Christ (*extra Christum*) we have no knowledge and, therefore, no

love of God. There is ample evidence that Staupitz thinks in terms
of a Covenant, but not the *bilateral* Covenant between God and his
partners, the *Covenant of Works* in which the partners have to fulfill
the Covenant law—as is the case with Holcot and Biel. For Staupitz
it is the *unilateral Covenant* which God has made with his elect, a
Covenant of Grace, because it provides for the works of justification.
Boldly he says that God made Christ a debtor to the elect so that He
owes them the gift of His righteousness.

Man is not called by God on the condition that he first be penitent
or that he first give his best effort, but on grounds of God's uncondi-
tional and eternal election. Through this call the marriage with
Christ takes place which is the temporal implementation or "execution" of God's eternal Covenant; the soul receives Christ's justice and
Christ receives the sins of the soul. Such a conjugal exchange of possessions with Christ is the chief basis of the salvation of the elect, and
not God's acceptance of their works. Staupitz would not deny that
the Christian can perform good works; on the contrary, he argues,
once the vocation has taken place and the elect soul is married to
Christ, these works follow spontaneously and without fail.

At one point (Chapter VII), Staupitz argues that there is a twofold
acceptance. On grounds of the finite works of the elect, the fruits
of his vocation are graciously accepted by God as full merit (*de
condigno*). At the same time, acceptance is founded on the infinite
merits of Christ which transfer the soul, married to Christ, to the
kingdom.

Closely related to the theme of double justification, this idea can
be traced to the Cardinals Gasparo Contarini (†1542) and Hieronymus Seripando (†1563), Vicar General of the Augustinian Hermits,
and is more typical of reform Catholicism than of the Protestant Reformation. On the other hand, Staupitz's strict confessional theology,
his requirement of self-accusation as the beginning of justification,
and his emphasis on faith in Christ as the only condition for salvation
allow us to understand why Luther claimed that Staupitz had initiated Reformation theology. Indeed, no other pre-Reformation treatise so closely equals in teaching and spirituality Luther's first
commentary on the Psalms, the *Dictata super Psalterium* (1513–

1515). Since, however, this treatise is a reworking of Staupitz's Advent sermons in Nuremberg, December 1516, it is impossible to determine with certainty who is the teacher and who is the student. On internal evidence, not to be presented here, we are convinced that a valid claim can be made that Staupitz's treatise reflects a theological position that shaped Luther's early thought and ultimately put him on the road to the Reformation. The footnotes will call attention to the striking parallel between this treatise of Staupitz and Luther's 1518 (1519?) sermon on "The two kinds of righteousness."

While the mystical elements in the theology of the young Luther remind one of Staupitz's teaching on this matter, it is precisely here that the distance between the two men becomes evident. For the Luther of this period, mystical experience is, as with Staupitz, founded on Scripture and enriched by tribulation and temptation; it is "practical" rather than speculative mysticism, a (spiritual) means to an end, not an end in itself.[21] For Staupitz, however, it is "practical" in the sense that the experience of sweetness is a sign of election; mysticism is the basis of certitude of salvation. For Luther mysticism is "practical" in the sense that it enlarges the capacities of man to understand and to appropriate the message of Scripture. Mysticism, the fruit of meditation on Scripture, leads back to Scripture. Not the sweetness of Christ's mystical embrace but the appropriation through faith of Christ's Person and Work forms the basis of Luther's certitude. For Staupitz the gift of grace is the soul inflamed by charity; for Luther the mark of the gift of grace is faith illumined by Scripture.

In 1520 Johann von Staupitz was accused of heresy, and abdicated as Vicar General of the Augustinian Hermits. He spent his last years as court chaplain to Cardinal Archbishop Matthew Lang, as Abbot of St. Peter's, a Benedictine monastery, and died in Salzburg at the end of the year 1524.

As a Forerunner in the sense defined at the beginning of this book, he did not associate himself with the Protestant Reformation, nor did he live to take a stand vis-à-vis the Tridentine Reformation, but his Augustinian and mystical theology represents a new search for doctrinal reformation which was a life option in the early decades of the sixteenth century before the confessional demarcation lines had been hardened by mutual condemnation.

Notes

1. *WA* 2. 394.
2. See for documentation *Harvest*, p. 144.
3. *Luther's Works*, 31, ed. H. J. Grimm, Philadelphia, 1957, p. 322.
4. See p. 265.
5. *WATR* I, no. 526.
6. *Text and Studies*, IX, 1–3, Cambridge, England, 1922–1932. Further Pelagian writings were identified by G. de Plinval, *Essai sur le style et la langue de Pélage*, Fribourg en Suisse, 1947.
7. "Da quod iubes et iube quod vis"; *Conf.*, Bk. X. ch. 29; *PL*, vol. XXXII, col. 796 ff. Augustine describes this occasion of Pelagius' irritation in his *The Gift of Perseverance*, ch. 53, where he goes on to explain: "What else does God command most of all and very especially than that we believe in Him."
8. Cf. H. A. Oberman, "Das tridentinische Rechtfertigungsdekret im Lichte spätmittelalterlicher Theologie," in *Zeitschrift für Theologie und Kirche*, 61, (1964), p. 277.
9. Arthur Landgraff, *Dogmengeschichte der Frühscholastik*, I, 1, Die Gnadenlehre, Regensburg, 1952, pp. 238–302.
10. P. de Letter, *De ratione meriti secundum sanctum Thomam*, Rome, 1939. Esp. pp. 110 ff., 121 f.
11. W. Dettloff, *Die Lehre von der Acceptatio Divina bei Joh. Duns Scotus*, Werl, 1954, esp. pp. 160 ff.
12. In his impressive study of this problem in the fourteenth century Paul Vignaux has argued for the basic alliance between Duns Scotus, William of Occam, and Gregory of Rimini against pelagianizing tendencies. *Justification et prédestination en XIVᵉ siècle*, Paris, 1934, esp. pp. 187 f.
13. For bibliography and an introduction to his thought see H. A. Oberman, " 'Facientibus quod in se est Deus non denegat gratiam': Robert Holcot, O.P., and the Beginnings of Luther's Theology," *HTR*, LV (1962), 317–342.
14. *De Causa Dei*, Book II, ch. 32, p. 613.
15. *Ibid.*, II, 32. 614.
16. Romans 9:16.
17. *De Causa Dei*, I. 35. 308 C–D.
18. *Sermones de Festivitatibus Christi*, Hagenau, 1510, Sermo XIV.
19. *PL* Vol. CLXXXIII, col. 383 ff.: reflected by Biel, *op. cit.*, S. II. 10 E.
20. Staupitz, Chapter XVII.
21. *WA* 55. 2.1, 48. 15; 55.20, 57. 3–6, 124. 9.

ROBERT HOLCOT

Lectures on the Wisdom of Solomon

Chapter III, Lecture 35

Question

Can man assisted by grace earn eternal life by his own full merit (*ex condigno*)?

Objections

(1) One could argue the negative position thus: First by the authority of St. Paul's Epistle to the Romans, ". . . the sufferings of this present time are not worth (*condigna*) comparing with the glory that is to be revealed to us."[1] Since the sufferings of the saints are worthy of the highest possible merit—and even these sufferings are not held to be comparable to future glory—no work of man can be worthy of (*condigna*) eternal life.

(2) Furthermore, he who merely repays someone for a debt earlier incurred does not earn anything by this transaction. Despite all we can do for God we are in His debt and would be even if we could do more. As Aristotle has said, "It is impossible for us to repay fitting honors to the gods and our parents because their favors always exceed ours,"[2] and, ". . . When you have done all that is commanded of you, say, 'We are unworthy servants, we have only done what was our duty.' "[3]

(3) Furthermore, whoever merits something from someone else makes him his debtor. But God neither is the debtor of any man nor can He ever be; therefore we cannot merit anything from Him.

Opposite authorities: sed contra

However, the contrary position draws its proof from the following authorities:

(1) Jeremiah 31:16: ". . . your work, says the Lord, shall be rewarded." The reward which is given for man's work corresponds to its worthiness, therefore since eternal life is the reward for the work of a man living in grace, such a man can fully earn eternal life by his own full merit (*ex condigno*).

(2) II Timothy 4:8: ". . . there is laid up for me the crown of righteousness, which the Lord, the righteous judge, will award to me on that day." Now what is awarded as the result of just judgment is a full worthy (*condigna*) reward. Therefore, man can earn the crown which is justly and fully deserved, that is, eternal life.

Solution

Now as to the original question, we can answer that the statement, man assisted by grace can earn eternal life by his own full merit, can be understood in two ways. It can be understood according to the natural value of man's action or according to its contracted value. Man would earn salvation according to natural value if his merit were, by its very nature and existence, such that eternal life would be suitable payment for it. According to contracted value, the value of one's merit would be determined by legal arrangement in the way that a small copper coin which, in natural value, has not the same weight or worth as a loaf of bread is assigned this value by the law of the land.

Now if we understand man's merit according to the first interpretation, the natural goodness of our works does not earn eternal life fully (*de condigno*) but only partially (*de congruo*), since it is appropriate (*congruens*) that if man has done all that he can with his finite resources God should reward him with His infinite resources.

But according to the second understanding of merit we can say that our works are fully worthy of eternal life, not because of any merit inherent in the acts themselves but because of grace, since our Lord has established that he who does good works in a state of grace shall receive eternal life. Therefore, through the law and grace of our ruler Christ we merit eternal life by our own full merit (*de condigno*).

Answer to the objections

(1) The first objection is answered by saying that although sufferings are not, by their natural value, deserving of eternal life, they have a contracted value.

(2) In answer to the second objection, we *do* earn something when we perform that which we owe to God, because Christ has established and ordained thus. The reward is not an absolute based on natural value, as the argument assumes, but it is, rather, dependent on its contracted value.

(3) To the third objection it is answered (as Peter Lombard has said)[4] that our Lord becomes a debtor because of His own promise, not because of what we do.

Chapter III, Lecture 52

Question

Are mercy and justice both conjoined in every work of God?

Objections

(1) One could argue the negative position thus: In the justification of the sinner, only mercy is present, since justice presupposes merits and the sinner is without merit before his justification.

(2) Moreover, in the work of creation one finds neither justice which presupposes merit, nor mercy which presupposes misery. Indeed creation does not presuppose anything.

(3) Another argument points out that baptized infants have been struck down with sickness and death. In such cases there is no justice, because the infants were free from every sin and do not deserve punishment. Therefore, they suffer unjustly.

(4) Furthermore, it does not seem just that one should be punished for the sins of another, and this is what God frequently does. For example, Canaan was cursed for the sin of Ham, his son.[5] Because of David's sin in arranging a nationwide census, the people were killed.[6]

(5) Furthermore, both Aaron and the people sinned when they worshiped the golden calf; the people were punished but not Aaron.[7] Therefore, God is shown to be a respecter of persons.

(6) Furthermore, the Apostle Paul has said, "I tell you that Christ

became a servant of the circumcized . . . in order to confirm the promises given to the faithful of the Old Covenant and in order that the Gentiles might glorify God for his mercy."[8] Therefore, in the conversion of the Gentiles, only mercy was present, while in the conversion of the Jews, only justice was present.

(7) Furthermore, in predestination there is no justice and in reprobation there is no mercy, for, as St. Paul has said, ". . . though they were not yet born and had done nothing either good or bad . . . not because of works but because of His call she [Rebecca] was told . . . 'Jacob I loved, but Esau I hated.' "[9]

(8) Furthermore, it would seem to be unjust to give to a good man more evil and less good while giving to an evil man more good and less evil. And, indeed, God does distribute temporal things in this fashion which involves neither mercy nor justice.

Opposite authorities: sed contra
However, the contrary position is argued as follows. The whole life of our Lord was mercy and truth.[10]

Solution
To answer the question one should begin by distinguishing between mercy and justice understood in a broad sense and in a strict sense. According to the broader definition, God's mercy is taken to mean His desire to benefit His creature, and God's justice is said to be the way He identifies Himself with His creature. According to the broader definition it is undoubtedly true that mercy and justice are joined together, because in all His works God acts according to this identification and desire to benefit the creature, so that even punishment of the reprobate works for the good of the elect. Thus understood justice and mercy are not at all opposed to each other. Moreover, St. Anselm teaches that mercy is the fruit of justice, since it is just for God's goodness to lead to forbearance. Anselm thus held that the entire life of our Lord is mercy and truth: at the same time the Lord is just in all His ways.[11]

When mercy and justice are defined in a narrower sense, mercy refers to God's will to alleviate misery irrespective of merit, while justice refers to God's will to reward according to merit. Since only a rational creature has the capacity to merit good or to incur punishment it is obvious that mercy and justice are not present in all of God's works but only in His work of retribution, which is directed toward man and which is based on God's covenant of mercy.

Answer to the objections

(1) The answer to this argument is that the justification of the sinner is preceded by a spontaneous act of attrition. For this reason, there seems to be a certain justice in the infusion of grace. Similarly, on the part of God, justice seems to be present, since He has, in some way, made Himself a debtor to the penitent by the commitment "that thou mayest be justified in thy works, and prevail when thou art judged."[12] God promised this so that He could bestow forgiveness on penitent sinners. And thus, when one examines the justification of the sinner, one finds there are on both sides—on God's and on man's —actions based on justice.

(2) To the second argument it is answered that in terms of the previous distinction (according to the broad not the strict sense), both mercy and justice are found in the works of creation.

(3) From original sin follows twofold punishment. The first is the corruption of the person, so that he loses the vision of God, and the other is the corruption of nature, which is a result of the loss of original righteousness, as has been explained earlier.[13] Baptism compensates for the loss of original righteousness, that is to say the corruption of the person is cured, but not the corruption of nature. Therefore, if the infant should die, baptism restores his vision of God. But the washing away of original sin does not remove the punishments which result from the damage done to the higher parts of man's nature. Thus baptism frees us from being condemned to eternal death but not from being condemned to corporeal death and to the other punishments that accompany our physical existence.

(4) Augustine answers this objection by saying that eternal punishment is never imposed on anyone for his own good but rather to pay for guilt. Temporal punishment, however, is often given for the benefit of the one who receives it or for the benefit of others who thus see how important it is to flee sin, since the sin of one can strike down many.[14] Thus the punishment was intended to put them all on their

guard against sin, and to make them concerned that their neighbor not sin lest everyone else might be punished for the sins of one. Furthermore, in regard to his body, a man is either the lord of another or his subject; for example, the son to the father or the servant to the master. And thus it may well happen that the son receives a temporal punishment for the sins of his father, just as the servant may be held responsible for the sins of his master. On the other hand, when it is a question of the good of the soul, every man is alone. In this case the father or the master is punished only insofar as he himself is guilty. In this sense, the son Canaan was punished for Ham. And the interpretation of the curse on Canaan for Ham's guilt is, "Your son will be of no pleasure to you just as you are of no pleasure to me."

Finally, according to Gregory, when someone is an accomplice in the guilt of another, as, for example, when God allows a prelate to fall into sin because of the guilt of those entrusted to his care, the prelate deserves only temporal punishment for the sins of the people.[15] And in this sense, whereas David committed the sin the people were punished.

(5) Moreover, Aaron was punished, as were the people, but not with public chastisement. Thus it is established that prelates should not be punished publicly but in private so as to avoid scandal. The punishment was imposed on Aaron and his sons because in the sacrificing of the bloody calf they were made unclean.[16]

(6) The Apostle speaks in this fashion because a certain kind of justice was present in the conversion of the Jews which does not apply to the conversion of the Gentiles. The justice in the conversion of the Jews was the fulfillment of the promises made to the faithful of the Old Covenant through the prophets. But in both conversions a condescension of divine goodness took place by which Gentile and Jew were called to the reward and in this sense justice was served. Moreover, since Gentile and Jew were insufficient in merits, in this sense mercy was served.

(7) In answer to this objection it can be said that the effect of predestination and reprobation on man most certainly combines justice and mercy not according to the strict but rather to the broad definition.

(8) In answer to this objection it can be said that such a seemingly unjust distribution serves the advancement of a true Christian in re-

gard to his spiritual benefit which, in an absolute sense of the word, is the main benefit for man.

Chapter XII, Lecture 145

Question

Is God required to give grace to the man who prepares himself for its reception?

Objections

(1) It seems that this thesis might be rejected on the following grounds. To whomever God gives grace He gives it for nothing and freely, out of His mercy alone. Therefore, no matter how much man tries to dispose himself for grace, whether or not grace is given to him depends on the free will of God.

(2) Man is related to God as clay is to the potter. "Like the clay in the potter's hand, so are you in My hand, O house of Israel."[17] But no matter how well the clay might be prepared, there is no necessity that it be given form at all by the potter. Likewise, there is no necessity that man receive grace from God, regardless of how much he prepares himself.

Opposite authorities: sed contra

(1) In support of the opposite position we may read in the gloss on Romans 5:1, "Therefore since we are justified by faith, we have peace with God."[18]

(2) And Augustine has said, "God receives those who take refuge in Him. To do otherwise would be unjust."[19] But injustice is an impossibility in God, therefore He could not refuse those who take refuge in Him, and therefore he who takes refuge in God necessarily receives grace.

(3) Furthermore, the Apostle has said, "Behold I stand at the door and knock. If anyone hears my voice and opens the door, I will come in to him and eat with him."[20] Therefore, when man disposes himself for grace by doing whatever he can and thus opens himself, God necessarily comes in to him. The following argument confirms this.

When man opens himself God must either enter or not enter; if He should not enter, He would have been practicing deception in knocking; to say which would be blasphemous. If He does enter, He gives grace.

(4) Furthermore, Anselm has said, "The reason the Lord did not give grace and perseverance to the devil was that the devil himself did not want to accept it,"[21] since whoever prepares himself to accept grace necessarily receives it.

Solution

To those who doubt such an affirmation, it may be said that there is a distinction between compulsory necessity and unfailing necessity [that is, consistency]. With God compulsory necessity has no place, but an unfailing necessity is appropriate to God because of His promise, that is, His Covenant, or established law. This is not an absolute but rather a conditional necessity. According to God's established law the pilgrim who does whatever he can to dispose himself for grace always receives grace. However, if He should choose to, God could deviate from His law for someone other than the pilgrim or the devil. Then, however much such a person [with whom God has not made His Covenant] might dispose himself for grace, he would not receive it. Man's disposition does not require the giving of grace except by congruency, because grace surpasses every natural act; it is impossible for man to fully merit (*de condigno*) through any natural act.

Answer to the objections

(1) It is conceded that God acts out of grace and mercy insofar as His law is established and observed by Him out of mercy. But on the basis of His established law He gives grace by unfailing necessity [that is, consistency or fidelity to His earlier promises].

(2) Although we are like clay in comparison to God one cannot by any means apply the analogy in every respect to man. Nor is the analogy totally correct, because there is no covenant between the potter and the clay; and even assuming that there could be such a covenant, the potter could very well break it without abrogating the Covenant law. But God cannot break His pact with man without the

Covenant being destroyed. Nor can the clay [like man] either partially or fully merit anything from the potter.

Now, one should deal with this issue reverently rather than with cold logic.

Notes

1. Romans 8:18.
2. Aristotle, *Nicomachean Ethics,* Bk. IX, ch. 1.
3. Luke 17:10.
4. This passage has not been found.
5. Genesis 9:20 ff. It should read "Ham, his father."
6. II Samuel 24.
7. Exodus 32.
8. Romans 15:8, 9.
9. Romans 9:11–13.
10. Psalms 24:10.
11. Anselm, *Proslogion,* Bk. IX and XI, in *Opera Omnia,* ed. F. S. Schmitt, vol. I, pp. 93–122.
12. Psalms 50:6. Holcot refers for his exegesis to the gloss on this passage.
13. *Sup. Lib. Sap.,* 13 C.
14. Augustine, *Questiones in Heptateuchum,* Bk. VI, ch. 8, in *PL,* vol. XXXIV, col. 778, 779.
15. Cf. Gregory, *Moral.* II. c.7. n. 10 in *PL,* vol. LXXV, col. 559 f.
16. Numbers 19.
17. Jeremiah 18:6.
18. The gloss says man is justified by truth and grace. *PL,* vol. CXCI, col. 1378.
19. Cf. Ambrosiaster, I Timothy 2 in *PL,* vol. XVII, col. 466 C. The opposite with Augustine; see e.g., *Enchiridion* 103, *PL,* vol. XL, col. 280, and *Contra Julianum,* IV.8, *PL,* vol. XLIV, col. 759 f.
20. Revelation 3:20.
21. Anselm, *De Casu Diaboli,* Ch. III.

THOMAS BRADWARDINE

The Cause of God
Against the Pelagians

The Pelagians now oppose our whole presentation of predestination and reprobation, attempting either to eliminate them completely or, at least, to show that they are dependent on personal merits.

(1) They use the following arguments: God does nothing unreasonable and there is no reason why He should predestine or reprobate one man rather than another. Therefore, He either predestines and reprobates everyone or no one. And since there is a consensus that not everyone is predestined or rejected, they conclude that no one is. Or, if they grant that there be such a thing as a reason for predestination or reprobation, this reason can then only be based on several different kinds of merit.

(2) Thus Abbot Joachim of Flora (†1202) in his dialogues with Benedict assigns two reasons or causes for the election, predestination, and mercy of God, of which the first is man's own capacity for mercy, salvation, and goodness, and the second is the good act itself. He assigns opposite causes and reasons for reprobation.[1]

(3) The Gospel of John states: "He gave them power to become sons of God."[2] Since, therefore, in accordance with predestination and grace men become sons of God, this lies within their own free power and occurs in no other way than by merits acceptable to God.

(4) The psalmist agrees with this when, after reciting certain sins, he says, "Let them [the sinners] be blotted out of the book of the living; let them not be enrolled among the righteous."[3]

(5) Again the Apocalypse says, "Hold fast what you have, lest any-

one should seize your crown,"[4] which is the crown God has promised
to His elect.

(6) Likewise, if Adam had not sinned no one would have been
reprobated. Therefore, predestination or reprobation corresponds to
individual merit.[5]

(7) Likewise, since it would be unfair and cruel for either man or
an angel to harm someone without provocation, and such an action
would be necessarily unjust, how much less befitting would such action be for a God who is the most right and the most righteous? Nor
would it befit God that anyone should be reprobated and predestined
to eternal fire unless it were done on account of preceding guilt.[6]

(1) The first of these arguments is unreasonable and can be answered with complete clarity by referring to the argumentation of
previous chapters [that is, the sovereign God, creator and redeemer,
cannot be dependent on anything outside of Him].

(2) Now turning to the support drawn from Joachim, it should be
pointed out that although Joachim was a great doctor, he did not have
great authority. He was an Arian in his Trinitarian doctrine, as is
clear from the book he wrote against Peter Lombard, *On the Trinity,*[7]
and from his condemnation by Innocent III at the Fourth Lateran
Council.[8] And just as he was an Arian in Trinitarian doctrine he was
a Pelagian in attributing the original cause of predestination and
reprobation, not to the God who predestines and reprobates but to
man's own capacity and to the actions of the men predestined or
reprobated, as indicated above.

Nevertheless he tried to avoid the most extreme Pelagian position
by asserting that the cause of divine election and reprobation was
man's own capacity for mercy or wrath, not his capacity for works or
acts themselves. When Benedict asks what the capacity for good and
evil might be if not for good and evil works, as the Apostle says about
Isaac and Jacob, Joachim answers that this capacity is not an act but
"a repository of grace or wrath from which the good and evil works
have their origin."[9] And farther on he says that when God elects certain men He does not look for righteousness in them, for He himself
will give them that. The only factors necessary are humility and
wretchedness, that is to say, "a propensity for mercy."[10] Thus in ap-

proaching too close to the banks of the Pelagian flood he slips over and is sucked completely into the whirlpool, when he says that one's merits are the cause of predestination and reprobation.

As I briefly reconstruct the diffuse course of his argument, he means to say that humility is the cause of predestination, and pride the cause of reprobation, for he claims that the state of despair and misery is the underlying cause of divine election—as the Apostle says, "Brother, look to your calling because not many are wise according to the flesh but those whom the world thinks foolish, God chooses."[11]

As one reads farther it becomes clear that man is claimed by God, not for his righteousness but for his wretchedness, not for his works but for his need, not for his strength but for his weakness, not for his wisdom but for his foolishness, not for his high station but for his obscurity. "Just as the Pharisee of the biblical account is rejected for his righteousness, so the publican is chosen for his sin. This does not mean that God loves unrighteousness or hates the purity of innocence, but rather that he rejects self-righteousness and has mercy on the humble penitence of the sinner."[12]

And later Joachim says the causes of election are despair and affliction, "not because these things in themselves please God but because they give birth to humility, the sole virtue required by God of men and angels."[13] And again he says that because "the Lord had foreknowledge of the pride of the people of Israel he hated and rejected them."[14]

All of this makes it quite obvious that Joachim contradicts himself. How can it be possible for man's own capacity to be the cause of predestination or reprobation when sometimes, between two of equal capacity, one is chosen and one is abandoned or, at other times, the one of lesser capacity is chosen while the one of greater is abandoned? How can despair and misery be the cause of divine predestination when, as I suspect, many men who in this world live in despair, misery, and poverty are ultimately rejected, while others who have always enjoyed high station, prosperity, and wealth are predestined unto life? Among the holy angels who have been predestined and ultimately confirmed there was never any despair or misery, for they were never guilty or subject to punishment. And above all what is the misery and despair which, according to Joachim's theory, caused

Christ's predestination, He whom St. Paul calls the "Son of God in power"?[15]

Joachim's whole position could be "reprobated" by other arguments, but since so few of his arguments hold, these few of my rebuttals will suffice.

(3) Now when they bring forward the quotation from the Gospel of John, "He gave them power to become sons of God," they seem to wish to conclude from this that some become or can become the elect sons of God in the course of their life. That is, that from the number of those who are not predestined or who are reprobate, some at the present time can become predestined and at the same time cease to belong to the reprobate. This conflicts with what has been established in Chapters 23 and 45 and, furthermore, contains evident contradictions in itself as can plainly be shown from these chapters.[16]

The quotation from the Gospel of John seems rather to prove the opposite. For he did not say, "He gave them power to make themselves sons of God," but "to be made sons of God." But by whom? Not by themselves. Not out of their own will. Whoever has produced himself? Whoever was born out of himself? What son of the devil can give birth to himself and appear to be the son of God? Hear what follows: ". . . who are born not from human flesh or will but from God."[17] Therefore they do not make themselves sons of God. God does this.

Furthermore Aristotle shows that power, or capability, is of two kinds, active and passive.[18] Now that which is meant by the quotation, "He gave them power to become sons of God," is also asserted in Romans, "Whoever are led by the Spirit of God are sons of God."[19] God gives men power, that is to say, a rational soul and free will with which man can freely and voluntarily receive grace in the present and glory in the future so that, in both the present and the future, they might become sons of God. Thus in the present, as they are being made sons of God by faith and prevenient grace, which makes them into adopted sons of God, they freely accomplish the pleasing work of sons and so freely persevere in this to such an extent that no one could take away their sonship unless they would permit it.

Chrysostom supports this argument in his exegesis of the text which indicates that there is need of much zeal to preserve unspoiled the image with which man is endowed in the baptism of adoption. At the same time, however, he indicates that no one can take this power away from us but ourselves and that this grace comes to those who zealously desire it.[20] Indeed it is in the power of free will and grace to become sons of God by their joint operation.

And Augustine, commenting on John, asks, " 'Why were all born in sin?' That we are children of Adam implies damnation by necessity. But to be children of Christ is man's act through his will and through grace, since men are not forced to become children of Christ. Even though they did not choose to be born children of Adam, all of them are sinners in the true sense of the word. All those who are children of Christ are justified and are just, not because of themselves but because of Christ."[21] He does not say, "He gave them power to become sons of God," as if only man were included and God excluded in this process. Nor did he give man the priority while making God a subordinate factor. Therefore John says, "He gave them power to become sons of God," not "to make themselves sons of God."[22] And again, "They are born not out of the will of flesh nor out of the will of men but out of God who is the origin and author of this divine birth."[23]

Furthermore, Bede is quoted as saying, "The carnal begetting of each individual is due to the conjugal embrace, but his spiritual begetting is due to the grace of the Holy Spirit."[24] And Chrysostom said, "St. John the evangelist tells us this so that learning the weakness and humility of the first birth, which takes place through blood and the will of flesh, and knowing the sublimity of the second, which is through grace and excellence, we might receive from this text a profound understanding appropriate to the gift of Him who begets us, and show the appropriate zeal."[25]

And Augustine said, preaching on this passage from John, "To as many as received Him He gave power to become sons of God." If they became children, they were born. If they were born, whatever may have caused it, it was not flesh or blood or the will of flesh or the will of men but God. Let them rejoice, therefore, that they are born of God. Let them anticipate their return to God. Let them receive the proof because they are born of God.

And, "The Word was made flesh and dwelt among us."[26] If the

Word was not ashamed to be born of men, should man be ashamed to be born of God? Saying "He gave them power to become sons of God" does not at all mean, as Pelagius dreamed, that He gave them power to become sons of God by preceding works of merit. It is inconceivable that St. John could contradict his Lord, who said, as John himself reports, "No one is able to come unto me unless the Father who sent me draws him."[27] And "No one is able to come unto me unless it has been given to him by my father."[28] It is equally inconceivable that he could in such short compass make contradictory assertions. Since following hard on the above he says that the Word was full of grace and truth and then adds, "From this fullness we have all received grace for grace."[29] We have received first of all, as I say, grace freely given and truth because we receive grace promised of old and thus grace for grace, that is to say, grace given freely to fulfill the grace promised earlier through the prophets. Secondly, we have received according to our certain hope the grace of beatitude in the future for grace now operative during this dispensation.

Therefore Augustine commenting on John says, "He did not say, 'And from His fullness we all have received grace for grace,' but he said, 'And from His fullness we all have received, and, beyond that, grace for grace.'" Now I do not know what he wants us to understand with the words "have received from the fullness of His grace and, beyond that, grace for grace." Have we not received from his fullness first grace and then again grace for the grace we have received initially?

Does Augustine mean we receive faith before we receive grace? But we cannot walk in faith without being in grace. How would we ever have received this grace? By our preceding merits? Grace is *given* to you, it is not a payment. For this reason it is called grace, because it is freely given. With preceding merits you cannot buy what you have already received as a gift. Therefore the sinner has received first grace in order that his sins might be forgiven. What has he merited? When he demands justice he will receive punishment and when he asks for mercy he will receive grace. But this is exactly what had been promised by God through the prophets. Therefore when He comes to give what He has promised He gives not only grace but also truth. How is this truth manifested? When that which has been promised is fulfilled. What, in fact, does "grace for grace" mean? By faith we merit God.[30] That you received the immortal reward, that is, eternal life, is grace. On account of what merit do you receive eternal life? On account of grace. "God crowns His gifts, not your merits."[31] But this text can also very appropriately be exegeted literally by saying that those who are actually now children of God through faith and grace in this dispensation are granted the power, that is to say, grace helping free will, so that they might become children of God in the future, in the kingdom of heaven.

For this very reason he introduces the statement with "Whoever received Him," that is, by believing in Him through faith active in love, "He gave them power to become sons of God." Therefore Theophilus is quoted in the gloss, "Because we shall attain the most perfect sonship in the resurrection—as the Apostle says, we are awaiting the adoption of the sons of God, the redemption of our bodies—He grants us the power to become sons of God, that is, this grace will be consummated in future grace."[32]

(4) Let us turn now to the objection from Psalm 68 [69], "Let them be erased from the book of the living." If this is understood with superficial literalness, we must concede that predestination and reprobation are subject to change; it would imply that someone who was previously elected and not reprobated is now reprobated and not elected. If someone can at any time be erased from the book of the living, this contradicts everything which previously has been shown.[33]

It is necessary, therefore, to interpret the quotation in a different way. It can be understood as a deletion in accordance with present justice. Or "let them be erased" could be taken to mean "let them be regarded as erased," that is, "as never entered in the book," since the following statement actually says, "Let them not be written with the just." Or "let them be erased" could be taken to mean that their hope of being entered in the book is shown to be vain, just as God is said to feel regrets.[34]

Therefore when Augustine interprets this psalm he says, "Brethren, let us not take this to mean that God would have enrolled someone in the book of life and then erased him out of the book. If Pilate, a mere human, insisted that the inscription 'King of the Jews' should stay on Christ's cross once he said, 'What I have written, I have written,' is it not more certain that God would not change His mind?"

God knows in advance, before the foundation of the world He has predestined all who will reign with His Son in eternal life. Those whom He has enrolled are contained in the book of life. How can they be erased from a book where they were never written? This quotation expresses their hope, that is, they thought themselves to have been entered in the book of life. What does this mean, "Let them be erased from the book of life"? It is obvious they were never there to begin with.

Thus, therefore, those who had hoped, by reason of their righteousness, that they were written in the book of God, when confronted by their damnation, are made aware that they are "erased from the book of life," and they realize that they were never there. The second part of the statement ["Let them not be enrolled with the righteous"] explains the first part. As I have said, "Let them be erased" is to be understood to refer to their vain hopes. And this can correctly be summarized by saying, "Let them not be enrolled."[35]

(5) Likewise, to those who understand the Apocalypse literally, "Hold what you have" seems to say that it is possible for someone's crown to be taken away at any time and given to another man, and that, therefore, such a one can cease to be predestined and begin to be reprobated, while for the man who takes his place it is the other way around. But all that has been said does not allow of this. Neither John nor indeed the Spirit in John said or suggested that man through his own strength, without the help of God, holds or can hold his crown, that is, can persevere in a good life and good works until death. Nor did John say that anyone by himself and his own strength, alone without the special help of God, can receive the crown of predestination or grace in the present, or the crown of glory in the future.[36] The following trustworthy words confirm this conclusion: "Thus says the holy and true one who has the key of David, who opens and no one closes, who closes and no one opens: Behold, I have set before you an open door which no one is able to shut. Although you have little power, still you have preserved my word. Therefore I shall preserve you from the hour of temptation. Behold I come quickly.

Hold fast to what you have, etc."[37] Here it is clearly taught that perseverance depends first of all on divine preservation and secondly on human co-operation. How much the less does the beginning and attainment of an upright life depend on man alone! Therefore the quotation "Hold fast to what you have, etc." means that the good act is preceded and elicited by God's grace in order that man might persevere to the very end. Thus he who heard this exhortation was perhaps predestined [to life eternal] by means of this exhortation, be it from God or man, so that he might persevere to the end and hold fast to his crown.[38]

Augustine said that we should pray that those who have not yet been called might be called; perhaps they have been thus predestined to be won over by our prayers and to accept the grace by which they desire election and actually receive it. For God who has predestined all things will fulfill all.[39] It is possible to exegete the passage from Revelations just like the earlier one of the Psalms; it is possible for man to gain or lose the crown of life in terms of present justice, that is, in terms of certain hope.

Accordingly, Augustine proves that the gift of final perseverance cannot be lost and he suggests the following clarification for what we mean by its being lost. Because final perseverance actually means persevering until the end, it is possible for many to have it but, by definition, impossible for them to lose it.[40] Let us beware, however, of saying that the gift of final perseverance can never be lost once it has been granted, that is, once one had the ability to persevere until the end. Let us rather say that it is lost in that moment when man rejects the gift so that he cannot reach the goal—just as we say that the man who does not persevere until the end has lost eternal life or the kingdom of God. It is not that he ever actually had it but he would have had it if he had been able to persevere. And let us not quarrel about words, but let us simply say that there are things we can refer to as losing which, in reality, we do not possess but only hope to acquire.

(6) The argument that if Adam had not sinned, no one would have been reprobated but all would have been predestined does not prove at all that predestination and reprobation depend on merit. The opposite of this thesis follows obviously. As was shown above, God does

not predestine a certain end for man or man for a certain end; that is to say, God does not grant man eternal life on account of his future good works, but, on the contrary, He grants the good works that may bring him to eternal life. But it does not follow the other way around that if man had acted differently God would have drawn up a different eternal plan. The contrary is true.[41]

Take Christ as an example. If Christ had not done good works He would not have been predestined Son of God—this is obviously untenable! If Paul had not preached he would not have been elected—or was he elected in order that he might preach? No, the contrary is true. If the sun had never shone or the fire given heat, would they not have been predestined to do so? Have they now been predestined to do so because they actually do it? No, that the sun actually shines and the fire actually heats is because they have been predestined or preordained to do this. Moreover, it is by no means clear that if Adam had not sinned no one would have been reprobated. It seems possible that even if Adam had not sinned, all his descendants would not necessarily have been made sinless and confirmed until the end. Rather they would have had the freedom to choose or accept good or evil.

But even when we grant Anselm's point that if Adam had not fallen, all his descendants would have remained sinless to the end,[42] still we say with Gregory that none of the reprobate would have been born, but only the predestined.[43] Therefore, the sin of Adam is not the primary cause of reprobation, but rather, as said above, if Adam had not sinned, God would have ordained differently. And when you object to this argument on the grounds that a predestined son may sometimes have a reprobate father, and that such a son would not have had a father at all if Adam had not sinned, and, in that case, not only the *now* predestined but *all* who have been predestined would not have been born, you argue against St. Gregory, not against me. At the same time several things can be said in defense of St. Gregory's position. One answer would be that if Adam had not sinned, only those who are now elect would have been born, that is to say, only that number of those now elect would have been born. If Adam had not sinned, God would have created only those souls as are now given to the elect, although some he might perhaps have joined to other bodies than they have now. Or, if we wish to keep body and soul together as an elect unit, only those would have been born who are now elect. In that case an elect who has actually been born of a reprobate parent would have instead been born of another father who belongs to the elect.

(7) Now we turn to the argument which accuses God of injustice and cruelty. It should be noted that not every punishment appropriately given to one man by another is imposed because of preceding guilt. Sometimes the punishment is given as a warning or for other reasons, as many passages in divine as well as human writings show. As a certain law said, "No one who has not committed a crime ought to be punished unless there be a cause."[44] Both civil and canon law agree on this.

Furthermore, Peter Lombard shows that there are five reasons for man's punishment in this dispensation, which are: (1) the correction of sin, (2) the beginning of punishment for sin, (3) the growth in merits, as it was in the cases of Job and Tobith, (4) the avoidance of sin, as Paul says about the thorn in his flesh,[45] (5) the glory of God, as John makes clear in his passage about the man blind from birth.[46] One can also be publicly punished, to frighten others, to deter them from evil and strengthen them in goodness, in accordance with the laws, be they divine, canonical, or civil. If a man may undergo temporal punishment for the temporal benefit of others, why should he not be punished temporally and eternally for the temporal and eternal benefit of the elect, in order that they might all the more flee from evil and choose the good in the present, that in the future they might have greater joy, deeper love, and higher praise for God?

Thus great profit, both in the present and in the future, accrues to the elect from the reprobate, indeed the whole purpose of being for the reprobate is that they have been created for the sake of the elect. What injustice and cruelty can be charged to God because He chooses to predestine and create one of His creatures for the service of another creature and both of them for His own service, praise, glory, and honor? This is particularly true, since He punishes no man with eternal damnation unless such a man deserves it, that is to say, unless through his sins he deservedly and justly requires eternal punishment. And God always punishes most mercifully and appropriately because innumerable times he finds a way to punish less than is deserved.

If indeed, as Augustine seems to say, it is more desirable to be wretched than not to exist at all, what injustice or cruelty can be ascribed to God if He gives to some creature many and great goods, even though He may punish him with other of his creaturely goods, such as physical pain?[47] When all is taken into account, this creature's position is more attractive than repulsive, and, therefore, even for this state he owes God thanks as for a great gift.

Why do they not accuse God because He punishes innocent beasts and baptized infants with no small physical pain? Indeed He gave up his own most innocent Son, our Lord Jesus Christ, to a most painful, cruel, and tormenting punishment. But since God is omnipotent, completely free Lord of His whole creation, whose will alone is the most righteous law for all creation[48]—if He should eternally punish the innocent, particularly since He does it for the perfection of the universe, for the profit of others, and for the honor of God Himself, who would presume to dispute with Him, to contradict Him, or ask, "Why do you do this?" I firmly believe, no one! "Has the potter no right over the clay to make of the same lump one vessel for honor and another for menial use?"[49]

Notes

1. The text of this dialogue has been edited and attributed to Joachim by Johannis C. Huck in his *Joachim von Floris und die Joachimitische Literatur*, Freiburg i. Br., 1938, pp. 278–287. For a review of further literature on the authenticity and editing of this text see H. A. Oberman, *"De Praedestinatione et Praescientia*: An Anonymous Fourteenth-Century Treatise on Predestination and Justification," in *Nederlandsch* *Archief voor Kerkgeschiedenis*, 43 (1960), p. 216, footnote 3.

2. John 1:12.
3. Psalms 69:28.
4. Revelation 3:11.
5. Cf. Joachim's dialogue in Huck, *op. cit.*, p. 285.
6. *Ibid.*, pp. 279–281.
7. For a description of the unpublished life of St. Benedict, in which Joachim attacks Peter Lombard, see Huck, *op. cit.*, pp. 169 ff.

8. The chapter beginning "Damnamus" in "De Summa Trinitate et Fide Catholica," cf. *CIC*, vol. II, col. 6. Pope Innocent III (1198–1216) had Joachim's criticism condemned at the Fourth Lateran Council (November 1215). The text is available in *Enchiridion Symbolorum*, 32d ed., ed. Denzinger and Schönmetzer, 803.

9. Huck, *op. cit.*, p. 281.

10. *Ibid.*

11. I Corinthians 1:26, 27.

12. Huck, *op. cit.*, p. 282.

13. *Ibid.*, p. 283.

14. *Ibid.*, p. 285.

15. Romans 1:4.

16. Chapter 23 of Book I of *De Causa Dei* asserts that God's will and knowledge are immutable. God is eternal and does not, therefore, shift His loyalties. Election and reprobation stand from eternity and are independent of good and evil deeds.

17. John 1:13. Another English bishop would two centuries later opt for Joachim's side of the debate. An opponent of Luther, St. John Fisher of Rochester (1469–1535), deals with this text in his *Assert. Luth. Confutatio* in art. 36, Venice, 1526, fol. 167.

18. Aristotle, *Nicomachean Ethics*, Bk. 5, ch. 7, and Bk. 9, ch. 2.

19. Romans 8:14.

20. Chrysostom, *Homiliae in Joannem*, Homilia X in *PG*, vol. LIX, col. 76.

21. Augustine, *In Joannis Evangelium*, Tractatus III, 12, in *PL*, vol. XXXV, col. 1401.

22. Augustine, *op. cit.*, Tractatus II, 13, in *PL*, vol. XXXV, col. 1394.

23. *Ibid.*, Tractatus II, 14 and 15, in *PL*, vol. XXXV, col. 1394, 1395.

24. Beda, *Expositio in Joannis Evangelium*, ch. I, in *PL*, vol. XCII, col. 641.

25. Chrysostom, *op. cit.*, Homilia XI in *PG*, vol. LIX, col. 76.

26. John 1:14. Augustine, *op. cit.*, Tractatus III, 6, in *PL*, vol. XXXV, col. 1399.

27. John 6:44.

28. An allusion to John 6:45.

29. John 1:16.

30. Augustine, *op. cit.*, Tractatus III, 8, 9, in *PL*, vol. XXV, col. 1399, 1400.

31. *Ibid.*, Tractatus III, 10, in *PL*, vol. XXXV, col. 1401.

32. This quotation has not been found.

33. Bradwardine refers to Bk. I, ch. 5, of *De Causa Dei*, which deals with the immutability of God's will.

34. Bradwardine refers to Bk. I, ch. 7, which discusses anthropomorphic language applied to God.

35. Augustine, *Enarrationes in Psalmos LXVIII*, 13, in *PL*, vol. XXXVI, col. 862, 863.

36. Bradwardine refers to certain earlier chapters to support his thesis. Bk. I, ch. 2 establishes the necessity of God's preservation of His creation. Bk. I, ch. 9 shows that the divine will is the efficient cause of all human acts. Bk. I, ch. 25 demonstrates the necessity of the prevenience of grace. Bk. I, ch. 45 shows that God's predestination is independent of man's works.

37. Revelation 3:7; 10, 11.
38. Bradwardine refers to Bk. I, ch. 23, which argues that God's predestination is independent of man's good or evil deeds.
39. Augustine, "De Dono Perseverantiae," ch. XXIII, 64, in *PL*, vol. XLV, col. 1032.
40. Augustine, *op. cit.*, ch. III, 7, in *PL*, vol. XLV, col. 998.
41. Bk. I, ch. 45 asserts that no one is predestined or rejected because of future works.
42. Anselm, *Cur Deus Homo,* Bk. I, ch. 19, in *PL,* vol. CLVIII, col. 390, 391.
43. Gregory, *Moralium,* Bk. IV. Bradwardine apparently uses the old chapter divisions, since he refers to ch. 39. Cf. *PL,* vol. LXXV, col. 673.
44. "De Regulis Juris," ch. VI in *CIC,* vol. II, col. 928.
45. Cf. II Corinthians 12:7.
46. Bradwardine attributes this to Lombard's *Sentences,* Bk. IV, Dist. 15.
47. Bradwardine refers to two passages, *De Libere Arbitrio,* Bk. II, ch. 3, which does discuss the problem of evil, and also to *De Civitate Dei,* Bk. II, ch. 27, which is apparently a misquotation.
48. In Bk. I, ch. 21, Bradwardine contends that something is just because God wills it. This typically fourteenth-century emphasis has often been misunderstood as making out of God an arbitrary tyrant. Cf. *Harvest,* pp. 96 ff.; p. 111, n. 71.
49. *Romans* 9:21.

GABRIEL BIEL

The Circumcision of the Lord

"His name shall be called Jesus" (Luke 2:21).

A few days ago we celebrated that glorious day which the birth of our Savior has made so wonderful and lovely for us and which He gave us as an example for our imitation. To this rejoicing is now added a new exultation when today in the circumcision of the new-born King "that name" is given "which is above every name,"[1] which was chosen by the Father from eternity before all worlds, which was enunciated by angels, by the Mother and by Joseph, the legal father, which was according to Origen announced to them by the new man.[2]

On this day of His circumcision we have no less reason for wonder, praise, and imitation than on the day of His birth. On that day we marveled that the highest majesty appeared in the form of a servant. Today we marvel that this God who is born sinlessly, true God from God the Father and true man from the Virgin Mary, was circumcised just like a sinner.

On Christmas Day we, in our small way, gave thanks, expressing our love and praise for the Redeemer who came into the prison of this world to lead the captives out of this prison. Today we magnify Him with all our hearts because He put on our fetters and bonds and because He put His own innocent hands into our chains in order that we criminals might be set free.

At His birth we saw with the shepherds the Word which was abbreviated to fit the dimensions of the world; we saw lying in the manger the holy and tender child whose humility we are urged to

165

imitate. Today we see that He who gave the law made Himself subject to the law by His circumcision and thus we are instructed even more clearly in obedience of the law to which we are subject. And just as on that day at the moment of His birth, or beginning, He joined together the human with the divine, now at His circumcision He shows that He is truly man, while simultaneously "that name which is above every name" bespeaks the glory of majesty. In order that His divine nature by which He saves His people from their sins might be better known, He has, by His circumcision, destroyed sin in the children of wrath and infused His grace in them. Therefore, it is most appropriate that the text, "His name shall be called Jesus," is selected at the beginning as our theme. Pray now for the needed assistance of grace with a "Hail Mary!"

> "Unto us a Child is born, unto us a Son is given":
> that is Jesus.

He is called Savior. Not just through human preaching but through the message of the angels it is already well enough known to Christians that the Child Who has been born and the Son Who has been given to us is called Jesus, that is, Savior. Savior, not because of some limited and temporal salvation, as some men have sometimes been called "savior," but Savior because of that universal, spiritual, and eternal salvation which no one else has bestowed or has ever been able to bestow.

To resume, Gabriel said to Joseph, "You will call His name Jesus for He will save His people from their sins." In truth *He has already saved* His people by preparing medicine. *He continues to save* them daily by driving out disease. *He will save* them ultimately by giving them perfect health and preserving them from every ill. The preparation of the medicine is the task of the human nature of Christ, the driving out of disease the task of the divine nature, and the perfect health the task of both natures.

He prepared the medicine when He instituted and commanded the medicinal sacraments. To heal the wounds inflicted by our sins, He, through the effusion of His blood, earned efficacy for the sacraments. Since I remember having preached about this at length a year ago on this very day, I comment no further on this point and turn to another. In the present sermon three issues are to be raised.

First, in what does this driving out of disease consist? How does this accord with Christ's divine nature? *Second*, what is actually accomplished by grace? We ought to see what grace is and what its effects are. *Third*, some truths should be deduced regarding the significance of grace by which we can be exhorted to come to know and to praise the power of God.

I said that our Savior saves us daily by driving out disease, which is the task of His divine nature. Now it is obvious that this disease is sin, which He drives out when He forgives and ceases to impute to the sinner eternal punishment. As the prophet says, "Blessed is the man to whom the Lord does not impute sin, whose sin is covered."[3] And Jerome, commenting on that said, "When the Lord forgives sins He covers the sinner lest in the judgment it be revealed to his damnation."[4] For, as Augustine said, when God sees sins He charges them unto punishment. But when He forgives sins He also always restores the lost grace which is the health and life of the soul.[5] Since, now, "all the works of God are perfect,"[6] He does not imperfectly heal the disease by merely driving it out, but He also gives health by the infusion of grace. For a man does not enjoy perfect health when, although without pain in his body, he is unable to use it for the tasks of life. But this capacity is a gift of grace. This is what Augustine meant when he said, "The Lamb takes away the sins both by forgiving what has been done and by helping the sinner not to sin again."[7] This help is extended through grace.

Both operations are ascribed primarily to the divine nature. No one removes sins except God alone, Who is the lamp taking away the sins of the world, as Augustine said. For this reason, namely, that He forgives sins, the Jews accused Christ of blasphemy, since they did not believe Him to be God. Now no one confers grace except God. It is clear that grace comes into being only through God's creative action, since grace cannot be acquired through our works like other moral habits which, as Aristotle said,[8] are naturally engendered in us by repetition of our own moral actions. The Apostle Paul said, "But if it is by grace, it is no longer on the basis of works, otherwise grace would no longer be grace."[9] Because nature cannot make something out of nothing, that which is created comes from God alone. If grace could come from the creature, a grace which would suffice unto salvation, then any creature would be able to save himself by his own natural powers, that is, do what only grace can do. That is the error of Pelagius. Therefore, the prophet said, "The Lord will give grace and glory."[10]

In order that we understand with what great kindness God saves us by His justification of sinners or the forgiveness of sins (and thus understand the mercy of the Lord), let us be found even more acceptable to Him and let us in gratitude prepare for the reception of even greater gifts.

Now we must see just what this grace is by which the sinner is justified and what is actually accomplished in us. The grace of which we speak is a gift of God supernaturally infused into the soul. It makes the soul acceptable to God and sets it on the path to deeds of meritorious love.

There are many other supernatural gifts which are also infused into the soul. The Apostle Paul says, "There are varieties of gifts but the same Spirit," and goes on to enumerate gifts of the Spirit—wisdom, knowledge, faith, healing, miracles, etc. "To one is given through the Spirit the utterance of wisdom and to another the utterance of knowledge, etc."[11] But none of them make the man who receives them acceptable to God, nor does it make his work worthy of merit.

Now the many praiseworthy effects of grace can be summarized under three headings: (a) making acceptable, (b) justifying, and (c) making the works which result meritorious and worthy of eternal life, of grace and glory.

a. Grace makes acceptable for this reason alone, that it is present in and is part of that nature which can be beatified, that is, man. According to Scotus, grace is an enrichment of nature that is pleasing to God's will.[12] Grace makes human nature acceptable to God by adorning it not with an ordinary acceptation but with that special acceptation by which man is according to God's decision ordained toward life eternal. For to be acceptable, to be beloved by God and to be His friend, means to be in such a state that one will attain eternal life unless one loses this state through sin. For example, in just this way, grace makes acceptable to God children who neither desire nor are able to desire the good. This is what the Apostle Paul said to Timothy, "So that we might be justified by His grace and become heirs to a firm hope of eternal life."[13] And Peter said, "Through the grace of our Lord Jesus Christ we believe unto salvation."[14]

b. And because grace makes the sinner acceptable to God it follows that it also justifies him. Justification has two aspects: remission of guilt, and acceptation to eternal life, since it is impossible for one who is going to be accepted to eternal life to be at the same time condemned to eternal punishment. If it were otherwise, the same person would be both worthy and unworthy of eternal life. Therefore, it is necessary that he who has been accepted unto life have his guilt forgiven (if he has any).

But if grace is infused into someone who is already justified, that which it accomplishes is not justification. An example would be the grace once given to the holy angels and now daily given to those who are upright of heart, who through their good works earn an additional gift of grace above and beyond the grace already in them. About this justification by grace Paul writes, "They are justified by His grace as a gift through the redemption which is in Christ Jesus."[15]

c. Thus God makes these our works meritorious and acceptable for eternal reward, not actually all our works but only those which have been brought forth by the prompting of grace. It is assumed of a meritorious work that the person who performs it is accepted, since the acts of a person who has not been accepted or of an enemy cannot please God. As Genesis says, "The Lord had regard for Abel and his offering,"[16] that is, God's acceptance went first to the person of Abel and only secondly to his gifts. And this acceptance is due to the mere presence of grace in a person, as we saw above.

But an act is not meritorious just because it is performed by one who has been accepted, since such a person can commit venial sins or perform morally indifferent [neutral] acts. Therefore, a meritorious act must be brought forth by the prompting of grace. This grace prompts us to love God above all things and in all things, that is, to seek after the glory of God as the goal of every action, and to prefer the ultimate good, God, ahead of one's self and everything else. Therefore, all those things which are not directed consciously or unconsciously toward God do not come from the prompting of grace and therefore are surely not worthy of eternal life.

And although, according to some doctors, man can love God above everything else with his natural powers alone [without grace], this applied particularly to man before the fall; but man can never love God as perfectly and easily as with grace. Moreover, without grace it is absolutely impossible for him to love God meritoriously. Such is the rule established by God that no act should be accepted as meritorious unless it be prompted by grace. Therefore, the Apostle said, "We are not sufficient of ourselves to claim anything as coming from us, our sufficiency is from God." And again after having said that he had worked hard for others, the Apostle quickly added, "Though it was not I, but the grace of God which is within me."[17]

Thus, as Lombard said, meritorious acts depend on two factors, our free will and grace.[18] There is no human merit that does not depend partly on free will. The principal cause of meritorious moral action, however, is attributed to grace. But grace does not determine the will. The will can ignore the prompting of grace and lose it by its own default. The prompting of grace is toward meritorious acts for the sake of God. Therefore, the act as such stems primarily from grace. This is the case because it is performed by someone who has grace in accordance with the prompting of grace. Augustine speaks in this way when he says that the will is related to grace like a footservant to her lady—it accompanies but does not precede grace.[19] And in his book on free will he says that grace is related to free will as a rider to the horse. The rider guides the horse and chooses the direction in which to go. Indeed it is in this way that grace steers and prompts the will to direct itself toward God.[20]

Thus it is clear that grace is nothing other than infused love [charity], because the same effects are attributed to both. For love [charity] is that which prompts us to love God above everything else, which makes us beloved to God, without which no one is beatified. Now this is exactly what grace does, therefore both Holy Scripture and the Fathers identify love with grace. What love accomplishes they attribute to grace alone and vice versa. So the Apostle says that no gifts are of benefit without love. And again the Apostle reported that the Lord had spoken to him, "My grace is sufficient for you."[21] Now these two assertions are consistent only if love and grace are exactly the same.

Augustine, too, says, "The whole difference between salvation and perdition is grace alone," and elsewhere: "It is love alone that makes the difference between salvation and perdition."[22] This thesis rests not only on authorities but also on reason based on Scripture, for if grace and love were different they could be separated by God. Then it would be possible for a man to have grace but not be a friend of God, or man could even be an enemy of God, if he had grace and not love, or, again, man could be a friend of God but not accepted by God, if he had love but not grace. Therefore, we conclude that it is one and the same to be accepted, beloved, and a friend of God.

Scotus, however, argues for a rational distinction between the two. Grace, he says, refers to God as the loving subject,[23] on the grounds that the word grace is used when God loves someone. Love [charity] on the other hand refers to God as the object of love, because this word has the connotation of love for God.[24]

Likewise it is clear why the doctors call grace a habit, although it is not acquired but infused. Grace accomplishes in the soul something similar to the effects of a naturally acquired habit, although in a far more perfect fashion than an acquired habit. The naturally acquired habit is a permanent quality in the power of the soul which stems from frequently repeated acts. This habit prompts and urges the man to repeat the same act. As Aristotle says, "Experience teaches us with certainty that all these acts leave behind a capacity which allows us to do these acts with greater care, readiness, pleasure, and correctness."[25]

But grace elevates human power beyond itself, so that acts which had turned by sin toward evil or inward toward one's self now can be meritoriously redirected against the law of the flesh and toward God. Grace leads, assists, and directs in order that man may be prompted in a way which corresponds with divine charity. And thus grace weakens the remaining power of sin, not—as many doctors say —because it forgives or wipes out sins, but because it strengthens human power.

We could use the illustration of a bird that has a stone tied to it so that it could scarcely fly away. Now if this bird's wings were strengthened, then we would say that the impediment to flight had been lessened, although the weight of the stone had not been lessened. Thus the Apostle knew that he was assisted by grace when he cried out against the law of the flesh by which he was tortured, "Wretched man that I am! Who will deliver me from the body of death? The grace of God through Jesus Christ our Lord."[26]

The preceding has made clear how much the grace given to us by Christ excels the original righteousness we lost in Adam. Because, although original righteousness completely subdued the tincture of sin and ordered the lower powers of man in perfect obedience to the higher powers, it did not give to human power the capacity to perform meritorious works. Nor could Adam have been saved by original righteousness alone without grace. From this we can understand how great a gift that grace is by which Christ saves in the present dispensation.

Grace is a gift above every created thing, as the Apostle makes clear. Referring to this the Lord said to the disciples, "No longer shall I call you servants but friends."[27] Augustine says, "Behold the gifts given to the Church, and know that from among them all, the most excellent is the gift of love." Grace is "the gift by which alone we are made good, as by no other created gifts."[28] Whatever you want, have this. This is the only gift which is indispensable, without which all the others are useless. "Even if you do not have the others, knowledge or prophesy, having this you have fulfilled the law."[29] Not only is this gift more glorious than all others, it is so great that it is never given unless the Holy Trinity gives Itself with it. The Trinity never gives Itself without this gift nor the gift without Itself. As the Apostle has said, "God's love has been poured into our hearts through the Holy Spirit which has been given to us."[30] And the Gospel of John asserts that the Holy Spirit is not given without the Father and the Son.[31]

In all these things, my beloved, magnify and praise the loving mercy and goodness of our Lord Jesus Christ which is shown in the justification of the sinner. He could very well have forgiven sins by abstaining from punishment for them, without going so far as embracing the sinner as a friend—for this is all that man usually does. But God thought it too little to forgive the sins of him who had lost God's friendship through sinning, without also restoring (*reformaret*) him to His personal friendship.

But even this does not exhaust the infinite mercy of the Savior; He also gives a special aid of grace. By this grace we are able to remain without difficulty in His friendship, and to grow continually through good works. On such a foundation we can easily overcome the on-slaughts of the devil, the world, and flesh, and gain a great reward in store for us.

No doubt He could have simultaneously made us His friends and accepted our work as meritorious without this gift of grace. But how could we have remained in friendship with God without the assistance of grace? Thus God has established the rule [covenant] that whoever turns to Him and does what he can will receive forgiveness of sins from God. God infuses assisting grace into such a man, who is thus taken back into friendship. As is written in John: "Grace and truth came through Christ."[32]

So that this might be more easily understood I shall tell a parable: Let us say that there is a most lenient king who shows so much mercy to his people that he publishes a decree saying that he will embrace with his favor any of his enemies who desire his friendship, provided they mend their ways for the present and the future. Furthermore, the king orders that all who have been received in this fashion into his friendship will receive a golden ring to honor all who are dedicated to his regime, so that such a friend of the king may be known to all. The king gives to such a man by way of delegation of his royal au-thority such a position that every work done to the honor of the king, regardless of where performed or how large or small it is, shall be rewarded by the king above and beyond its value. And to give him extra strength to perform this kind of meritorious work, precious and powerful stones are inserted in the ring to encourage him who wears it, so that his body does not fail him when he needs it but increases in ability to gain further rewards the more the body is exercised and accustomed to resist every adverse force.

How could one ever praise highly enough the clemency and the preciousness of the gifts of such a king? Behold, such is our King and Savior! The gift is grace, which is bestowed abundantly on us, which is to the soul what the ring is to the body in the parable.

Therefore, it is indeed fitting that the name of such a great Savior be Jesus, because He alone can save His people by His gift of grace. We pray that He deign to give us this grace in the present and glory in the future. Amen.

Notes

1. Philippians 2:9.
2. It is possible that Biel refers, in this text, to Origen's homily which says that the Savior was a new generation not born of man and woman but of the Virgin alone. *PG,* vol. XIII, col. 1837, Homilies on Luke (ch. 2).
3. Psalms 32:1.
4. In Jerome's comments on the Psalms it is the sins which are covered, not the sinner. *PL,* vol. XXVI, col. 967.
5. Biel paraphrases Augustine's interpretation of Psalms 32:1, *Enarrationes in Psalmos, PL,* vol. XXXVI, col. 264.
6. Deuteronomy 32:4.
7. Biel paraphrases Augustine, *Contra Julianum,* Bk. II, in *PL,* vol. XLV, col. 1176.
8. Aristotle, *Nicomachean Ethics,* Bk. 2, 1.
9. Romans 11:6.
10. Psalms 84:11.
11. I Corinthians 12:4-8.
12. Biel refers this to the *Commentary on the Sentences* of Scotus, Bk. III, dist. 17, q. 1. See Vivès edition, vol. 23, 135a.
13. Titus 3:7.
14. Acts 15:11.
15. Romans 3:24.
16. Genesis 4:4.
17. II Corinthians 3:5; I Cor. 15:10.
18. Lombard, *Sent.,* Bk. II, dist. 27, in *PL,* vol. CXCII, col. 714–717.
19. Augustine, *Enchiridion,* ch. 32, in *PL,* vol. XL, col. 248.
20. The simile is found in the Pseudo-Augustinian *Hypognosticon* III. ii. 20 in *PL,* vol. XLV, col. 1632. Cf. *Harvest,* p. 162, note 52.
21. II Cor. 12:9.
22. Augustine, *op. cit.,* ch. 30, and *Commentary on John, PL,* vol. XXXV, col. 1809, 1846.
23. Scotus, *op. cit.,* Bk. II, dist. 27.
24. *Ibid.*
25. Aristotle, *Nicomachean Ethics,* Bk. II, 1.
26. Romans 7:24, 25.
27. John 15:15.
28. Augustine, *Enarrationes in Psalmos CIII, PL,* vol. XXXVI, col. 1543, 1544.
29. Augustine, *Commentary on John, PL,* vol. XXXV, col. 1845, 1846.
30. Romans 5:5.
31. Cf. John 14.
32. John 1:17.

JOHANN VON STAUPITZ

Eternal Predestination
and its Execution in Time

I. The Goal of Creation and Redemption

God is the creator of heaven and earth and all things contained in them. Each individual work is full of the glory of the Lord. He himself knows all there is to know, and perceives it in the mirror of eternity, and grasps the past, present, and future all at once. No thought escapes Him nor is any work hidden from Him. Not by chance, therefore, but by His bidding did He fashion the universe. With His wisdom He adorned and made attractive each and every thing so that each was very good but not, however, the best. It is impossible for the creature to be the best, since to be a creature means to tend toward nothingness, and to return to nothingness unless upheld by the One Who created him.

Indeed, goodness is not possible unless it be given by the Best, nor can it have any meritorious power unless done by the grace of the Best. Hence the Lord has made all things in and for Himself, whether by creation He provides for life or by redemption for good life. For just as He creates all things in such a fashion that their existence might derive from Him, so also He restores the fallen ones that their goodness and righteousness derive from Him. As the Lord says according to Scripture, "I, I am He who blots out your transgression for My own sake, and I will not remember your sins."[1]

Since God is infinite perfection, and nothing better than He can be conceived, nothing more or less, nothing further is required than praise, honor, and glory. In order that we might know and love God,

He has made the saints relate all His marvelous acts which He, the omnipotent Lord, has established in His everlasting glory. To the degree He is known He is loved, and to the degree He is loved He is praised. Therefore, the goal of creation and restoration is the praise of the Creator and Redeemer.

II. The Utility of Praising God

Provided one praises in the proper manner, the praise of God is never without beneficial effect. By praising God, immense in Himself, we make Him great in us, and by comparison with Him we reduce the created universe to its own proportions, to nothingness. Thus we prepare a worthy habitation for God and we erect a temple for the Holy Spirit, full of God and empty of all creatureliness. And so it happens that we, who have our origins outside ourselves (*extra nos*), cease to be what we were and begin to be what we were not. For surely by nature we were children of wrath but by grace we are children of God. We were cursed in Adam, but we are blessed in the promised Son.

Nothing, therefore, is more felicitous for the creature than to return with praise to his origin, to abandon himself and approach God. Nor can anyone praise God worthily without reducing himself to nothing. Hence, the more one is freed from himself the more felicitous it is for him. Indeed, eternally felicitous is he who does not cease to praise God.

For this purpose the Spirit of the Lord comes to our hearts saying, "How lovely is thy dwelling place, O Lord of hosts, My soul longs, yea, faints for the courts of the Lord, My heart and flesh sing for joy, they jump (*extra se*) to the living God."[2] And a little farther this is added, "Blessed are those who dwell in Thy house, ever singing they shall praise Thee."[3]

Nor should this be forgotten, namely, that praise is required from the mouth and heart of every rational creature for the gifts of the whole creation which are put at man's disposal and were created for his benefit. But man should praise God most of all for the gifts personally given to him, so that amid this accumulation of gifts, man's responsibility grows, since they put the recipient under obligation.

III. The Deficiency of Man's Praise Without Christ

Just as we do not love unknown things and insufficiently love that which we insufficiently know, so we are unable to praise that which we do not know at all and have no reason to love. Nor can we worthily praise that which we can see only dimly and love only half-heartedly. Since, however, no one knows the Father except the Son and the man to whom the Son wishes to reveal Him, no one can rightly praise God who does not believe and confess Christ to be the true Son of God.[4] He who sees Him sees the Father, since the Father is in the Son, and the Son in the Father. Now he sees in faith, but ultimately he will see face to face, just as he himself is seen.

That Christ is believed, acknowledged, and worshiped as the Son of God is not due to flesh and blood but rather to revelation by the Heavenly Father. Those who believe in Him are already saved in hope, since we are able "to comprehend with all the saints what is the breadth and length and height and depth, and to know the love of Christ which surpasses knowledge that we may be filled with the fullness of God."[5]

Undoubtedly it is necessary for him who desires to praise God rightly to know in what ways God wants to be praised and ought to be honored. There are four principal ways. First, we ought to acknowledge God as omnipotent, of infinite power and majesty. This is the "breadth," which transcends all measure and dimension. A second confession is necessary, that is, that God's wisdom cannot be measured; it stretches from pole to pole and establishes a perfect harmony in all things. This is the "length," which must be comprehended by anyone who wants to praise God rightly. Thirdly—more necessary than these—is to understand the sublimity of the infinite mercy of God and that His compassion overshadows all His other works [the "height"]. Nor should the fourth be forgotten, that is, that His justice is infinite and inflexible and His judgments are unfathomable [the "depth"].

These are the "unsearchable riches of Christ, the mystery hidden for ages in God, who created all things that through the Church the

manifold wisdom of God might now be made known to the principalities and powers in the heavenly places. This was according to the
eternal purpose which He had realized in Christ Jesus our Lord, in
whom we have boldness and confidence of access through our faith
in Him."[6]

From the preceding we conclude that if we are to fulfill our debt
of praise to God we must know Him, and we cannot know Him if we
do not know Christ, because the sublimity of God's mercy is not
seen, indeed, *cannot* be seen apart from Christ (*extra Christum*). The
guardians of truth among the Jews perceived this when they established the rule that no one with the exception of the Messiah was
allowed to use the four letters of the Hebrew name for God, so that
neither in writing nor in thought could anyone articulate the name
God apart from the Messiah.[7] This was most appropriate, since only
in Christ are the four previously stated incomprehensible conditions
found all togther.

IV.   The Predestination of the Saints

From the foregoing it is clear, I think, that it is impossible to praise
God without knowledge and love of Him. Nor is it possible to praise
God worthily without absolutely certain knowledge of Him, which
is attainable only through faith in Christ. For faith means just this,
that where knowledge fails and scientific proof is out of the question,
nothing remains except faith, hope, and love.

Since faith in Christ is so necessary that without it, it is impossible
to please God, and since we are unable to acquire faith by our own
means, it is clear that what flesh and blood does not reveal is, doubtless, a gift of God and not the result of our works. Therefore, let no
one pride himself that it is because of his merits that he is enrolled
among the faithful and let no one claim for nature what properly belongs to grace.

If, however, you attribute your election to nature, and accept your
heritage from Adam, you are left, not with faith, hope, and love but
with a half-dead man, lame, weakened by wounds, and powerless to
perform even his natural tasks, to say nothing of those works which
are beyond us and which transcend our every faculty, namely to know

God as the Three in One, and to know the Son of God, God of God, Light of Light, who was incarnate, suffered, was crucified, and died.

For even our Augustine, notwithstanding the great reach of his natural insight, had no idea of the depths of mystery of the Incarnation. Therefore, it is most certain that no one can attain to true faith in Christ by his or anyone else's natural insights.

Originally God decided that for His praise and glory men should be created and that all corporeal things should be put at his disposal, but soon the nothingness of His creature came to light. Left to his own devices this creature could not avoid slipping, falling, and reverting to nothingness in his very existence, in his natural capacities, and in his natural actions. And it proved to be even less possible for him not to be deficient in morally good actions.

In order that the whole plan of creation should not be frustrated, there has been ordained preservation by divine power for nature and for free will the grace of the divine Incarnation; and thus natural life is upheld by preservation, a morally good life is sustained by grace, and both by God Himself. Accordingly, before the creation of the world it was determined that no one would be able to do morally good works without the grace of Christ.

Because mercy and justice contribute equally to the praise of the Almighty it has been decreed that some should be elected and predestined to conformation with the image of the Son of God and to faith in our Lord Jesus Christ.[8] But those who do not have faith are judged already.[9]

This [election] is the first grace which precedes nature and works. No one elicits or merits this grace, nor is this grace due to merits foreknown by God, nor to good use of reason in the future foreseen by God, nor to merits already performed. Rather, the sole source of this grace is the most kind and generous will of God.

Once this first grace is given, other graces follow one by one without fail, and Christ is put under obligation to save the elect. That is exactly what He said to Zacchaeus, "It is necessary that I stay in thy house,"[10] implying that even this Israelite, this son of Abraham, was elected according to promise. Necessity in the same sense of the word led to Christ's passion, crucifixion, and death for sinners.

These now are the eternal decrees, but beware lest you think you can order them chronologically, for you are limited by the deficiency of human speech. The earthly language that comes from earth is limited to earthly things.

I now ask, faithful soul, that you consider well the things that have been said; truly, you also shall experience this truth which Christ himself taught, namely, that "the highest joy on earth is to know that your name is written in heaven."[11]

V. The Call to Faith and Salvation

Paul, illustrious doctor of the Church, tongue of Christ, and the most direct disciple of the most Holy Trinity said: "Those whom He predestined He Himself also called." He did not say, "He *had* them called."[12] Many are called by "the light that has arisen over us,"[13] others by the law, by prophets, by gifts, by tribulations, by Apostles or preachers of the faith. But not all are elected. However, those who are freely predestined are called without fail in their lifetime unto faith by God's powerful will. For indeed this is not done by Moses nor by the prophets nor by the Apostles, but by God Himself Who speaks to the heart.

Concerning this call the Son said, "No one comes to Me unless the Heavenly Father draws him."[14] Paul also preached this in an excellent manner: "I planted, Apollos watered, but God gave the growth."[15] For indeed he who plants is nothing, nor he who waters, but He who gives the growth, that is God, is all.

Provided the exterior call is efficacious, then you could certainly say that all who are called will doubtless be justified. For just as God is committed to call all who are predestined, so He is committed to justify all who are called. This is not a natural obligation but an obligation of grace which the Apostle fully appreciates when he says, "He who did not spare His own Son but gave Him up for us all, will He not also give us all things with Him?"[16]

For just as the knowledge of natural things flows from the knowledge of the first principle, so also each individual grace flows from the grace of predestination. In this and through this, as I have indicated above, Christ has been made the servant of our salvation and "has come into the world not to be ministered to but to minister and to give His life as a ransom for many."[17]

Hence the well-known saying attributed to our own Augustine is by no means defensible in the way in which it is put: "If you are not predestined make yourself predestined." For the gifts and call of God are not the result of penitence. How and by what means God calls men in the Spirit is known to the Spirit of God, which searches the very depths of God, and perhaps to the spirit of the man who is called.

VI.   Justification of the Sinner

Those whom He called He also justified. From the beginning God created man righteous and good according to the image and likeness of Christ and in conformity with Christ Who is the luster of the glory of God and the form of His substance. Man has, however, by his own free will involved himself in endless questions, and from that time has fallen and, alas, continues to fall.

First, as you know, man began to question why God had commanded him to abstain from one tree of paradise, while all the others were at his disposal. He pondered whether perhaps it had rotten fruit which looked horrible or tasted bitter. But he saw that the forbidden fruit would be good to eat and was beautiful to the eye and that it was, so to see, delicious. The coldly calculating serpent insinuated himself into the thoughts of an innocent woman, since he knew well that the good of mankind, and indeed of every creature, consists in obedience to God alone. He raised the question of why God had commanded not to eat of the forbidden fruit, and when the wretched woman was caught in the first question a whole infinity of questions followed.

When she had heard that this was a tree of the knowledge of good and evil she did not want to be subject to God but rather she wanted to be like Him. Wrapped up in herself she broke the commandment and rejected obedience, whereby she was brought to naught and to subservience to the devil, the world, and the flesh. Damned to eternal death she was cast into such great misery that she became her own hell, perpetually tortured. She had neither the knowledge nor the will to be freed from this, let alone to free herself.

Oh woeful wretchedness! And worse, we bear this accursed damnation with joy, and serve sin with glee. But the hand of the Lord is not shortened—no, rather the earth is full of the mercy of the Lord and it reaches up to the heavens. Through eternity it was and is and shall be. As the prophet said, "The Lord is good, His mercy is everlasting."[18] Hence sin is less able to harm us than grace is able to benefit us.

Therefore, God owes to the elect not only the call but also justification. That is, justification by which transgression is reshaped into true obedience to God. This happens at that moment when the sinner's eyes are opened again by the grace of God so that he is able to know the true God by faith. Then his heart is set afire so that God becomes pleasing to him. Both of these are nothing but grace, and flow from the merits of Christ, be they foreseen or already displayed. Our works do not, nor can they, bring us to this state, since man's nature is incapable of knowing or wanting or doing good. For this barren man God is sheer fear.

The sinner is justified by regeneration when he is reborn through water and the Holy Spirit. This is not a carnal but a spiritual birth, since that which is born of the flesh is flesh and that which is born of the spirit is spirit. He is reborn "not of blood nor of the will of flesh nor of the will of man but of God."[19] He is reborn not by necessity but by God's free election, for the Spirit breathes where He will.

He is reborn unto heaven, therefore necessarily not to himself but to Christ. Indeed "no one ascended into heaven except He Who descended from heaven, the Son of man who is in heaven."[20] He is reborn unto Christ, not unto his own righteousness. Because "just as Moses lifted up the serpent in the wilderness, so the Son of man must be lifted up in order that those who believe in Him might not perish but have eternal life."[21] In this regeneration God is the father, the will is the mother, and the seed is the means by which the merits of our Lord Jesus Christ sprout forth.

Where these three come together a son of God is born, justified, and made alive through faith active in love: that is to say, active through the fire of our love, set afire by the love of Him who is the only perpetual fire, coming down from heaven. All other fires have lost their spell. This fire makes God pleasing and acceptable to us, so that not only what is contrary to God but also that which is not God becomes displeasing to us. This fire is the grace which makes acceptable (*gratia gratum faciens*). It does not, as many people say,[22] make man acceptable to God, since election itself has already done this; rather, it makes

God alone pleasing and acceptable to man through the love which
restores the obedience stolen by concupiscence. Through this love we
are and live upright and just, not for ourselves but for God.

VII.   The Elect on the Way to Glory

After the justification of the sinner his progress to glory follows
without fail. This progress of the justified ends in the state of glory of
the saints at that time when God most generously gives the eternal
reward to each one according to his labors. And faith declares that
those who do good works go forth into eternal life and those who do
evil, into eternal fire. No one receives less than he merits but often
more.

The Scriptures say that our perdition comes from ourselves and our
salvation comes from God alone. And the Gospel says that just as the
branches do not bear fruit unless they abide on the vine, so we do not
bear fruit unless we abide in Christ. Those who abide in Christ and
Christ in them bear much fruit.[23] St. Paul, the most profound of all,
says clearly in his writings that *we* do not live and even less do *we*
work but Christ lives in us.[24] From these and other passages wise men
conclude that God rewards only His own work, knowing that He
Himself gives grace and glory.

Scripture is clear concerning the first grace of justification, but regarding eternal life the diversity of witness raises some doubt. However, it ought to be remembered that God is the universal, principal,
and most immediate cause of each individual thing and the prime
agent of all actions. Therefore, though there are different kinds of
work, it is one God who works all in all.

Thus it is God's work to make heat in the fire, it is He Who laughs
in those who laugh, cries in those who cry, whinnies in the horse,
roars in the lion; these works flow from nature. And there are greater
works than these, namely, to know, to choose, and to do, but even
these works still flow from nature, though from human nature. Therefore, all these natural works fall short of deserving eternal reward.

God accomplishes other works in us, works informed by faith that
is alive and active in love. These works are more His than ours, for
in justification love is poured into man, his will is set afire by the

exceedingly great love of God and he receives the grace by which God becomes pleasing to him. As I said above, we call this the grace that makes acceptable not us to God but Him to us.[25] For by the grace of predestination we are made acceptable to God. Then certainly this fire kindled by the heavenly flame does not die down but surges up until it reaches its origin, the love of God, the very place of the aforementioned eternal fire. This place is Jesus Christ, God and man. Since all works which flow from this fire go out from Christ and return to Christ, therefore these works are in a very true sense the works of Christ. But they are executed by men and they are finite; they are only imputed to God.

Still other works are the works performed by Christ Himself, the personal actions and suffering of our Lord Jesus Christ which He did and sustained for our salvation. Such are the works of the infinite Divine Person.

If now it is asked whether Christ is obliged to reward our good works with eternal life or, to say it more emphatically, whether God is bound to give Himself for our works, I answer "No" with regard to the first kind of works [that is, the natural works]. Christ is not bound to do this because those works take place outside of faith active in love and do not deserve to be called good works.

As regards the second kind, in view of the fact that these are the works of a finite person they are finite by nature. Therefore it is impossible to found upon them a righteousness of infinite merit to which an infinite reward is due. If, then, God decreed to give himself as reward for such works, this is grace and not justice.

We ought not to doubt, however, the merits of Christ [that is, the third kind], knowing, as we do, that He is both God and man and that His claim to be equal with God was not presumptuous.[26] Therefore the merits of Christ entitle us to enter the eternal kingdom. It is with regard to the call of the elect soul to this kingdom that God has said: "Come quickly to me, my friend, my dear one, my dove."[27] He went on to say: "[Settle down] within the holes in the rock," that is, "in the wounds of Christ"[28] and "in the open cave," that is, "in the opening to the heart of Christ," whence the power of the sacraments bursts forth; and then added: "Show me your face, and make your voice heard in my ears, your voice will be sweet and your face beautiful."

VIII.   The Works of the Justified Man

The man who is predestined, called, and justified surely does not live his life without good conduct and holy works. The justified man cannot but love. He loves God above all things and his neighbor according to the law. He has a love which is impatient with idleness. But granted by grace, this love brings Christ into the heart and in Christ obedience, contrition, and righteousness and thus a renewal of life. Christ is put on and Adam is cast out. He magnifies the life of Christ and damns the life of Adam, with its disobedience, iniquity, and self-indulgence. Those things that had characterized Adam he does not imitate, he hates them; and spontaneously he begins to follow the goodness, obedience, and resignation of Christ, so that just as through grace he holds Christ in his heart, so even more abundantly he strives to show Him in his action.

From Adam we inherit self-love, self-interested love, a distorted sense of values, blindness in judgment, and thus wickedness in works. From Christ comes love of God to the point of disregard for one's self, love of justice to the point of disregard of one's own life, clarity of judgment to the point of realization of our own stupidity, and hence goodness in our works.

Our hearts are fired to do these things by the inestimable love of God Who offered up to a most shameful death Christ burning with love for us. Our hearts are fired to the works of Adam by the accursed concupiscence, through which true goodness becomes odious to us, the contrived things seem delightful, the eternal things are without savor, temporal things do not satisfy, the inner life is not considered; only external things console.

Thus our thinking is enslaved and our will is bound, so that all wisdom of the world, all intelligence, knowledge, and prudence become so subservient to concupiscence that it seems they were meant to serve only its purposes.

Quite rightly, therefore, is the wisdom of this world, even its highest achievement, deemed folly by God. Indeed, what serves concupiscence cannot be elevated to the knowledge of God, for he who begins with self-love cannot get beyond himself. Therefore, human acts performed without faith in Christ (*extra fidem Christi*) cannot serve God but only mammon. Hence I shall not even consider such works but pass them by as useless, not to say, impediments to salvation.

Rather let me now turn to those works we do in Christ renewed by grace, works that issue from the love of God and are directed to it. These works are not self-centered but Christ-centered. The mind is rededicated to God, the works start to become good and now possess characteristics of goodness which they never had without faith (*extra fidem*). These works display love which makes faith alive, faith which without works is said to be dead[29] and indeed is dead. No predestined adult ever dies without having performed such works, because they issue from God and return to God. They please the Most High and are graciously accepted as worthy of eternal reward.

Far more exalted are the merits of Christ Himself, His actions, sufferings, and death, for by nature He was and is the Son of God. His merits are given to us to be ours and on them we found and build our firm hope, for we know our hope is firmly founded on them.[30] Only Christ's own merits can one call merit of full worthiness (*meritum condigni*). They are sufficient alone to save all Christianity or indeed the whole world. Through them the little children are saved and sometimes those still in the womb are sanctified. Through them guilt is absolved, and punishment is mitigated and remitted.

Since justification is due to grace and not to nature, since acceptation of works performed in grace is grace, and since it is again grace that the merits of Christ are made ours, it is appropriate to attribute the whole Christian life to grace. And thus the claim for man, namely, that he is master over his works from beginning to the end, is destroyed. So, therefore, the origin of the works of Christian life is predestination, its means is justification, and its aim is glorification or thanksgiving—all these are the achievements not of nature but of grace.

IX.   The Marriage of Christ and the Christian

Perhaps you would like me now to state briefly how the merits of Christ really become ours. As you know, between Christ and the Christian there is a true, nay the truest, marriage of which our earthly marriage is the sacrament, and but a shadow in comparison with the sacred marriage of Christ [with the Church]. Hence the uprightness of human marriage consists in conformity to the true marriage of Christ and the Church. For, as the Apostle said: "Husbands, love your wives just as Christ loved the Church."[31]

In human marriage there are two in one flesh. In the marriage with Christ there are no longer two, but there is one flesh—Christ and the Christian are one flesh, one spirit. And just as Christ left his father and mother to join his spouse, the Christian, so the Christian leaves father and mother to join Christ.

For the following reason, however, the contract between Christ and the Christian differs greatly from that between man and wife. The contract between man and wife requires that each one gives himself to the other, so that the man belongs to the woman and the woman to the man by free consent, and man has power over the body of woman as woman has over the body of man. But they wield no power over each other's spirit, nor does the one have the other as a servant. Rather, they are partners and help each other in procreation. The marriage claim which the spouses have on each other is therefore limited and not all-embracing.

The contract between Christ and the Church is consummated thus: "I accept you as Mine, I accept you as My concern, I accept you into Myself." And conversely the Church, or the soul, says to Christ, "I accept You as mine, You are my concern, I accept You into myself." In other words Christ says, "The Christian is My possession, the Christian is My concern, the Christian is I"; so the spouse responds, "Christ is my possession, Christ is my concern, Christ is I."

The first vow is the same as human marital vows, but the other two transcend them. By virtue of the first vow the Christian receives that which every spouse ought to give the other according to matrimonial law. By virtue of the second the Christian receives all the benefits, none excluded, that come to him from Christ himself; and by virtue of the third vow he is Christ as much as he is himself.

The first vow:[32] Concerning the betrothal to Christ and the marriage with Him the prophets Isaiah and Jeremiah have spoken and David has sung: "He has set His tabernacle in the sun and He Himself comes as a bridegroom to His marriage bed. He exults like a giant as He goes on His way. His going out is from the highest heaven and His meeting with the heights of it."[33]

The second vow: Regarding "His concern with me and not with himself," the bride has explicitly said, "My beloved is my concern and I am His."[34] I am His by right and He is mine by grace. And later she said more modestly, "I am my beloved's and His desire is toward me."[35] And Isaiah says, "Unto us a Child is born, unto us a Son is given."[36]

The third vow: Concerning His becoming one with us, all Scriptures agree that Christ is in us and we in Him, especially where Christ said that He gave himself up for His disciples so that they might be one. To which he added, "I am in them, as You, O Father, are in Me, so that they might be completely one."[37]

From all this it follows that all things which Christ, the Incarnate Word, possesses, He makes ours by the assumption of human nature. He has given us all things for our salvation, as Scripture says: God, Who did not spare His own Son but delivered Him up for us all, will He not surely give us all things with Him?"[38]

Finally, if Christ is I, I have a claim to heaven, I have hope, and I glory in that hope which belongs to the children of God; and more than that I also glory in all things which directly or indirectly foster hope.[39]

X. The Correlation

Between the Extremes of Mercy and Misery

The lowest point of misery is called guilt. The highest point of mercy we steadfastly believe to be the Incarnation of our Lord. Only when we connect the nadir of misery and the apex of mercy do we extol God's compassion above all His works.

Theologians marvel at the hypostatic union of divine nature with human nature, immortality with death, immunity with suffering. As for me, I marvel at the fusion of the extremes of mercy and misery; as I say, I marvel and give thanks, because out of this union comes salvation for the sinner, out of this union proceeds the Savior's highest glory; through it God has become pleasing to us, and through it the sinner is accepted by God. Therefore I give thanks and will sing forever of the mercies of the Lord.

And how would my God be known, how would I have grasped Your mercies, O God, better, clearer, and more intimately, if You had had no compassion on sinners? In order to have mercy on all, You have consigned all men to unbelief.[40] In order that the promise which comes from faith in Jesus Christ might be given to all believers, Your Scripture has consigned all under sin, so that where sin abounded grace might much more abound.[41]

For that reason You have come, Lord Jesus Christ, to call not the righteous but sinners. You have come, O greatest physician, not to those who are well but to those who are sick. Clearly it is not our sacrifices but Your mercy which draws You to us.

It is Your office, O sweet Savior, to seek and to save that which is lost. By this You make the angels in heaven rejoice, You rejoice, Your friends and neighbors rejoice. They have more cause for rejoicing over "one sinner who repents than over ninety-nine righteous who need no repentance."[42] This is because the joy over the penitent one is based on the mercy of the Most High, while the joy over the righteous is based on the works and merits of man.

Already you can see how appropriate it is that the tax collectors and prostitutes precede us into the kingdom of heaven. And you can see why sins have been permitted and that all have sinned and fallen short of the glory.

It follows, therefore, that those have nothing in common with their Spouse who do not participate with Him in sin, who claim righteousness for themselves, who spurn sinners. After all, this marital love is the highest mercy, which applies itself immediately to the deepest misery, concerned as it is before everything else with the extinction of sin. For this purpose "He gave himself up for the Church that he might sanctify her, having cleansed her by the washing with water in the Word of Life, that the glorious Church might be presented before Him without spot or wrinkle or any such thing, that she might be holy and without blemish."[43]

XI. The Transference of Our Sin to Christ

If you think that the mercy of the Lord has not been given its due by showing how He justifies us through His own righteousness and how He did not shun marriage with sinners, you must realize that He goes even further. He makes our sins His own. Just as the Christian is just through the righteousness of Christ, so Christ is unrighteous and sinful through the guilt of the Christian.

Whereas the Jew would say "blasphemy" and the Greek "madness" the believer says, "You are right." The Jew is affronted, the Greek ridicules, the believer rejoices. Thus "we preach Christ crucified, a stumbling block to Jews and folly to Gentiles, but to those who are called, both Jews and Greeks, Christ, the power and wisdom of God."[44] For it pleased God to overcome strength by weakness, to subjugate wisdom by foolishness, to condemn righteousness by sin "so that no one might take pride in himself before God."[45]

For the time being let us be silent about other issues and let us see whether He who is sinless by nature can be convicted as a sinner. He stands clearly convicted by his own confession: "God, my God, why have You forsaken me? Why are You so far from helping me who is involved in transgressions?"[46]

How can these be Your words, dearest Jesus? I see the answer clearly: God has placed upon You the iniquity of all and You alone are the Lamb of God Who bears the sins of the world. You are like the two goats at one and the same time.[47] In Your human nature You are sacrificed by lot to the Lord for sin; as immortal God You live in eternity and hence are like the goat that was sent out. They put on Your head all the iniquities of the sons of Israel and all their trespasses and sins. You were sent forth into a barren land where no one dwells except God.

You are that matchless Spouse that is my possession, that is my concern, that is I. Therefore, You are mine and everything You have is my own and I am Yours and whatever there is in me is Your own. And because we are one, things which are Yours become mine while yet remaining Yours, and, likewise, things which are mine become Yours while at the same time they remain mine.

Therefore I am righteous because of Your righteousness and a sinner because of my guilt.[48] You are a sinner because of my guilt and righteous because of Your own righteousness. By the same token, I am strong through Your power but weakened by my own feebleness. You are weakened by my feebleness and strong in Your own power.

I am wise in Your wisdom and foolish in my stupidity. You are wise in Your wisdom and foolish in my stupidity.[49]

XII. The Condemnation
of the Sins of the Elect

There is, therefore, no condemnation for those who are in Christ Jesus, who do not live according to the flesh. For God sending the Son in the likeness of sinful flesh condemned sin by sin.[50] As you just saw, the sins of the Christian are transferred to Christ and become the sins of Christ, who came not in sinful flesh but in the likeness of sinful flesh.

He became subject to death and suffering and He could suffer and die because of His likeness to sinful flesh. He could bear sins because He was not merely a pretender to the throne of God, but He was by nature unlimited, infinite, and eternal.[51]

Because of His likeness to sinful flesh He could make satisfaction for sins, since He could fast, pray, give alms, and offer himself as a sacrifice to God. Each and every one of these penitential duties of all the elect the Lord imposed upon His own head.

Because of His equality with God He was able to condemn and bear, to annihilate and extinguish every fault and sin. Indeed, as God He made the sins of all men His sins by imposing on himself penance for all, while, as man, by suffering and dying He made satisfaction for all.

Hence by the imposition of sin on Christ He condemned sin. For the violation of the law ceased when the Son became a sinner. The disruption of sin in man is eradicated when the highest mercy is united with the lowest misery. The sentence to punishment for sin is void when the infinite God suffers and frees man from his punishment, finite both in quantity and quality.

Since beyond these three things [the violation of the law, the disruption in man, the sentence], there are no aftereffects of sin, it follows that when sin is transferred to Christ, sin's claim on man has no legal basis. Thus you see that by the sin of Christ all the sins of the Christian are condemned.

Nor should it escape you that the suffering of the Son of God is sufficient for all, though it was not for all but for many[52] that His blood was poured out. Remember also that His power not only heals but also prevents sin; in other words one and the same cause underlies the remission of sins which have been committed and those which may be about to be committed, that is, the sins which have not been committed but would have been if the power of the cross had not intervened.

Thus it can happen that he who has done less evil is forgiven more, since he might have been about to do greater evil. This clarifies what Scripture means when it says, "[. . . her sins (Mary Magdalene), which are many, are forgiven, for she loved much; but the one] to whom less is forgiven, loves less."[53]

Therefore, less was forgiven to Mary Magdalene when God cleansed her sin, than to the Virgin Mary when God prevented her from sining [by purifying her at her Conception]; for the Virgin had a greater love than Mary Magdalene, her elect sister.

XIII.   The Durability of Christ's Love

God loves the elect with a lasting passion. The biblical concept of the wrath of God does not apply to the sinner but to the sin committed. However, "he who continues to be a sinner continues to be punished. But he who sins only for a time is punished only for a time. Once one is predestined, it follows that one sins for a time and does not continue to do so. He will only be chastened by temporal punishment."

XIV.   The Return of Peace
to the Heart of the Justified Sinner

The elect may receive punishment, sometimes even tougher punishment than the reprobate, but Christ grants him the peace that the world cannot give. That which undermines the peace of heart is the tension between the mercy and the justice of God. "For that reason mercy and truth [= justice] have met in our Savior."[55] According to truth man is a sinner; "mercy agrees" and suggests a way which does

not undercut truth and yet makes the salvation of the sinner possible:
the infinite God atones for finite man. In this way "justice and peace
have kissed each other."[56] "This is the complete restoration of internal
peace, which nobody finds outside Christ (*extra Christum*), Who is
our peace."

XV.   The Foretaste of Salvation

Mystical experience, which cannot be taught but only tasted, provides further consolation. There are, according to four stages of mystical experience, four kinds of soul. The first does not receive special
tokens of God's love but is so enraptured by God that evil cannot take
hold. The second is the mystic in the world. God calls him every now
and then away from his job to nourish him. "I believe to have the
evidence that those spent in the sweat of labor have a more ecstatic
enjoyment of sweetness in Christ than others in more advantageous
conditions." The third group—the contemplatives, not involved in the
active life—are the "queens who nakedly copulate with the naked
Christ. They know that there is no sweetness but Christ, and enjoy this
sweetness continuously. The naked Christ cannot deny himself to
these naked ones . . . these are certain of their salvation." On the fourth
level stands the Virgin Mary alone, "who is the only one to know how
sweet Jesus is."

XVI.   The Easing of the Burden of the Law

You have now grasped that Christ reveals the sweetness of His love
to the innermost soul by certain signs. Not the least of these signs is
that He makes the burden of law easy and the yoke light, even though
every law is harsh, heavy, and unbearable to our nature.

Indeed, when we compare the several kinds of law—the law of
nature, the law of Moses, the law of Christ—we see that the law of
nature is harsh and the law of Moses harsher, but harshest of all is the
law of Christ. This law is harsh because it strips away man's self-
identity, drives him out of his mind, destroys his freedom, increases
his burden, and imposes the yoke. There is no question that this is a
hard lot.

But the law of nature, being the dictates of reason, is relatively light because everyone is bound by his own judgment, that is, he binds himself. As Paul likes to say, one is a law unto one's self.[57] It is indeed hard to be bound, but it makes it easier if one is bound by one's self.

The law of Moses, which requires that the exterior man be taken into almost total captivity, is an unbearable yoke. As Peter said in the apostolic council, "Why do you tempt God by imposing on the necks of the disciples a law which neither we nor our fathers were able to bear?"[58] In the Old Testament there were so many ceremonial and judicial rules that it deserves its name "law of fear," under which we, children of a slave, are born for servitude.

But the law of Christ, read according to the letter, is the harshest of all because it seizes the whole man and terminates man's self-control completely. It was said of old, "Whoever kills shall be liable to judgment." The law of Christ says, "Everyone who is angry with his brother shall be liable to judgment, whoever shows wrath shall be liable to the council, whoever insults by words shall be liable to hell fire."[59]

It was said of old, "You shall not commit adultery."[60] The law of Christ prohibits all lewd thoughts, all lascivious glances, and, what is more, all foul language, all concupiscence of eyes and flesh and likewise all pride of life.[61] Thus the Christian is bound in every aspect, so much so that he ought to hate himself, lose and deny himself, and daily follow Christ with the cross.

These things are extremely difficult to carry out: until the beloved puts his hand secretly through the opening and touches the belly of the spouse. At this touch, the soul, suddenly changed, says, "My belly began to tremble, for after extreme weakness it sensed immense strength."[62] Such was the change in Peter, whom first a single servant girl frightened with her question, but who, after the Spirit had touched him, had the strength of princes.[63]

This touch of the Spirit, the love from the groom, is directed toward the love of the bride, spirit reaching to spirit. The bride's spirit, warmed by that Spirit which is by nature warm, is kindled and indeed set on fire so that nothing is sweeter for her than to abandon herself because of the overwhelming love of God.

Thus fear is transformed into love, and the burden of Christ is made very light, the yoke very easy. The fundamental reason the law is a burden is that you lose title to yourself, but this fundament is destroyed when our Lord Jesus Christ becomes acceptable and pleasing to us so that He ranks above ourselves and all other things.

Again, you see that grace which makes acceptable does not make us acceptable to God but makes God acceptable and pleasing to us.[64] Therefore, attribute to divine, eternal election the grace which makes you acceptable to God, attribute to justification the grace which makes God acceptable to you.

How great are the joys of the heart, the exultation, the jubilations which come from this touch! If possible, let him who has experienced this touch speak out: "Since I have experienced it, therefore, I witnessed to it."[65]

XVII.   The Sweetness of
the Message of Christ for the Soul[66]

It is a rare sign of His love when Christ speaks to the soul. This is always revelation of truth, but basically one hears two things: God is power and God is mercy. "To *believe* these is necessary for salvation; to *know* them is a foretaste of eternal happiness."[67]

XVIII.   Christ's Banquet With the Christians

Through the Incarnation, Christ has provided Himself as food and drink for the faithful. In an even greater act of mercy He brings the elect in ecstasy so that the soul receives a foretaste of eternal sweetness. "These are great things but not necessary for salvation. Therefore Christ does not owe these to the elect, and when He grants them it is sheer generosity."

XIX.   The Beneficial
Vision of God in This Life

To search the face of God belongs to the Christian life. But it is often the pseudo prophets who proclaim their own greatness by claiming all kinds of visions: Sometimes they see Christ, sometimes they claim to have had a vision of God Almighty as a venerable old man with a beard. These external visions do not profit us: "Therefore let us always look for the face of God in ourselves and in our works." God becomes visible in our life when we are so intent to execute His will that we are not concerned about outcome and reward, whether life or death, salvation or damnation.

XX. The Discovery of the Spirit of Christ in the Hatred of Sin[68]

The first sign of true faith is the battle against the demons. The love of justice and the hatred of sin go together, or rather have been joined together by the Spirit. "From this it follows that we should choose and even cherish to shoulder punishment for sin, which God has imposed on us. . . . Hence it is better and more useful to remove sin through one's own satisfaction than through indulgences."[69]

XXI. The Christian Language

The second sign of true faith is the gift of a new language. At the inside it is the language of the Spirit; the outer language expresses itself in speech and works, which makes for unity in the Church. The language of works, such as humility, love, and patience is internationally understood. The Pentecostal gift of tongues "lasted till all countries had their own doctors."

XXII. The Protection of the Christian Against Diabolic Poison

The third sign of the faith is immunity against serpents, which implies—as the fall of Eve indicates—immunity against the temptation of curiosity. Knowledge is dangerous without knowledge of God. Curiosity—hunger for knowledge—may seem useful to society, but it should not endanger one's salvation. Unless called by God, one should not aspire to public office. "Obedience to God is the test here. If called by God serve others. . . . If, however, you enter into public affairs without a call from God and buy the First See with money and favors, you may serve others but you neglect your own salvation; you have already received the reward for your work, since you looked for honor and honor you received; man you served, by man you are rewarded; you obeyed yourself, yourself is all you have."[70]

XXIII. The Certitude of Salvation

It says in the Gospel of Mark that if they [the faithful] should drink something poisonous it will not hurt them; we find the literal interpretation of this in the Gospel of John and elsewhere.[71] This was a manifestation of the Spirit for the benefit of the Church. Understood mystically it serves as a test of our faith and gives not a little consolation to the believer.

Poison of the soul is a mortal threat and draws it to sin. He is free from such poison who has complete faith in Christ "out of whose hand no one can snatch the Christian."[72] Since he has Christ the Christian lacks neither grace nor instruction; he has, thereby, everything necessary for salvation. For truly "God did not spare His own Son but gave Him up for us: will He not give us all things with Him?"[73]

The Christian has God for him—who can be against him? There is no prosecutor any more, because it is God Himself Who justifies. There is no place for a judge to condemn, because the Christian has Christ to intercede for him. Therefore, he has unwavering love and a living hope. Although it is not his own investigation that enables man to ascertain whether "he is subject to the hate or love of God,"[74] he is able through the unfailing signs given for this purpose to have a sure hope and to cast off despair; this despair arises from questions regarding one's election and is the greatest tribulation of the soul.[75]

Through Baptism, hope overcomes tribulation.[76] Through Confirmation, hope drives away the anxiety of temptation. Through Holy Communion, hope stills the hunger for eternal food. Through true Absolution, hope reclothes the nakedness that results when righteousness is lacking. Through the Sacrifice of the Mass, hope lifts up the believer thrown into peril by his deficient merit. Through Holy Matrimony, hope halts the persecution by the flesh. Through Extreme Unction, hope dulls the sword of suffering and death.

Therefore, who shall separate us from the love of Christ? Tribulation? No, because we are baptized. Anxiety? No, we are confirmed. Hunger? No, we eat the Flesh of Christ and drink His Blood. Nakedness? No, we are absolved in confession and dressed in righteousness. Peril? No, the sacrifice has been made. Persecution? No, through matrimony we are wedded to Christ and through the solemnization of our marriage joined together. The sword? No, we are anointed with the oil of mercy. Therfeore the Christian is certain that "nothing can separate him from the love of God which is in Christ Jesus our Lord."[77]

There are still some things that give offense (scandals), which drive us into sin. However, Mark the Evangelist reassures us that even these cannot overwhelm us, although the impressionable are easily swayed, especially when these temptations come from those who are most elevated in the hierarchy of the Church and who, as it were, by their authority cause scandals.[78] Thus we read concerning Peter that he forced the Gentiles into literal obedience to the Jewish law, which God overruled by the mouth of Paul.[79] To cause such scandals is absolutely forbidden; but they do not corrupt unless the impressionable comply. [These scandals poison the weak] when they do not realize the seriousness of imitating them, and they sin with all the more abandon when they see others, especially clerics, on the same road to damnation. In the end they are corrupted, not by the sins of others, but by their own sins.

Others spread poison by boasting of the exceptional degree of their own righteousness. If they are not exceptional, if they have superiors or even peers in virtue, they are thoroughly offended. They have more of an eye for the sins of others than for their own, and they wish to purify sinners completely without realizing that "the just man is first of all his own accuser"[80] and that true love starts with one's own sins. One ought not throw stones at the adulteress[81] when one is one's self also a sinner. It is necessary, first, "to take the log out of your eye before you take the speck out of your neighbor's.[82]

Thus they sin who hate the sins of others but neglect their own; who observe disease in their neighbor but do not discover death in themselves; wishing to judge the innermost thoughts, they place themselves next to God in their pride. According to the just judgment of God they are contaminated by the very things of which they stupidly presume to clean others. Christ taught us not to be concerned with the scandals these cause, because they result from blindness.

Since works of nature certainly do not displease God, and questionable actions should receive the best possible interpretation; since impulsive actions do not implicate us, ignorance excuses sins of omission, and venial sins are not crime, very little is left over to be damned by human opinion.

Admonition and correction are appropriate only when they deal with that sin and offense to the impressionable which results from measuring the status of others. But since they can cause joy as well as frivolousness, and a talking-to can lead to error as well as to fabrication, one should rather watch and scrutinize one's self.

Therefore, if anyone is condemned by you, it should be yourself not your neighbor. And if anyone is commended by you, it should not be yourself but your neighbor. You do not know his guilt, but your own you know very well. See in conclusion: Great certitude of salvation awaits him who ponders the good in others, who often contemplates his own evil deeds, and who makes it a habit to condemn himself and justify others.

XXIV. Self-resignation for the Benefit of the Church and the Praise of God

The last sign of true faith is the gift of healing, which spiritually seen is the mutual assistance Christians give each other, since they are united in Christ, in one Spirit and one Baptism. The sole purpose of this mutual aid is the increase of the praise of God. If it furthers this purpose to yield our merits to others, we should be prepared to abandon everything that nature and grace have bestowed upon us, even Christ Himself.

"See, with this apex of obedience and resignation, man powerfully created out of nothing and mercifully redeemed from sin, reduced to nothingness by himself, return to his origin with constant praise, through Jesus Christ our Lord."

Notes

1. Isaiah 43:25. This sermon by Staupitz is full of biblical references in addition to actual quotations. Some of the more significant references are given in the notes, together with the actual quotations. More of the references can be found in the margins of the Latin text: *Tractatus de executione aeternae praedestinationis fratris Ioannis de Staupitz, Theologi et Augustinensium Vicarii*, Nuremberg, 1517. The most important discussion to date on Staupitz's relation to Reformation theology is Ernst Wolf, *Staupitz und Luther*, Leipzig, 1927. Bibliography there.
2. Psalms 84:1, 2.
3. Psalms 84:4.
4. Cf. John 5:37; II Corinthians 5:7.
5. Ephesians 3:18, 19.
6. Ephesians 3:8-12.
7. The Jewish tradition has at times forbidden the enunciation of the name of God (YHWH). For a discussion of this, see the article, "Names of God," in the *Jewish Encyclopedia*, New York, London, 1905, vol. IX, pp. 162, 163.
8. Cf. Romans 8:29.
9. Cf. John 3:18.
10. Luke 19:5.
11. Luke 10:20.
12. Romans 8:30.
13. This quotation from Psalms 4:7 is in scholastic theology widely interpreted as proof-text for the innate or natural knowledge of God. In RSV it is rendered in Psalms 4:6 as "the light of Thy [i.e., God's] countenance."
14. John 6:44.
15. I Corinthians 3:6.
16. Romans 8:32.
17. Mark 10:45.
18. Psalms 100:5.
19. John 1:13.
20. John 3:13.
21. John 3:14, 15.
22. The schools of Scotus and Occam. Staupitz also dissociates himself from the teaching of Aquinas, for whom the *gratia gratum faciens* is the habit, or form, of grace which God loves in man (*Summa contra Gentiles*, III 150), by which man is related to God (*Summa Theologica*, or *ST* I. II, q. iii, art i). It is crucial that Staupitz does not refer to the concept "habit" at all but actualizes grace to the point where it does not differ from love. What he teaches is therefore *gratia* [= election] *faciens* [bringing forth] *caritatem* [love for God by the elect].
23. Cf. John 15:4, 5.
24. Cf. Galatians 2:20.
25. Cf. notes 22 and 61.
26. Cf. Philippians 2:6.
27. Song of Solomon 2:14.
28. With this reference to the wounds of Christ, Staupitz advised Luther

to abandon speculation about predestination. See Luther's Table-
talk, *WATR* II. 1490 (April
1532): "He [Staupitz] answered
me: 'In the wounds of Christ predestination is grasped and found,
nowhere else . . . God does not
want to be understood apart from
Christ [*extra christum*].'" Cf.
ibid., 1820 and 2654a. In his commentary on Romans (1515-1516),
Luther warns against the danger
of speculation about predestination: "For us the wounds of
Christ are sufficient safety," and
refers to exactly the same wording
as in the Song of Solomon (2:14)
which Staupitz here adduces.
(Commentary upon Romans
9:19, *WA* 56. 400.) See the excel-
lently annotated edition of *Luther: Lectures on Romans,* Library of Christian Classics, XV,
by Wilhelm Pauck, Philadelphia,
1961, p. 271. The same words,
"the holes in the rock," occur in
Exodus 33:22 and were in medieval exegesis widely applied (inter-
linear Gloss and Lyra, *Postilla,
ibid.*) to the Passion of Christ.

29. James 2:26.

30. Cf. Contarini's *Epistle on Justification,* dated May 25, 1541, written in Regensburg. After having
distinguished two kinds of righteousness, the righteousness of
Christ, given and imputed to us,
and the righteousness which in-
dwells in the faithful through the
habit of grace, he links the Christian hope only to the first kind:
"Therefore we should rely only on
this certain and stable one and
believe that through it alone we

are justified before God [*coram
Deo*]." Ed. F. Hünermann, *Corpus Catholicorum,* VII, Münster
i. W., 1923, pp. 29-30. This Epistle is an elaboration of the fifth
article of the declaration of reconciliation accepted twenty days
before, May 5, by Gropper, Contarini, Melanchthon, Bucer, and
others. Luther was not impressed,
and a papal consistory rejected
this last concordat on May 27.
Staupitz's marriage theme allows
him to relate Contarini's two
kinds of righteousness much more
intimately.

31. Ephesians 5:25.

32. This subtitle and the two following are not in the text but are
added in the translation for clarity.

33. Psalms 19:4-6. Cf. *Vulgate* Psalms
18:6, 7.

34. Song of Solomon 2:16; 6:2.

35. Song of Solomon 7:10.

36. Isaiah 9:6.

37. John 17:23. The usual medieval
exegetical device, according to
which the same truths apply allegorically to the Church that
apply tropologically to the individual Christian, facilitates the
smooth transition from the
Church to the soul, in evidence
throughout this section. Since in
modern biblical studies this
method of exegesis has been abandoned, such a text as John 17:23
is usually understood to refer to
the Church. This text could thus
become the basis of the Ecumenical Movement. See further the
introduction to chapter VI, p. 286.

38. Romans 8:32.

39. Such as tribulation and temptation, cf. Romans 5:2, 3. Gerson,
Biel, and later Luther regarded
temptation as a sign that the devil
had discovered a challenging target. To be without temptation
could therefore be understood as
a danger signal rather than as a
sign of optimal sanctification. For
Gerson and Biel, see *Harvest*, pp.
231 f. For Luther see ed. Pauck
pp. 156 ff.

40. Romans 11:32.

41. Cf. Galatians 3:22.

42. Luke 15:7.

43. Ephesians 5:25, 26. The Latin text
reads *sacrificaret*, but on the assumption that this is a mistaken
copying of *sanctificaret*, which is
the Vulgate reading, the passage
is translated as "sanctifies."

44. I Corinthians 1:23, 24.

45. I Corinthians 1:29.

46. Psalms 22:1; Vulgate 21:1.

47. Leviticus 16:9-11 describes an
atonement rite in which one goat
is offered and the other one is
sent out into the wilderness.

48. Here again Staupitz's independence of the medieval tradition is
in evidence. Though articulated
in many different ways, basically
all schools agree that guilt and
righteousness are two successive
stages separated by Baptism or
Absolution. For Staupitz they are
two *aspects* of the life in Christ.
This is, as far as I know, the
closest parallel in pre-Reformation
documents to Luther's "*simul iustus et peccator*" [at once sinner
and justified].

49. Chapters IX, X, and XI find their
close parallel in Luther's 1518

(1519?) sermon, "Two Kinds of
Righteousness," *WA* 2, 145-152.
Translated by L. J. Satre, in *Luther's Works*, Vol. 31, *Career of
the Reformer* I, ed. Harold J.
Grimm, Philadelphia, 1957, pp.
297-306. The same use of the
marriage theme, the identical biblical references, and the same
transition to the vocation of public office, as in ch. XXII are too
striking to assume coincidence.
Different is, e.g., Luther's further
elaboration of Staupitz's point in
ch. VIII according to which the
justified one shows forth Christ
in his works: The "second" righteousness is the Christian's responsibility for his neighbor. See further my "'Iustitia Christi' and 'Iustitia Dei': Luther and the Scholastic Doctrines of Justification," in
The Harvard Theological Review,
59 (1966), pp. 1-26, esp. p. 25.

50. Cf. Romans 8:1-3.

51. Cf. Philippians 2:6.

52. Mark 10:45.

53. Luke 7:47. Staupitz's emphasis on
the interdependence of God's
mercy and man's sin required a
clarification of the status of the
Virgin Mary. Although many
Dominicans and their supporters
had not accepted the Council of
Basel's (1439) promulgation of
the dogma of the Immaculate
Conception, there was agreement
that the Virgin Mary never committed sin but was cleansed by
grace, at or immediately after
conception.

54. Chapters XIII, XV, XVII-XXII,
and XXIV are reproduced in abbreviated form. The résumés and

translations should allow the
reader to follow the line of argument.

55. Psalms. 85:10a.
56. Psalms 85:10b.
57. Romans 2:14.
58. Acts 15:10.
59. Matthew 5:21, 22. The Latin text
reads "counsel," but it is assumed
that this is a misreading of the
Vulgate's word for "council."
60. Matthew 5:27.
61. Cf. Matthew 5:28–30 and I John
2:16. This "pride of life" is, according to Aquinas, *Summa Theologica,* I.II.q.77 art 5, ad 1, "the
inordinate appetite of excellence."
62. Song of Solomon 5:4.
63. Cf. Luke 22:54 ff.
64. Cf. notes 20 and 24.
65. Cf. II Corinthians 4:13 = Psalms
116:10.
66. See note 54.
67. Staupitz is more positive in his
evaluation of the auditive mystical
experience than of its visual
counterpart. See ch. XIX.
68. In the final five chapters XX–
XXIV, Staupitz discusses the five
signs of faith as enumerated in
Mark 16: 17, 18.
69. The same pastoral concern about
indulgences is in evidence in Luther's attacks on indulgences in
his first thesis and in his Leipzig
disputation with Eck (1519): It
undercuts satisfaction—the third
part of the Sacrament of Penance
following contrition and confession—and obscures what God
intends with his punishment,

namely, to further the health of
the soul.
70. Staupitz's reference to "the First
See" may be a general one. But it
may refer to the First See of Germany, the archbishopric of Mainz,
which Albrecht of Brandenburg
(1490–1545) had acquired in 1514.
Indebted to the Fugger bank because of the necessary payment of
Pallium dues to the pope, Albrecht undertook the sale of the
Jubilee indulgences for the curia
for half of the profits. John Tetzel (†1519), appointed by Albrecht in 1517, preached in Jüter-
borg close to Wittenberg in the
same year. Against Tetzel's sales
of indulgences, Martin Luther directed his ninety-five theses in
1517.
71. Mark 16:18, John 10:28. See note
65.
72. John 10:28.
73. Romans 8:32.
74. Ecclesiastes 9:1.
75. This is a further elaboration of
ch. XIV.
76. This whole section refers to Romans 8:35–39. It applies the seven
sacraments—notably replacing ordination by the sacrifice of the
Mass—to the seven kinds of poison
which cannot, according to St.
Paul, separate the Christian from
Christ.
77. Romans 8:39.
78. Cf. note 76.
79. Galatians 2:12 ff.
80. Proverbs 18:17.
81. John 8:7.
82. Luke 6:42.

Chapter Four
The Church

Introduction

A comprehensive history of the late medieval disputes on the nature of the Church is yet to be written. It is certain that the twin movements of conciliarism and curialism will occupy a central place in any such enterprise; it is equally certain, however, that there are numerous shadings of thought not easily classified under these headings. One of the best articulated among these is formulated in Jan Hus's treatise *On the Church,* completed in 1413.

Until the fourteenth century the discussion of the nature of the Church had been largely left to the canon lawyers. Other problems, especially those related to the Sacrament of Penance and the Sacrament of the Eucharist, had seemed more essential and had absorbed more interest than answers to ecclesiological issues. But, on the subject of the Church's nature, the answers of the thirteenth century had to stand the test of the times—and this test proved to be formidable, especially in view of the duress resulting from the exile in Avignon of the papacy (1309–1377) and the shocking confusion of the Great Western Schism (1378–1417).[1]

Although Avignon itself belonged to the King of Naples, Clement V and his successors could not avoid being identified with French political interests when that city was chosen as Papal See (1309). In the following period profound administrative changes, affecting primarily the fiscal policy of the Church, were to lead to high taxation by the extension of papal prerogatives. Although during most of this time England and France were involved in a series of campaigns and battles usually referred to as the Hundred Years' War, the relation between the curia and the English crown remained surprisingly intact. In England, aversion to papalism was not so much due to high taxation; this fattened the pockets of the king, the barons, and the clerks; but here it was primarily a reaction against the extension of papal prerogatives. This furthered the indigenous legal tradition established in the Constitutions of Clarendon in 1164 and thus prepared for the *Statutes of Provisors* and *Praemunire*.[2] The statute of 1353 forbade the withdrawal from England of cases which should be decided by the royal courts. In 1391 the prescribed penalties were extended to all those who would promote a papal bull or papal excommunication. In the elimination of the possibility of a higher appeal, these statutes form the secular counterpart of the famous bull *Execrabilis,* which was more than a century later to be promulgated by Pope Pius II (1460).

Against this background are to be understood the two works of Wyclif which form the introduction to his later writings on the Church. In his treatise *On Divine Lordship*[3] (1375) Wyclif argues that whoever has received from Christ some office in the Church holds this as a temporary charge with limited jurisdiction, since as a "steward of the Supreme Lord" he remains subject to the will of his master. *On Civil Lordship* (1376)[4] gives this principle a revolutionary potential by claiming that possession or power in Church and State are rightfully held only by one in a state of grace.

In his discussion of the nature of the Church (1378)[5] the contrast between office and spiritual relationship with God is discussed in terms of the difference between the visible Church, with its formal membership and offices, and the invisible Church, defined as "the totality of the elect" (*universitas fidelium praedestinatorum*). The pope is not the head of this communion of saints but at best the head of the Roman part of the visible Church, which comprises, besides the elect, the "body of the devil," the reprobate.

The main question in determining Wyclif's orthodoxy is undoubtedly whether he went so far in requiring for the *gift of office* the *gift of personal sanctity* that he can be accused of Donatism, in other words, whether he holds that sacraments administered by a "wicked priest" are invalid. The Council of Constance (1414–1418) claimed this was indeed Wyclif's position when it condemned, in its eighth session (1415), forty-five conclusions of Wyclif, among them: "If a bishop or priest lives in a state of mortal sin, he does not ordain . . . nor baptize."[6]

All these ideas are reflected in the treatise by Hus *On the Church*. As a matter of fact for a long time[7] Hus has been regarded as a mere copyist of Wyclif. It is certainly true that Hus heartily welcomed the works of Wyclif and never dissociated himself from the Oxford master even after the general prohibition and burning of Wyclif's works in 1410 in Prague, and 1413 in Rome. But recent research strongly suggests that Hus made a selective use of Wyclif's arguments and changed or omitted the more extreme statements. Furthermore it has become clear that Hus stands in a succession, or school, of Czech reformers: he had therefore already available a blueprint for reform in which Wyclifite ideas could conveniently be sketched in, but he was not completely relying upon the import of English ideas.

It can be shown that Hus, from his first writing until the final interrogation in Constance in 1415, has rejected the Donatistic position. In the Sentences Commentary, his first work, he states explicitly that a priest in a state of mortal sin can administer Baptism and so cleanse the baptized of the stain of sin, "since he performs a ministry through which the power of God, the omnipotent first agent, operates."[8]

He makes exactly the same point during an interrogation in the last days of his life: The wicked priests are unworthy servants as far as their moral stature is concerned, but, nevertheless, as far as the office is concerned, God uses them as his instruments in the administration of the sacraments.[9]

In the same interrogation, however, it becomes clear that what is said about the *sacerdotal power* does not apply to the *power of jurisdiction*: "No one represents Christ or Peter unless he follows him in his moral action, since this is exactly the condition on which he has received this representative jurisdictional power. To be such a representative one needs both morals of high quality and legal permission. The pope is not the clear and true successor of Peter, the first among the Apostles, when he lives in a way contrary to Peter. When it is greed that motivates him, then he is the vicar of Judas Iscariot, because of the way in which this greed affects him. Just the same applies to the cardinals..."[10]

Although "the good life cannot be the ultimate proof of belonging to the true Church as the fact of Judas' inclusion among the Apostles before his betrayal documents,"[11] displaying the "wicked life" strongly suggests that one belongs only to the visible, nominal Church and to the "body of the devil." Hus's treatise *On the Church* does not want to argue that this diabolic power requires secession from the Church of Rome, as his radical successors in Bohemia later understood it. In spite of the fact that Hus is willing to argue that "even when Rome would be destroyed like Sodom, the Christian Church would still continue to exist,"[12] and that as Holcot before him, he can refer to "the modern prelates" as "the hands of the Antichrist" greedily grasping the reins of the Church, wickedness does not imply exclusion from the true, invisible Church of the elect. The telling point of his doctrine of predestination is *not* to draw a visible demarcation line between the pure Church and the wicked Church, that is, in his own words, the hierarchical Church of the pope, his cardinals, and prelates. Hus is too much intent on showing that one can be and often is at once just and unjust (*simul et semel iustus et iniustus*).[13] This does not have the Lutheran connotation that the justified sinner continues to be subject to the power of evil (*simul iustus et peccator*), but implies that one can live for a long time in a state of sin and still belong to the elect (*secundum praedestinationem tantum*) or, vice versa, that one can belong to the reprobate and still live for a time in a state of grace (*secundum presentem iusticiam*).[14]

Hus's main point is that no obedience is due to a wicked prelate, since there is no reason to assume that he belongs to the true Church. A sinful life does not interfere with the priest's power to administer the sacraments (*potestas ordinis*)—and in this Hus is, as we saw, anti-Donatistic—but it does interfere with his jurisdictional authority (*potestas iurisdictionis*), and to this extent Hus can be conveniently labeled at least semi-Donatistic: "When their behavior is contrary to the divine counsels and precepts they have to be publicly resisted."[15]

As regards jurisdiction, no clear distinction is made between office and private life, as is apparent from the way in which the discussion freely moves from prelates who live a sinful life to prelates who establish laws contrary to the law of Christ—both are "wicked priests." Notwithstanding the many references to fornication and avarice, this latter issue is the test case: "Therefore, O true lovers of the law of Christ, first note their works and see whether they incline to the world; second, analyze their commands, whether they savor of avarice or the gain of this world; third, consult Holy Scripture, whether their commands are in accordance with Christ's counsel. In the light of this counsel believe them or disbelieve them . . ."[16] One can argue that, although third in the order of enumeration, the law of Christ is the first in the order of evaluation; a sinful life is a warning; Scripture is the final test. Since jurisdictional power implies teaching authority, Hus's semi-Donaticism provides a critical stand both against curialism, "one highest prelate," and against conciliarism, the authority of the "gathered prelates."

Since "the law of Christ" stands for the Old and New Testaments, for doctrine and discipline, for Gospel and law, we see that Hus makes the issue of Scripture and Tradition a central aspect of his thought regarding the Church. He does not pit Scripture against Tradition but rather, as the upholder of Tradition I, he argues on grounds of Scripture and its doctoral exposition against the extrascriptural tradition of the authority of canon law.[17] It is therefore not his doctrine of predestination, prominent as it is in his work *On the Church,* but his understanding of the relation of Scripture and Tradition which gives the revolutionary edge to this chief work of Hus. This underlies his appeal to the spiritual authority of Christ and his critical evaluation of "ecclesiastical obedience" defined as "obedience to the inventions of the priests of the Church, beyond the explicit warrant of Scripture."[18]

Thus Hus articulated a reform program which ran equally counter to curialist and conciliar principles. Charges were lodged against him in Rome and he was requested to appear before the great conciliar Council of Constance. Hus arrived there with a safe-conduct on November 3, 1414, but was soon to be imprisoned under the pretext that he had tried to escape in a haycart.[19]

The final condemnation of Hus on July 6, 1415, was based primarily on propositions derived from his treatise *On the Church.* The same morning that Hus was burned at the stake a copy of this work was symbolically destroyed by fire. Not because of Hus's understanding of the law of Christ, nor his way of contrasting the visible and invisible Church, but probably due to his opposition to the authority of extrascriptural canon law could Luther, who received a copy on October 3, 1519, write with so much enthusiasm: "I have taught and held all the teachings of Jan Hus, but thus far did not know it. Johann von Staupitz has taught it in the same unintentional way. In short we are all Hussites and did not know it. Even Paul and Augustine . . ."[20]

While Hus's treatise *On the Church* had been most explicit in its attack on the papal and curial position, his attack on canon law implied doubts about the legislative power of the Church itself even when assembled in general council; in other words he opposed the two major ecclesiastical forces of his time, curialism and conciliarism, all at once. Contemporary research has shown that conciliarism should no longer be regarded as merely the religious expression of late medieval secular nationalism but rather, drawing on the canon law tradition just as much as the curialistic party, as the "logical culmination of ideas that were embedded in the law and doctrine of the Church itself."[21]

Hus's direct appeal to the authority of Christ meant not only a bypassing of the pope but also of the council. Since an appeal from the pope to his successor proved to be useless and "to appeal from a pope to a council is to rely on a far future and to call upon an uncertain aid in a serious doctrinal issue, therefore I have ultimately appealed to the Head of the Church, the Lord Jesus Christ."[22]

It is an irony of history that Hus, condemned by a conciliar council, uses here exactly the same argument against conciliar arbitration as half a century later would be employed in *Execrabilis,* the coup de grâce for conciliarism administered by a pope.

On May 29, 1453, Constantinople had fallen, with the result that Christian Europe was not only politically jeopardized but also painfully reminded of the failure of its Holy War, the Crusades. In the fall of the same year Pope Nicholas V (1447-1455) was able to bring the chief Italian powers together in a planning conference but, although a joint military command could be set up (1455), it was obvious that the major non-Italian military powers would have to participate if there could be any hope of successful armed intervention.

Enea Silvio (Aeneas Silvius) de' Piccolomini, choosing the name of Pius II (1458–1464), saw as his immediate task the reconquest of Constantinople, which had fallen under the onslaught of Islam in 1453, and the mobilization of the European nations for this purpose.[23] Until shortly before his elevation to the papal throne he had not, to say the least, lived up to the standards of Hus, and his personal conduct very closely answered Hus's understanding of the papacy of his day. Originally Piccolomini had been regarded as a conciliarist, and his involvement in the Council of Basle (1431–1449) documents this abundantly. The choice of his name, suggestive of Pius Aeneas (Vergil), is an indication of his involvement in the development of Italian humanism, which soon would be spreading north of the Alps. Yet the leading humanists were to be disappointed in Pope Pius as a Maecenas and supporter of their cause. Ever since the fall of Constantinople, Piccolomini had been very much concerned with the necessity of organizing a crusade, and upon elevation to the papal throne he gave this campaign—not only politically but also financially—first priority. It may well be that the immediate goal of *Execrabilis* was to secure the financial basis for a new crusade. Several nations showed little enthusiasm for the crusade taxes Pius II presented them with at the congress which opened at Mantua on September 29, 1459: 1/10 for all churches in papal service, 1/30 for all laymen, and 1/20 (!) for the Jews. As had happened in the past, there was good reason to expect that the French especially might appeal from this papal decision to a council since, according to Gallican principle, "the advise and consent" of the French Church was required for the levy of any tax. But beyond this immediate concern, *Execrabilis*, promulgated a few days after the termination of the Mantua meeting, had a larger scope and would actually prove to be a turning point in the medieval history of reform. By forbidding "henceforth" (*deinceps*) any appeal from the pope to a council under the severest possible ecclesiastical punishments, it struck at the heart of conciliarism. It thus declared[24]—with more vigor than Pope Martin V before—null and void the two famous decrees of Constance: *Sacrosancta* (the superiority of the council over the pope—April 6, 1415) and *Frequens* (at least once every ten years a council as highest court of appeal—October 9, 1417).

It was not as successful in its short-term objective as Pope Pius II had hoped. Throughout the century to come, many ways to arrange for a crusade were sought, but the spreading missionary movement was already absorbing the religious sentiment a former age had invested in its Holy Wars.

Initially also the attack against conciliarism seemed to be abortive; in France and Germany *Execrabilis* met with stiff political resistance where leading theologians could discard it as invalid on grounds that it obviously ran counter to natural law.[25] Yet barely two years later Gabriel Biel would appeal in his *Defense of Obedience to the Pope* (1462) to *Execrabilis*[26] in support of Adolph von Nassau, papal appointee to Germany's first See, Mainz, against Diether von Isenburg, who in 1450 had been elected to the position by the cathedral chapter of Mainz.[27]

The Conciliabulum of Pisa (1511–1512) shows that conciliarism remained a political power, and the writings of the Parisians Jacob Almain and John Major remind us that, theologically, conciliarism continued to draw supporters. As late as March 27, 1517, the Sorbonne decided to appeal from the pope to a future council, to be repudiated the next year by a papal bull which reiterates and reinforces the principles of *Execrabilis*.[28]

It is useless to speculate what might have happened if Luther had not compromised conciliarism and called for an adjudication by a nonpartisan council on German soil. We can note that, notwithstanding its continuing relevance to conciliar principles, even after the Council of Trent (1545–1563) and the First Vatican Council (1869–1870), the principles contained in *Execrabilis* mark the shift from a conciliar to a papal reform movement. Pius II did not merely reject conciliarism and therewith its solution for the need of reform but left just before his death his own reform program, *Pastor Aeternus*, which closely resembles the plan for reform drawn up by another famous convert from conciliarism, Nicholas of Cusa (†1464).[29]

Only recently published in its entirety, *Pastor Aeternus* shows that in rejecting his conciliar past Pius II had not therewith abandoned its goal of reform "in head and members."[30] Without compromising the dignity and authority of the pope, the principle of curial reform as the basis of a general reform of the Church is clearly enunciated, a reform which would apply to the pope himself moral standards which would have satisfied both Hus and his conciliar judges at Constance.[31]

The medieval quest for reform has in *Pastor Aeternus* found expression on the highest hierarchical level of the Church. Not implemented, however, it could not stem the tide of passionate reform zeal which in the century to come would change priorities and regard as its first objective a doctrinal rather than a moral reformation of the Church.

Notes

1. On the Western Schism see Walter Ullmann, *The Origins of the Great Schism*, London, 1948. On the relation of canon law and conciliarism see Brian Tierney, *Foundations of the Conciliar Theory: The Contribution of the Medieval Canonists from Gratian to the Great Schism*, Cambridge, 1955. On aspects of conciliarism see Ernest F. Jacob, *Essays in the Conciliar Epoch*, Manchester, 1953. For a concise presentation of the background of Hus's *On the Church*, see *Magistri Johannis Hus. Tractatus de Ecclesia*, ed. S. Harrison Thomson, Cambridge, 1956, pp. vii–xxii. For more extensive analysis and a defense of Hus, see Paul de Vooght, *L'Hérésie de Jean Huss*, Louvain, 1960, and the companion volume of documentation, *Hussiana*, Louvain, 1960. Less passionate is Matthew Spinka, *John Hus's Concept of the Church*, Princeton, N.J., 1966. On the Council of Constance and its quest for reform, see John H. Mundy, Kennerly M. Woody,

The Council of Constance: The Unification of the Church, New York, 1961, esp. pp. 3–49. For a collection of English translations of ecclesiological discussion by conciliarists—Henry of Langenstein, John Gerson, Dietrich of Niew, John Major—see *Advocates of Reform: From Wyclif to Erasmus*, ed. Matthew Spinka, The Library of Christian Classics, XIV, Philadelphia, 1953, pp. 91–184. Here also Hus's treatise *On Simony*, pp. 196–278. On Hus and the Reformation see Jaroslav Pelikan, "Luther's Attitude Toward John Huss," *Concordia Theological Monthly*, 19 (1948), pp. 747–763.

2. Text available in *Documents of the Christian Church*, 2d ed., ed. Henry Bettenson, London, 1963, pp. 232–242.

3. *Johannis Wycliffe, De dominio divino*, ed. R. L. Poole, London, 1890.

4. *Johannis Wycliffe, De civili dominio*, I, ed. R. L. Poole, London, 1900; II, ed. J. Loserth, London, 1904.

5. *De Ecclesia*, ed. J. Loserth, London, 1886.

6. *Enchiridion Symbolorum*, 32d ed., ed. H. Denzinger, A. Schönmetzer, Freiburg i. Br., 1963, No. 1154.

7. Since 1884 when J. Loserth, the editor of Wyclif's *De Ecclesia*, discovered striking parallels with Hus: *Hus und Wyclif, Zur Genesis der Hussitischen Lehre*, Prag, 1884; English translation by M. J. Evans, London, 1884.

8. "Super IV Sententiarum," *Opera Omnia*, II, ed. W. Flajšhans and M. Komínková, Prague, 1905, IV Sent. d 5 q 3, p. 542. See also ch. 10, *De Ecclesia*, ed. S. Harrison Thomson, Cambridge, 1956, pp. 73, 88.

9. *Documenta Magistri Joannis Hus*, ed. F. Palacký, Prague, 1869, p. 302, quoted by de Vooght, *Hussiana*, p. 214.

10. *Documenta*, pp. 226 f.

11. Ch. 3 in *De Ecclesia*, ed. Thomson, p. 17.

12. *Ibid.*, ch. 18, p. 172.

13. "Hic dicitur quod debet concedi, quod idem simul et semel est iustus et iniustus . . . idem homo est iustus ex gracia predestinacionis et iniustus ex vicio deperdibili . . ." *Ibid.*, ch. 4, p. 27.

14. Cf. *ibid.*, ch. 4, pp. 27 ff.

15. *Ibid.*, ch. 19, p. 177.

16. *Ibid.*, p. 181.

17. *Ibid.*, ch. 18, p. 157. Cf. ch. 16, p. 121.

18. *Ibid.*, ch. 17, p. 156.

19. In "Richental's chronicle" in *The Council of Constance*, p. 113, it is suggested that Hus broke by this action his safe-conduct; see, however, p. 130 where the reason indicated is that "there could be no law by which a heretic had safe-conduct." See also p. 195, note 77.

20. *WA* Br 2. 42; quoted from *Luther's Works*, Vol. 48, Letters I, ed. G. G. Krodel, Philadelphia, 1963, p. 153; cf. p. 155.

21. Brian Tierney, *op. cit.*, p. 13; cf. p. 246.

22. ". . . a papa ad concilium appellare est in longum et in incertum auxilium in gravamine postulare, ideo ad caput ecclesie dominum Ihesum Christum ultimo appellavi," *De Ecclesia*, ed. Thomson, ch. 18, p. 165.

23. For primary sources and nineteenth-century secondary sources see F. Zöpffel (Benrath), "Pius II," in *Realencyklopädie*, Vol. 15, col. 422 f., and Ludwig von Pastor, *Geschichte der Päpste seit dem Ausgang des Mittelalters*, II, Freiburg i. Br., 1886, pp. 49–81. For general setting see Hubert Jedin, *Geschichte des Konzils von Trient*, I, *Der Kampf um das Konzil*, Freiburg i. Br., 1953², pp. 50 ff. On *Execrabilis*, see G. B. Picotti, "La pubblicazione e i primi effeti della *Execrabilis* di Pio II," in *Arch. della soc. Romana di storia patria*, 37 (1914), pp. 5–56. Picotti builds a strong case for the thesis that *Execrabilis* was particularly directed against Sigismund of Tyrol and was redated for this purpose. Nevertheless, it contains the major papal argument, first against conciliarism and secular rulers, and then

against Luther and the German Reformers.

24. Confirmed by Julius II, *Suscepti regiminis,* 1 July 1509; Benedictus XIV, *Altissimo,* 26 June 1745; Pius IX, *Apostolicae Sedis,* 12 October 1869, I, n. 4; VI, n. 1.

25. Jedin, *op. cit.,* p. 53.

26. Biel, *Defensorium obedientie apostolice,* Hagenau, 1510, II. I, col. 2. Critical edition in press.

27. See further *Harvest,* p. 13.

28. P. Feret, *La Faculté de Paris,* I, pp. 204 ff.

29. See "Der Reformentwurf des Kar-dinals Nikolaus Cusanus," ed. St. v. Ehses, *Historisches Jahrbuch,* 32 (1911), pp. 281–297.

30. "Reformentwurf Pius des Zweiten," ed. R. Haubst *Römische Quartalschrift,* 49 (1954), pp. 188–242.

31. "Cumque Romanorum praesulem, quanto prae aliis sublimiorem sortitus est cathedram, tanto mundiorem et nitidiorem esse conveniat, studebimus omni conatu omnipotenti Deo castum servare pectus . . ." Ed. Haubst, *loc. cit.,* 10, p. 208.

JAN HUS

The Church

Chapter I

. . . The holy, universal Church is the sole bride of Christ, a virgin
perfectly spotless until the end, whom the Son of God united with
Himself in marriage out of eternal love and through the grace of
adoption. We believe this Church as we say in the Creed: "I believe in
the holy, catholic Church," to which is added in the second Creed:
"and apostolic." It is called "apostolic" because the Apostles, purified
in the Spirit, are true partners of this same Mother Church which
they established by means of the teaching of Christ and His Blood,
and on the basis of their teaching and authority Christ's vicars rule
the young bride who seeks only the Bridegroom of the Church . . .

The unity of the Catholic Church consists in the bond of predestination, since her individual members are united by predestination,
and in the goal of blessedness, since all her sons are ultimately united
in blessedness. For the present time her unity consists also in the unity
of faith and virtue and in the unity of love, even as Augustine interprets the words of John 18:21, "that they all might be one," and John
18:14, "it was expedient that one man should die for the people."
"Caiaphas," says Augustine, "prophesied that God would gather together his children unto one, not," he said, "he has gathered them together in one Spirit, whose head is Christ."[1] The Apostle Paul refers
to this same unity in his letter to the Ephesians: "Eager to maintain
the unity of the Spirit in the bond of peace—one body, one Spirit, one

Lord, one faith, one baptism, one God and father of all."[2] There is no doubt that without this aforesaid union there is no salvation . . .

Chapter III

. . . It is one thing to be of the Church, another thing to be in the Church. Clearly it does not follow that all living persons who are in the Church are of the Church. On the contrary, we know that tares grow among the wheat, the raven eats from the same threshing floor as the dove, and the chaff is harvested along with the grain. . . . Yet the relationship between these things is subtle, and thus we ought to conceive of the holy Mother Church as the text from I John directs us, "How many Antichrists have come . . . They went out from us but were not of us . . . for if they had been of us they would have continued with us."[3] For just as excrements proceed from food and the solid members of the body but are not identified with them, so the refuse of the Church, the reprobate, proceed from the Church but are not of it and are not real parts, since no true members of the Church can permanently fall away from it, because the bond of predestination binding them to the Church never fails, as Paul said to the Corinthians.[4] And in his letter to the Romans he says: "We know that in everything, God works for good with those who love Him, who are called according to His purpose, namely predestination. For those whom He foreknew He also predestined to be conformed to the image of His Son in order that they might be first born among many brethren. And those whom He predestined He also called and those whom He called He also justified."[5] And Paul concludes his extended argument on behalf of the predestined, "For I am sure that neither death, nor life, nor angels, nor principalities, nor powers, nor things present, nor things to come, nor fear, nor height, nor depth, nor anything else in all creation will be able to separate us from the love of God in Christ Jesus our Lord."[6] Moreover, it should be noted, as many say, that the relation of the pilgrim to the holy Mother Church is fourfold. Some are in the Church in name and in reality, as are predestined Catholics obedient to Christ; some are neither in name nor reality in the Church as are reprobate pagans; others are in the Church in name only, as are, for example, reprobate hypocrites; and still others are in the Church in reality and, although they appear to be in name outside it, are predestined Christians, as are those who are seen to be condemned by the satraps of the Antichrist before the Church. In this fashion high priest and Pharisees condemned our Redeemer to a most shameful death, as if He were a blasphemer, and consequently condemned Him "who is predestined to be the Son of God."[7]

Furthermore, it should be noted that neither status nor human prerogatives can make anyone a member of the holy, universal Church, but only divine predestination can, as it does for everyone who steadfastly follows Christ in love. Moreover, according to Augustine, predestination is the election by the divine will through grace; or, as it is usually said, "predestination is the preparation for grace in the present and for glory in the future."[8] But, as it is said in canon law, predestination is twofold: "by the one, man is preordained to receive righteousness and forgiveness of sins in the present." This preordination does not include the attainment of eternal life and hence is not consonant with the latter definition stated above. "By the other predestination man attains eternal life in the future."[9] The first preordination follows this predestination, not vice versa. For if anyone is predestined to eternal life, it follows by necessity that he is predestined to righteousness. And if man attains eternal life, he necessarily attains righteousness, but not vice versa. For many are "participants in present righteousness but not participants in eternal life, because they lack perseverance. Hence many seem to be predestined in regard to present righteousness but not in regard to eternal glory."[10] Gratian establishes this position in the words of the Apostle: "Blessed be the God and Father of our Lord Jesus Christ who has blessed us in Christ with every spiritual blessing in the heavenly places, even as He chose us in Him before the foundation of the world, that we should be holy and blameless before Him in love. He predestined us in Him unto the adoption of sons through Jesus Christ, according to the purpose of His will to the praise of His glorious grace, which He freely bestowed on us in the beloved, in whom we have redemption through His Blood, the forgiveness of our trespasses."[11]

Furthermore, it is evident that men can belong to the holy Mother Church in two ways. They can be of the Church according to predestination to eternal life. In this way all who are holy until the end are of the holy Mother Church. The other way in which men can be of the Church is according to predestination unto present righteousness alone; for example, all who in some way receive grace for the forgiveness of their sins but who do not persevere until the end.

And beyond this it is clear that there are two kinds of grace. The one is the grace of predestination, from which the preordained can never ultimately fall away. The other grace is according to present righteousness which is present today and gone tomorrow, effective today but failing tomorrow. The first kind of grace makes sons for the holy, universal Church infinitely more perfect than the second kind of grace, because it bestows an infinite good, which can be enjoyed forever, while the second kind of grace cannot do this. The first kind of grace makes sons of an eternal inheritance, the second makes officials temporarily acceptable to God. Hence it seems probable that while Paul was a blasphemer according to present righteousness and at the same time a member of the holy Mother Church, and thus one of the faithful, in grace according to predestination to eternal life, Judas was in grace according to present righteousness, and at the same time never a member of the holy Mother Church according to predestination to eternal life, since he did not have this latter kind of predestination. And thus although Judas was chosen by Christ as an Apostle and bishop (which is the name of an office), he never was a member of the holy, universal Church; and thus, Paul never belonged to the devil, although some of his actions were similar in all respects to acts of the Church of the wicked; and likewise Peter was permitted by the Lord to speak a serious falsehood in order that he might come back from the experience all the stronger, since, as Augustine says, it is advantageous for the predestined to fall into sins of this kind.[12]

From these considerations it is clear that separation from the holy Church is twofold, either permanent or temporary. All reprobates are separated from the Church permanently. Some heretics, separated from the Church by a sin that can be overcome, are separated only temporarily, since they can, by the grace of God, return to the fold of Jesus Christ. Christ said concerning these latter ones, "And I have other sheep that are not of this fold; I must bring them also."[13] He had other sheep which were His according to predestination, but they were not of His fold, that is to say, they were not in His Church according to present righteousness. These were brought to life through His grace.

This distinction between the grace of predestination and that of present righteousness should be given serious attention, because some are sheep according to predestination but ravening wolves according to present righteousness ...

Chapter IV

Now we turn to the objection that no reprobate is a member of the holy Mother, the Catholic Church. There is only one holy Mother, one Catholic Church from the beginning of the world which was held in unmixed purity by the right hand of the Bridegroom out of His perpetual love. As is clear from the aforesaid, this same Church will have no other members after the day of judgment than it has and has had before the day of judgment. Rather, all who are to be saved after the day of judgment are now predestined. Therefore, none of them are reprobate before the day of judgment and consequently no reprobate is a member of the holy Mother, the Catholic Church.

Likewise, it is impossible that Christ should ever not love His bride or any part of her, since He necessarily loves her just as He loves Himself. But it is impossible for Christ to love any reprobate in this fashion; therefore, it is impossible that any reprobate would be a member of the Church. The premise is proved by that famous principle of Augustine, namely, that it is impossible for God to begin to know or love someone He has not known and loved before.[14] For God cannot begin or cease to know or will something, because He is immutable and because divine knowledge and volition would then be determined by an outside factor ...

The objection now might be made that the reprobate living for a time in a state of grace has this bond of union with Christ just as the predestined living for a time in a state of sin lacks this bond of union with Christ. However, it is clear that the body of Christ is like the human body, in that the human body has some liquids which flow in and out, while other liquids are the lifeblood of the body, and so in the mystical body of Christ there is grace according to present justice and also final grace. Therefore, just as an abscess is a growth upon the body but not a part of the body itself, since it is essentially different from the body, so the members of the devil may temporarily adhere to the body of Christ as they live in present righteousness. The predestined, on the other hand, although they may be temporarily deprived of the flow of grace, have their roots in grace, from which they cannot fall away. And thus the predestined who are now righteous are bound by a twofold bond.

But against this another objection is made that if one grants the aforesaid, it is necessary to concede that a man could be at one and the same time righteous and unrighteous, faithful and unfaithful, true Christian and heretic, in perfect grace and without grace, and be entitled to other such opposing labels which obviously imply contradictions.

This I answer by granting that a man can at one and the same time be righteous and unrighteous. But I deny that this man can at one and the same time be righteous and unrighteous in the same respect, just as exact opposites cannot be present simultaneously in one person. But the aforementioned labels are not true opposites, since, according to the philosopher, only one aspect of a thing can be opposed to another. Thus the same man can be righteous due to the grace of predestination and unrighteous due to an insurmountable sin, such as Peter's denial of Christ and Paul's persecution of Him. For they at that time had not fallen away from the bond of predestination and thus, as a result of this bond of predestination, they were in grace and hence righteous. But because they were committing an evil deed and were thus, for a time, deprived of the flow of grace, they were from this perspective unrighteous. I deny that we can infer from the assertion, "Paul and Peter were at one time not righteous," the further assertion, "Paul and Peter were unrighteous."

It is invalid to argue from privation to negation unless we specify more exactly what is meant, as in my proposition: Paul and Peter were unrighteous, therefore, according to present grace, they were not righteous. The conclusion is true and thus properly conceded. Peter and Paul were righteous according to the grace of predestination, but

they were not righteous according to present grace. Likewise Paul
was faithful according to predestination and unfaithful according to
persecution, an Israelite according to predestination and a blasphemer
according to present righteousness; he had the love of predestination
but lacked the love of present righteousness. Paul's own words as he
quotes from Hosea affirm this distinction:

> "Those who were not my people
> I will call 'my people,'
> And her who was not beloved
> I will call 'my beloved.'
> And in the very place where it was said to them
> 'You are not my people'
> They will be called 'sons of the living God.' "[15]

This quotation and others like it can be understood by those who
know that there is a true contradiction only when opposites are
predicated of the same thing, regarding the same issue, and at the
same moment in time. Those who understand this, grant that Christ
was for three sacred days dead but yet alive. As Ambrose says, "He
was dead and not dead because He lived in the Spirit and was dead
in the body. He was dead as man and not dead as God."[16] But St. Paul
said that the widow "who is self-indulgent is dead even while she
lives,"[17] because she lives in the flesh but does not live in the Spirit.
Thus it is clear that neither opposing nor contradictory assertions
follow from the previous statements.

Finally it is clear that no reprobate is truly a part of the holy Mother
Church. If St. Thomas or anyone else should assert that a reprobate
is a member of the Church and in grace, then he contradicts Augustine
and Holy Scripture, following a superficial popular definition and
heeding only the standards of the militant Church. Hence we referred before to Augustine's assertion, "If they do not have true perseverance, if they do not persist in that in which they began, they are
not rightly named when they are named only in name and not in
reality. But nobody will do this who knows future events, who knows
how evil emerges out of good."[18] This quotation of Augustine should
suffice against any ambiguous objections.

Chapter V

. . . The exegesis of the Fathers makes it clear that in the parables of Christ the reprobate are symbolized by the evil fish, by the evil wedding guests, by the man not dressed in wedding garments at the wedding feast, by the chaff, by the tares, by the bad seed, by the evil tree, by the foolish virgins, and by the goats. On the other hand the predestined are symbolized by the good fish, by the good wedding guests, by the men dressed in wedding garments, by the wheat, by the good seed, the good tree, the wise virgins, and the sheep.

Having considered these things the faithful ought to be on his guard against the conclusion: the reprobate are in the holy Church of God, therefore they are part of it. For it has already been pointed ou that there is a difference between being in the Church and being of the Church or a part or member of the Church. Just as it does not follow that because the chaff or tares are in the wheat or mixed with the wheat the chaff is the wheat, so it does not follow that the reprobate are of the Church. Likewise, just as it does not follow that because some waste or infection is in the human body it is therefore part of the body, so also it does not follow that because the reprobate is in the mystical body of the Church he is therefore part of it. Again one cannot validly conclude that because someone is in grace according to present justice he is a part or member of the holy Catholic Church. But it can be most validly concluded that if someone is in the grace of predestination he is part or member of the holy Church.

Nor is it valid to conclude that because Peter has sinned he is not a part or member of the holy Church, but it does indeed follow that when Peter has sinned, then he is not in the Church according to the grace of present justice. Subtleties of this kind are understood by considering what it is to be in the Church and what it is to be a member or part of the Church and that predestination, which is the preparation for grace in the present and glory in the future, makes one a member of the holy Catholic Church. One is not made a member by high status or human prerogatives or any visible sign. For that devil Judas, in spite of his election by Christ and the transitory gifts given

to him for his apostolate or episcopate and even the reputation with
the people that he was a true disciple of Christ—in spite of all this he
was not a true disciple but a "wolf clad in sheep's clothing," as Augustine said,[19] and as a result was neither predestined nor a part of
the Church, the bride of Christ.

From this it is clear that it would be exceedingly presumptuous for
anyone without revelation or great caution to assert that he himself
is a member of this holy Church. For no one is a member of this
Church unless he be predestined and in due time without spot or
blemish. But no one without great caution or revelation could assert
that he is predestined or holy without spot or blemish. Hence the
argument is established. Thus we see what effrontery those have who
are deeply devoted to the world, who live a totally secular and indul-
gent life far removed from Christ's way of life and, even more, without even so much as a token fulfillment of Christ's commands and
precepts assert without great caution that they are the heads or the
body or the ruling members of the Church, the bride of Christ. How
can we believe they are without a spot of mortal sin or without a
wrinkle of venial sin when, by their abandonment of the counsels of
Christ, by their neglect of their holy office and by their works they
lead us to think just the opposite? For the Bridegroom of the Church
says, "You will know them by their fruits," "believe the works," and
"so practice and observe whatever they tell you but not what they do;
for they preach but do not practice."[20]

The first objection to this is the following: Every priest who in the
judgment of the Church has been stamped by his bishop with visible
sign of character of his priesthood is a part of the holy Mother Church.
Only the totality of these is called by *antonomasia* the Church.[21] We
ought to give special honor to his body because otherwise it would
follow that Christians would not know their own Mother. And if
they did not recognize their Mother, then they would not fulfill their
duties to her, such as offerings and tithes, and great confusion in the
Church militant would result.

To refute their argument an example is furnished by Judas who was
called to the episcopal ministry by Christ, who could not err. But that
reprobate was never a true disciple of Christ, as Augustine establishes,

but he was a wolf dressed in sheep's clothing and he was always chaff, the bad seed of the weeds and the tares.

In a similar way the second part of the previous argument is refuted. The Church, by *antonomasia,* is called the bride of Christ, which is the totality of the predestined, as has already been said. For if this totality is the most excellent bride of Christ, then this totality is by *antonomasia* the holy Church, since she is the only dove and queen, standing at the right hand of the King to whom young virgins shall be led. In the case of the clergy Christ met when He was on earth, who had established themselves as high priests, priests, Pharisees, and various ranks of priests observing traditions they had developed themselves, they claimed God as their Father and that they were the seed of Abraham. They were never subject to anyone, even enjoying good repute among the people. But all this did not imply that this clergy was truly the holy Church by *antonomasia.* And concerning these clergy, Christ said that the disciples should not allow them to become a scandal because "they are blind leaders of the blind."[22] In the same manner it now holds true that no group of clergy is called by *antonomasia* the holy Church simply because this group asserts that it is the holy Church.

Furthermore it is clear that three conclusions are not valid. The first conclusion stated that "otherwise it would follow that Christians would not recognize their own Mother," but we must know our Mother by faith just as we know by faith the triumphant Church, Christ, His mother, and His Apostles together with the blessed angels and many saints. But the living and the dead we know only very vaguely and imperfectly, "But when the perfect comes, the imperfect will pass away,"[23] because in heaven we shall see our Mother face to face with each of her individual members. Let not the faithful complain but rather rejoice in this truth, that the holy Mother Church is thus hidden from him during his pilgrimage, because on that the merit of the Christian faith depends.

According to the Apostle Paul, "Faith is the substance of things hoped for, the evidence of things not seen,"[24] that is, things not visible to our corporeal eyes during our pilgrimage. During our pilgrimage we cannot see with our eyes the basis of this predestination or love which does not fail, which is the wedding garment distinguishing a member of the Church from a member of the devil. According to Augustine, "The act of faith is to believe what you do not see."[25]

Furthermore it is clear that the opposite of the second conclusion is established because we fulfill our duties to the holy Church when we, who have Christ as our high priest, provide with temporal things for physical sustenance His ministers whom, on grounds of their works, we with our imperfect faith hold to be ministers, and the poor whom we, without certitude, suppose to be members of Christ.

Now it might be objected that every layman is required to believe of his prelates that they are heads of the Church and parts of the Church according to predestination or present justice. But here it is answered that the layman is required to believe only what is true. This is obvious because one is required to believe only what God moves one to believe. God, however, does not move man to believe anything which is false, although there may be times when good does result from a false faith; God moves man only in regard to the substance of an act; God does not move man so that he should be led astray. Hence, if a layman should believe regarding his prelate that he is a holy member of the Church, when in fact he is not, then his faith or act of believing would be false. Therefore, the pastor is required to instruct his flock by his own virtuous works so that in this way they may see that he is holy. Hence if one of the flock does not see virtuous works on the part of the pastor, he is not required to believe that the pastor is a holy member of the Church insofar as present justice is concerned. But, insofar as predestination is concerned, he should hold this view conditionally and with great caution. Moreover, if the faithful know with certainty that the pastor has committed sin, then they ought to presume that the pastor is not righteous but rather an enemy of Jesus Christ.

Finally it is clear that the conclusion of the third argument is false. For no confusion results in the Church militant from the fact that we cannot without revelation clearly discern the true members of the mystical body of Christ so long as they are still in the course of their earthly pilgrimage.

But still another objection is raised. Since grace makes sons of the Church, while sin makes members of the devil or unfaithful ones, it appears that a man can become a member of the Church after he has been unfaithful, or a member of the Church after he has been a member of the devil. For who doubts that Judas when he was a true Apostle was also a member of the Church just as Paul when he was a blasphemer was separated from the holy Mother Church? Here it is answered that the Church can be defined in a true sense and a nominal sense. In a true sense the Church is the Church of the predestined. In a nominal sense the Church is the congregation of the reprobate, although it is plainly an error on the part of those still on their pilgrimage to reckon the reprobate in the holy Mother Church. Thus many are, according to worldly reputation, heads or members of the Church, even though according to the foreknowledge of God they are members of the devil, those who for a time believed but later fell away, or those who now and always have been unfaithful. Of such kind were those who, as we said above "according to Augustine," were disciples of Christ but who "turned away and no longer walked with Him." Likewise with Judas who was a false disciple of Christ about whom Augustine remarks to point out how the sheep hear the voice of Christ, "But what are we to think? Are those who heard the sheep? After all, Judas heard and he was a wolf. He followed, but he was merely dressed in sheep's clothing and he conspired against the shepherd."[26] In this way therefore, many can be said to be of the Church nominally according to present righteousness but not truly according to predestination to glory. Augustine teaches who these are: "The Lord knows who are His, who will endure to the crown, who will endure till the flame, He knows the wheat in his threshing floor, He knows the chaff, the seed, the tares. But to others it is not known who are the doves and the ravens."[27]

Chapter VII

We have stated that Christ alone is the head of the holy, universal Church and that all the predestined of the past and the future are His mystical body and each of them is a member of the same body. Now our task is to consider whether the Roman Church is that holy, universal Church, the bride of Christ. And it would appear to be so on the basis of this argument. There is only one holy, Catholic, and apostolic Church. But there is no other Church than the Roman Church. Therefore the Roman Church is the holy, universal Church.

The first premise is proved by a quotation from Pope Boniface: "We are impelled by faith to believe and hold that there is only one holy, Catholic, and apostolic Church."[28] And the second premise is proved similarly from the same source. "The Church has only one body and head, it does not have two like some monster. That body, that head, is Christ, that is to say Peter, the vicar of Christ, and the successors of Peter. For the Lord Himself said to Peter, 'Feed my sheep.' He said this with reference to all sheep. He did not single out some. Clearly it means that all sheep were put under Peter's care. Therefore if the Greeks or any others claim that they are not subject to Peter and his successors, they thereby of necessity confess that they are not sheep of Christ, since the Lord said, 'there shall be one flock, one shepherd.' "[29]

These authorities establish that the holy Roman Church is the holy, universal Church because all the sheep are Christ's. There is one fold with one shepherd. This is the point of Boniface's decretal which ends thus: "We declare, assert, and define that it is absolutely necessary as a condition for salvation that every human creature be subject to the Roman pontiff." If, therefore, every human being is as a condition for salvation subjected by this definition to the Roman pope, then indeed it follows that the Roman Church is the universal Church.

But now we state the argument which denies this conclusion. The Roman Church is a Church constituted by the pope as head and the cardinals as body. But this Church is not the holy, Catholic, and apostolic Church. Therefore the Roman Church is not the universal Church. The first premise is proved by certain doctors who say, among other things, that the pope is the head of the Roman Church and the College of Cardinals its body. And the second premise is evident from this consideration, namely, that the pope together with the cardinals is not the sum total of all predestined.

To understand this problem one should consider this Gospel passage: "Simon Peter replied, 'You are the Christ the Son of the living God,' and Jesus answered him, 'Blessed are you, Simon Bar-Jona! for flesh and blood have not revealed this to you but My Father who is in

heaven. And I tell you, you are Peter, and on this rock I will build
My Church and the gates of hell shall not prevail against it. I will give
you the keys of the kingdom of heaven and whatever you bind on
earth shall be bound in heaven, and whatever you loose on earth shall
be loosed in heaven.' "[30] The Gospel speaks here of the Church of
Christ, its faith and its foundation and authority. The Church is referred to by the words, "I will build my Church." "You are Christ the
Son of the living God" refers to faith. And "I will give you the keys
of the kingdom of heaven" refers to authority. These four things—
the Church, its faith, foundation, and authority—should be briefly discussed.

Regarding the first point, if we go beyond what usually presents
itself as the Church and is referred to as the Church, then it can be
said that she can be defined in three ways. First the Church is defined
as the congregation or convocation of faithful, the faithful understood
in a relative sense, namely, faithful for a time or merely according to
present righteousness. According to this definition those who are reprobate, who possess grace only in the present time, do belong in the
Church. But such a Church is not the mystical body of Christ nor the
holy Catholic Church nor any part of it.

The second definition posits a Church which contains a mixture of
those who are reprobate, who are in a state of grace only according
to present righteousness, and those who are truly predestined. This
Church coincides partially but not completely with the holy Church
of God. It is called "mixed" because it contains both grain and chaff,
wheat and tares. For the kingdom of heaven is like a net cast into the
sea which gathers up fish of all kinds. The kingdom of heaven is like
the ten virgins, of whom five were foolish and five were wise. This is
the Church Tyconius erroneously called the "bipartite body of
Christ."[31] Erroneously because the reprobate are not the body of Christ
nor any part of it.

The third definition includes in the Church the whole convocation
of the predestined who will be in a state of grace ultimately, regardless of whether or not they are now. This was the definition used by
the Apostle Paul when he said, "Christ loved the Church and gave
Himself up for her that He might sanctify her by the washing of

water with the word, that the Church might be presented before Him in splendor, without spot or wrinkle or any such thing, that she might be holy and without blemish."[32]

This is the Church the Savior called His own in the previously quoted passage, "On this rock I will build My Church." That he refers to this Church is made clear by the next phrase, "and the gates of hell shall not prevail against it." Since Christ is the rock and foundation on which this Church is built according to predestination, therefore this Church cannot be overcome by the gates of hell, that is by the scoffing of persecuting tyrants or malignant spirits. For Christ, the King of Heaven and Bridegroom of the Church, is more powerful than the princes of this world. In order to declare His power, foreknowledge, and predestination, with which He so powerfully edifies, protects, foreknows, and predestines His Church and to give His Church hope that it will persevere He added, "and the gates of hell shall not prevail against it." Regarding this, Nicholas of Lyra says, "From this it is clear that the Church is not made up of men with reference to their authority and ecclesiastical or secular status. For many princes and popes and others of lesser office have been found to be apostates from the faith."[33] A supporting example for Lyra's statement is Judas Iscariot. Both Apostle and bishop, he was present at the very moment when Christ said, "On this rock I will build My Church and the gates of hell shall not prevail against it." But Judas was not built upon the rock, that is, Christ, according to predestination. Therefore in the end the gates of hell prevailed against him.

From these words of the Lord it becomes clear that the Church is understood in this particular way. It includes all who after Christ's resurrection were built upon Him in faith and perfecting grace. To Peter, as representative of the universal Church and confessing its faith, "You are the Christ the Son of the living God," he directed these words of praise, "Blessed are you, Simon Bar-Jona!" The commendation befits Peter and the whole, holy Church which is blessed in this life because it begins by confessing humbly, obediently, lovingly, and steadfastly that Christ is the Son of the living God. For neither flesh, that is, worldly wisdom, nor blood, that is, pure philosophical knowledge, reveals a thing about such a hidden article but only God the Father. Thus, because of this confession, which was so clear and firm, Christ said to Peter, the rock, "I tell you, you are Peter" (that is, the confessor of the true rock which is Christ), "and on this rock" (which you confessed, that is, on Me) "I will build" (through steadfast faith and perfecting grace) "My Church" (that is, the convocation of the predestined who after this life are appointed to receive glory). Therefore "the gates of hell shall not prevail against it."

Thus far we have drawn these assertions from the words of the Savior: There is one Church (from the word "Church"), it is Christ's (from the word "My"), and it is holy (from the promise, "and the gates of hell shall not prevail against it"). From this we conclude that there is one, holy Church of Christ, called catholic in Greek or universal in Latin. It is apostolic because it was through apostolic words and acts that it was established and "founded upon the rock, Christ," as Jerome says.[34]

Therefore I submit that this universal Church should be called the holy Roman Church, for canon law says, "Although there is only one marital bed for the universal Catholic Church of Christ throughout the world, nevertheless many synodical decisions attribute to the Roman Catholic and apostolic Church a superior rank to that of other Churches."[35] And farther on in canon law this Church is called "the Roman Church, primal apostolic see, having neither spot nor blemish." But the Church thus understood cannot be said to be a pope with his cardinals and his household, because they all come and go. The gloss says about this text, "The argument is that wherever the good are, there is the Roman Church. This argument should give the believer full confidence that he knows where the Roman Church is."

A second quotation from canon law should be understood in the same fashion: "This is the holy and apostolic Church, Mother of all the other churches, the Church of Christ, which has been proved by the grace of God, the omnipotent, never to have deviated from teaching nor to have succumbed to the perversion of heretical novelties."[36] This quotation cannot be understood as referring to the pope or his household. For the gloss says, "What Church do you mean when you say 'it cannot err'"? Certainly canon law states that the pope can err. Therefore, neither the pope nor his household can be that Church which cannot err.[37] Rather the gloss says that "by the Church here is meant the congregation of the faithful." This is the way one should interpret the assertion by Jerome. He says, "The holy Roman Church, which has always remained spotless, will in the future—by the providence of the Lord and the help of St. Peter—remain free from the scoffing of heretics and will stand firm and unmoved forever."[38] This cannot be said of any pope or College of Cardinals, for these are often stained by common deceitfulness and sin. An example was the English Pope John, a woman with the name Agnes. How could one ever say that the Roman Church remained immaculate while she and her college ruled, since she gave birth?[39] The same goes for other popes who were heretics and were deposed because of their many enormities.

Therefore when the decretals say that the Roman Church has in God's eyes primacy and worthiness above all other Churches, clearly this should be read as referring to the entire militant Church, which God loves more than any one part. Thus it follows obviously from the truths of faith that it is not a particular part of the Church but the whole Mother Church, dispersed among every nation of every tongue, which is the holy Roman Church. It is this church to which both canon law and the holy doctors refer.

In order that this position might be impressed on our minds this hymn has been given by Ambrose and Augustine for use in the Church, "The holy Church throughout the world confesses Thee." And in the canon of the Mass we pray first and foremost for the holy Catholic Church that God might deign to keep her and grant her peace and support her throughout the whole world. Hence without doubt a prayer is offered for the foremost Church militant, which I take to be the Roman Church. But when we rank the various parts of the Church, the pope and his college are given the places of highest worthiness only as long as they follow Christ closely and, by forsaking pride and ambition and insistence on their primacy, serve their Mother effectively and humbly. If they do the opposite they will be transformed into an idol of desolation and into a college opposed to that humble college of the Apostles and of the Lord Jesus Christ.

However it should be noted that the Roman Church properly speaking is the congregation of those faithful to Christ, who live in obedience to the Roman bishop, just as the Antiochian Church is said to be the congregation of those faithful to Christ who are subject to the

Bishop of Antioch; and the same holds true for Alexandria and Constantinople...

A second definition of the Roman Church asserts that it is the pope together with his cardinals, regardless of where they live or whether their way of life is good or evil. A third definition equates the Roman Church just with the pope alone. But these last two definitions are the products of academic distortions. For other reasons one should call the Roman Church our Mother, not on account of the vain gesture of the emperor to make this concession to the Church, nor on account of the haughtiness of papal ostentation in regard to authority based on his primacy or lordship; nor is this third reason a sound one, namely that it is necessary, as some believe, for every Christian to have recourse to the pope and as a necessity for salvation to recognize him as head of the Church and most holy father. Since the Roman Church as such does not occur in Scripture, it is sufficient that there is a probable reason for its existence. Although the Christian Church began in Judea and the head of the Church, Christ, was killed in Jerusalem, nevertheless there are three good reasons why the Church of Christ is called the Roman Church on account of its pre-eminence. The first reason is that Christ knew that the Gentiles would be engrafted in the place of the unfaithful, unbelieving Jews, as the Apostle says. The second reason is that more martyrs died in triumph there than in any other city. Just as man is named after the city in which he is born or achieves great triumphs, so, since many parts of the holy Church came forth out of the womb of the synagogue in Rome and triumphed there by growing among all peoples, it was appropriate that she should take as her name Rome, from that metropolitan city of many peoples. . . . The third reason, already mentioned, is that it is neither location nor antiquity but rather faith active in love which founds the Church. In regard to both location and time the Church of Christ was established earlier in other sees . . .

From what has been said it is clear what is the answer to the question stated in the beginning of this chapter. It ought to be conceded that the Roman Church is the holy Mother, the Catholic Church, the bride of Christ. Now there is the opposing position which argues that the Roman Church is the Church whose head is the pope and whose body is the cardinals. Now this argument is granted if the Church is defined according to the second definition above, that is, the pope with his cardinals, wherever they may live. But it is denied that this is the holy, Catholic, and apostolic Church. Thus both premises are granted, but the conclusion is denied. Now it might be stated as a presupposition that the pope and all twelve cardinals living with him are holy—an assumption which could very well be true. This line of argument concludes that the pope himself is the holy, Catholic, and apostolic Church. Again I deny the conclusion. It does indeed follow that the holy pope with his holy cardinals are a holy Church which is *part* of the holy, Catholic, and apostolic Church. The first conclusion is established as firm faith for believers in Christ, but the second is not. The first conclusion is verified by Christ's promise, "the gates of hell shall not prevail against it." The second conclusion is doubtful to me and to any pilgrim unless divine revelation elucidates him.

Thus the pope is not the head nor are the cardinals the entire body of the holy, Catholic, and universal Church. For Christ alone is the head of that Church and all predestined together form the body, and each alone is a member of that body, because the bride of Christ is united with Him.

Notes

1. *PL,* vol. XXV, col. 1920 ff.; cf. vol. XXIII, col. 846.
2. Ephesians 2:3–6.
3. I John 2:18.
4. I Corinthians 13:8.
5. Romans 8:28–30.
6. Romans 8:38, 39.
7. Romans 1:4.
8. Augustine, *De Predestinatione Sanctorum, PL,* vol. XLIV, col. 959 ff. The reference is less a quotation than a summary of the treatise.
9. *CIC,* vol. I, col. 1235.
10. *CIC,* vol. I, col. 1233.
11. Ephesians 1:3–7.
12. Cf. Augustine, *De Corruptione et Gratia,* C-9, in *PL,* XLIV, col. 930, 931.
13. John 10:16.
14. Augustine, *De Trinitate,* Bk. VI, ch. 10, in *PL,* vol. XLII, col. 931, 932.
15. Romans 9:25, 26.
16. This passage has not been located.
17. I Timothy 5:6.
18. *De Penitentia,* IV, c. 8, in *CIC,* vol. I, col. 1232.
19. Augustine, *In Joannis Evangelium,* in *PL,* vol. XXXV, col. 1723.
20. Matthew 7:20; John 10:38; Matthew 23:3.

21. *Antonomasia* is the use of a name to denote a class of persons.

22. Matthew 15:14.

23. Hebrews 11:1.

24. I Corinthians 13:10.

25. Cf. Augustine, *De Unitate Ecclesiae Contra Donatistas*, in *PL*, XLIII, col. 432.

26. Augustine, *In Joannis Evangelium*, in *PL*, vol. XXXV, col. 1723.

27. This quotation has not been found.

28. *CIC*, vol. II, col. 1245 ff.

29. John 10:16.

30. Matthew 16:16–19.

31. Augustine, *De Doctrina Christiana*, III, ch. 32, in *PL*, vol. XXXIV, col. 82 ff.

32. Ephesians 5:25–27.

33. *Biblia cum Postillis Nicolai Lyrae*, Basel, 1498–1508, vol. IV. Cf. the commentary on Matthew 16.

34. Cf. Jerome, *Epist.* 15, in *PL* XXII, col. 355.

35. *CIC*, vol. I, col. 70, dist. XXI, c. 3.

36. *CIC*, vol. I, col. 969, qu. I, c. 9.

37. Hus refers to two passages in canon law, dist. XIV, c. 9, "Anastasius," in *CIC*, vol. I, col. 64, and dist. XL, c. 6, "Si Papa," col. 146.

38. XXIV, qu. I, c. 14, in *CIC*, vol. I, col. 970.

39. Hus here refers to a thirteenth-century legend that claimed that after the death of Pope Leo III (816) a woman ruled as pope for a brief period.

POPE PIUS II

Execrabilis

Pius, bishop, servant of the servants of God, for perpetual remembrance.

A horrible and in earlier times unheard-of abuse has sprung up in our period. Some men, imbued with a spirit of rebellion and moved not with a desire for sound decisions but rather with a desire to escape the punishment for sin, suppose that they can appeal from the pope, vicar of Jesus Christ; from the pope, to whom it was said in the person of the blessed Peter "feed my sheep" and "whatever you bind on earth will be bound in heaven"—from this pope to a future council. How harmful this is to the Christian republic as well as contrary to canon law anyone who is not ignorant of the law can understand. For, not to mention all the other things which so clearly gainsay this corruption, who would not consider it ridiculous to appeal to something which does not now exist anywhere nor does anyone know when it will exist? The poor are heavily oppressed by the powerful, offenses remain unpunished, rebellion against the first see is encouraged, license for sin is granted, and all ecclesiastical discipline and hierarchical ranking of the Church are turned upside down.

(1) Desirous, therefore, of banishing this deadly poison from the Church of Christ, and concerned with the salvation of the sheep committed to us and the protection of the sheepfold of our Savior from all causes of scandal; with the counsel and with the assent drawn from our venerable Fathers of the Holy Roman Church, all the cardinals and prelates and all those who interpret divine and human law in accordance with the curia, and being fully informed, we con-

demn appeals of this kind, reject them as erroneous and abominable, declare them to be completely null and void. If any such appeals are found to have heretofore been made we declare and decree them to be of no effect but rather void and injurious. And we lay down that from now on, no one should dare, regardless of his pretext, to make such an appeal from our decisions, be they legal or theological, or from any commands at all from us or our successors, to heed such an appeal made by another, or to make use of these in any fashion whatsoever.

(2) But if anyone—regardless of his status, rank, order, or condition, even if he be distinguished by imperial, regal, or pontifical dignity—should violate this command when two months have expired from the day this bull has been published in the papal chancery, he, by this fact alone, incurs excommunication from which he cannot be absolved except through the pope and at the time of death. Moreover, the college or university should be subject to ecclesiastical interdiction and both the colleges and universities no less than the aforesaid persons and any others whatsoever will incur these punishments or censures. In addition, notaries and witnesses who give expert counsel, help, and assistance to those who make such appeals are to be punished with the same punishment.

(3) No one, therefore, is allowed to violate or daringly oppose this, our expression of what is to be desired, condemned, reproved, voided, annulled, decreed, asserted, and commanded. If, however, anyone should be presumptuous enough to attempt this he should know that he will incur the indignation of almighty God and of his blessed Apostles, Peter and Paul.

Dated: Mantua A.D. 18 January, 1460

Chapter Five
The Eucharist

Introduction

In the most elaborate of late medieval discussions of the Eucharist, the *Exposition of the Canon of the Mass,* Gabriel Biel (†1495) discusses not only eucharistic problems in the more limited sense of the word but he also relates this sacrament to the whole range of theological discussions of his day with constant reference to the preceding tradition. Even though a quarter of his book was still to be written at Christmas 1487,[1] by 1488 it had begun its influential pilgrimage through European presses and libraries. The work of Biel had already gone into the making of another important—more allegorical—interpretation, *The Fourfold Exposition of the Mass,* by Johannes Bechofen, an Augustinian monk writing in the last decade of the century,[2] and in years to come such representative theologians and leaders as Martin Luther and Johann Eck (†1543), as well as the influential Jesuit spokesman at the Council of Trent, Jacobus Lainez (†1565), would be raised on it. In spite of the fact that for some time the reliability of the *Exposition* as a dependable guide through the various late medieval eucharistic schools of thought has been doubted,[3] it can well be claimed that Biel, on all significant points summarized by Bechofen, not only intends but also succeeds in showing at what points the main lines of the medieval discussion cross, converge, or coincide.

The two issues that emerge as the dominant themes under which most other questions can be subsumed concern the relation of the elements of bread and wine to the eucharistic presence of Christ and the relation of the two offerings, in other words the relationship of

243

the cross and the altar. As background to the whole relationship is
to be assumed the doctrine of transubstantiation[4] or substantial conversion: After the words of consecration have been pronounced by the
priest the *substance* of bread and wine are converted into the Body
and Blood of Christ, whereas the *accidents* (which are the means by
which the presence of a substance is communicated to our senses)
remain unchanged.

Closely related to the Sacrament of the Eucharist, and to the doctrine of the sacraments as such, are the concepts *ex opere operato* and
ex opere operantis. The first term can be translated as "on grounds
of the performance of the rite," and designates the ability of an exterior rite to bring about what it signifies. The Sacraments of the New
Testament were regarded by most medieval doctors to have power
in this way to convey grace so long as the recipient did not provide
an obstacle and the administrant had the proper intention. *Ex opere
operantis* is the efficacy of a rite as determined by the interior disposition of the administrant or the recipient. The othodox interpretation
of *ex opere operantis* is that a proper disposition on the part of the
recipient will provide him with grace above and beyond the grace
received *ex opere operato*.

Within this context there are a series of questions which naturally
arise, both with respect to the Eucharist as offering and the Eucharist
as communion. When, after the consecration, the historical Body of
Christ becomes substance under the unchanged accidents, does the
offering on the altar repeat, re-enact, or recall the sacrifice on Calvary?
Is this a memorial of the offering of Christ or indeed a true immolation?[5] If Christ is, after the conversion, substantially present, does this
imply that when the Host falls on the floor and is eaten by a mouse,
the mouse actually eats the Body of Christ?[6] Such a question may
seem to modern ears the product of an irreverent mind, but in the
discussion of this issue by Albert the Great, Thomas Aquinas, and
Bonaventura it is clear that it leads inevitably to an analysis of the
duration of the presence of Christ in the consecrated Host and also
—more importantly—of the degree to which the disposition of the
recipient plays a role. Do the infidel, the heretic, the Christian in a
state of sin, and the Christian in a state of grace all receive Christ
in the same manner? Does the *ex opere operato* efficacy obliterate the

differences between these three groups? Or, to discuss the meaning of the exterior and interior presence of Christ in another way, is it more sinful to inattentively drop the consecrated Host or to pay no attention to the preached word?[7]

These were not abstract academic problems but rather religious questions of crucial importance on the lay and parish level. For proof of their importance we have only to look at the ramifications of these issues as discussed by Cardinal Cajetan, who deals with the real presence and immolation of the Body of Christ related to the devotion of the recipient, by Sylvester Prierias in his discussion of the relation between the Eucharist and the sermon, and by Cornelisz Hoen in his defense of the necessity of faith and the spiritual nature of communion against the "papal teaching" of transubstantiation.

James Cajetan (1468–1534), or Thomas de Vio as he was named after his entry in the Dominican Order (1484), came for the first time to general attention in 1494 when he crossed swords with Pico della Mirandola (†1494). Instrumental in the pre-Tridentine renaissance of Thomism and rising to places of high authority in his order, he wrote against Scotism and was himself attacked by the Parisian nominalist and disciple of Gabriel Biel, Jacob Almain (†1516). The main reason for the latter's attack was the curialism which led Cajetan to oppose the participation of Dominicans in the abortive council— depreciatingly referred to by the opponents as "Little Council," or Conciliabulum—convened in Pisa in 1511 by Maximilian and Louis XII against the wishes of the pope.[8] A year later, on June 10, 1512, speaking to the conciliar Fathers present at the Fifth Lateran Council (1512–1517) he stresses the image of the Church as the New Jerusalem, with the pope as the supreme ruler to "whom all citizens and inhabitants of the Jerusalem descending from heaven owe obedience, not only as individual persons but also all taken together."[9] The most precious treasures of this New Jerusalem are the holy things (*sacra*), the sacraments which are so powerful that through the Sacrament of Marriage, generations are brought into being, through the Sacrament of Baptism, children are reborn in God who then grow up through the nourishment of Holy Communion . . ."[10]

One is reminded of the maxim of reform formulated by Giles of Viterbo one month earlier: "It behooves men to be changed by the holy things (*sacra*), not the holy things by men."[11] Both the Augustinian Giles and the Dominican Cajetan addressed the Fifth Lateran Council, both chose for their presentation a text from the Apocalypse of John, and both emphasized the sacred things (*sacra*), together with the necessity of communion with the See of St. Peter, as the foundation of the Church and basis of renewal. But whereas for Giles there are times in which the bride (the Church) falls asleep and the Bridegroom (Christ) returns to heaven, Cajetan does not appear to allow such discontinuity in the history of the Church; he bases his vision of the Church on the unbroken continuous succession of the papacy. In contrast to Giles he places the Church's sanctity outside the reach of the assaults of impiety,[12] since they are organized by the exterior enemies of the Church of God, Who in His mercy, forces them back in the fold and into acknowledgment of the Holy See.[13]

In July 1517 Cajetan received from Pope Leo X the cardinal's hat and was given, a year later, the weighty task of representing the pope as his legate at the important Diet of Augsburg. As few others, he was equipped by his scholarship (his most recent book dealt with indulgences) and by his experience in Church politics to subject Luther to an intensive interrogation, which proved, however, to be of no avail. Until the end of his life he would serve his Church in many missions and charges, although in the history of theology he has come down to us as a great, if not always submissive, commentator on the *Summa* of Thomas Aquinas.

Our selection from Cajetan's writings is especially relevant to the discussion of the role of late medieval nominalism in its relation to sixteenth-century thought. It has been argued that nominalistic theologians such as Occam, Holcot, d'Ailly, and Biel are responsible for what is often called "the disintegration of the medieval synthesis." By undermining truly Catholic spirituality they prepared the ground for the Reformation and should therefore be allowed to claim the title Forerunners of the Reformation. One of the more explicit spokesmen for this view is Louis Bouyer. He imputes to nominalism "what was without doubt most irreparably vitiated and corrupt in Catholic thought at the end of the Middle Ages" and calls attention to "the utter corruption of Christian thought as represented by nominalist theology."[14]

Regarding sacramental issues, especially those related to the Mass, the following short treatise of Cajetan, written in Rome, December 1510, has played one role in the past and should play another in future research. In his important study, *Eucharistic Sacrifice and the Reformation*,[15] Francis Clark has shown how Cajetan's opening remark has been widely misinterpreted by English scholars. Cajetan refers here to the "common error of many" who think that the sacrifice of the Mass yields a limited amount of satisfaction *ex opere operato*.

This "error of many" has served Anglican scholars as documentation for the thesis that in the later Middle Ages Scotists and nominalists regarded the Mass as a mechanical device which functioned apart from the right intention and faith of the recipient. Thus B. J. Kidd inferred: "The very man who, on October 12, 1518, called upon Luther to revoke his assertion that faith is necessary to the effectual reception of the sacraments thought it necessary to raise his voice against the notion of their operating mechanically on the ground that it was a widespread delusion of his own side. Further proof that the later medieval doctrine of the Eucharistic Sacrifice had degenerated into a hard and perfunctory theory as to the mode of operation can hardly be required."[16]

As a matter of fact Cajetan does not oppose as "an error of many" the notion of *ex opere operato*, which means that the proper performance of the rite has objective effects independent of the subjective condition of the priest and the participants. He holds this doctrine himself and, far from seeing it as a sign of nominalistic decay, he regards it as the cornerstone for Tridentine and post-Tridentine Roman Catholic teaching. The "error" he criticized was the Scotist-nominalist assumption that the *ex opere operato* effect of the sacrifice of the Mass is necessarily limited, since it is less than the effects of the sacrifice of Christ on the Cross.

Cajetan holds with Thomas that the objective effects of the sacrifice of the Mass are as unlimited as those of Christ's death on the Cross. This scholastic debate has continued within Roman Catholic theology until modern times. Cajetan's term "error" should not be understood as "heresy" but as "untenable opinion," however much he might have been inclined to identify these two.

So much for the role of our selection in past scholarly discussion.

There is, however, another role which it has yet to play. It has been argued by the outstanding specialist in late medieval eucharistic problems, Erwin Iserloh, that nominalistic theology should be held responsible for the late medieval abuses surrounding the celebration of the Mass. In his last major study on this problem, Iserloh concluded from an analysis of their works that a considerable number of nominalist theologians such as Holcot and d'Ailly (the friend of Gerson and Biel's authority) influenced by their teaching the development of a totally *un*catholic doctrine: "The larger the number for whom the sacrifice is made, the smaller the fruit for the individual."[17] The final conclusion of Cajetan, the chief representative of the late medieval Thomistic revival, makes clear that this judgment of Iserloh does not merely apply to nominalistic eucharistic theology. For the nominalistic theologian, as for Cajetan, there exists a relation of diminishing returns between the number of those who stand to profit from the sacrifice of a particular Mass and the beneficial effects for each individual concerned.

However, while Cajetan and the nominalists reach a similar conclusion, their basis of argumentation is not the same. For the Scotist-nominalist school the limitation of the fruits for each individual is due primarily to the limited objective result, the *ex opere operato* result of a Mass compared to Christ's sacrifice on Calvary.[18] "Were it not so," Gabriel Biel argues, "one Mass would be sufficient for the redemption of all souls from all purgatorial punishments and for the conveyance of all gifts, just as Christ had to suffer only once for the redemption of the whole world. In that case all those priests and all those Masses prescribed by the Church for all kinds of purposes would be redundant." It was the long-standing practice of the Church to undertake private Masses for the living and the dead, and to this practice Biel refers time and again. This practice, he says, is due to the fact that "in the sacrament of the Eucharist there is the fullness of spiritual grace and merit—yes, Christ himself is contained in it, who is uncreated and infinite grace; yet the fruit of the satisfaction for punishment and the conveyance of gifts is limited to a certain amount and measure because the meritorious value of the oblation of Christ in the sacrament of the Mass is much less than that of his sacrifice on the Cross. On the cross, Christ offered himself immediately [that is, not through the mediation of his priests as in the sacrament]; He becomes a true sacrifice when He *once and for all* dies for the redemption of the elect, as Hebrews 9:11–12 says: 'Christ the High Priest of the good things that have come entered once and for all the Holy Place through the shedding of His own blood, securing eternal redemption.' Just so I Peter 3:18 says: 'Christ died for sins once and for all, the righteous for the unrighteous.' In the Mass, however, there is the same sacrifice and oblation, not through reiteration of His death but through commemorative representation of the death He suffered once and for all."[19]

A second limitation of the fruits of the Mass is due to the subjective factors (*ex opere operantis*) involved, the disposition of the celebrant and—in case of a public Mass—the disposition of the lay participants. The disposition of the celebrant does not refer to his moral status nor is it determined by his being in a state of grace, for it should be recalled that the priest does not offer as a private person but as a minister of the Church: "He may not always be pleasing to God, because he is often a sinner. But the Church who offers through him is always accepted by God, because she is always holy and the one and only bride of Christ . . ."[20] The subjective factor here is rather the intention of the priest who is to pray and apply the Mass he celebrates to particular people, dead or alive. This concept of the limited fruit of the Mass, because of the natural limitations of a priest's intentions, does not foster late medieval abuses. On the contrary they form the very basis from which Biel can attack such a long-standing abuse as the plurality of benefices or accumulation of pastoral charges.[21]

The other subjective factor is the proper disposition of the lay participants, who do not necessarily take communion but according to canon law should attend Mass on Sundays and feast days: "The priest offers sacramentally, the people present spiritually." They should be concentrated and devout "in order to become participants in the priest's intercession with the Lord, especially for those in attendance."[22] To receive the fruit of the Mass they should in the first place "believe that after the words of consecration the true Body and Blood of Christ is contained under the signs of bread and wine." Thus "they profit from the sacrifice offered, by which they are sacramentally united and joined to the other members of the mystical Body [the

Church] and to the Head of this Body, Christ." Secondly, the will to profit from the Mass is required by which the participants are united with God in loving devotion just as they are united with Him in faith by an act of the intellect: "and thus they are united [with Him] through intellect and will in truth and devotion. When faith and devotion are present in those who hear Mass they receive the fruit of this sacrament, divine grace, and that often more abundantly than the offering priest."[23]

Iserloh has pointed out that Luther's nominalistic opponent at the 1519 Leipzig Debate, Johann Eck, had to defend the abuse of multiplication of private Masses because of his assumption that the fruit of the Mass is limited. Eck argued this on grounds of the objective limitations, not on grounds of the subjective limitations: "Eck does not say a word about the faith and devotion of the priest and the faithful, which according to St. Thomas determine the efficacy of the Mass."[24] If we may interpret Eck's silence as implying rejection of the subjective limitations, he breaks on this point with the preceding scholastic teaching. This includes, as we saw, the teaching of Gabriel Biel, so highly esteemed and frequently quoted by Eck.

For our purposes it is important to point out that Cajetan has no quarrel with Biel regarding the subjective limiting factors, especially the importance of the devotion of the participants. It would be unreasonable to make the nominalists responsible for the multiplication of private Masses, not only because this phenomenon has roots which reach far back in the medieval history of the Mass but also because this practice does not have to be defended on grounds of the objectively limiting factors—*ex opere operato*—but can very well be supported by arguments drawn from the subjectively limiting factors related to the *ex opere operantis* aspect of the Mass. Cajetan's discussion of this central issue helps us to widen our perspective on the theological bases of devotional practices on the eve of the Reformation.

Whereas late medieval theologians tried to curb the *abuses* connected with the private Masses, the Thomists, Scotists, and nominalists defended the *practice* itself, each in their own way. The reform program of the important provincial Synod, Cologne 1536, documents the continuation of these reform efforts in a programmatic fashion. Private Masses if administered on Sundays or feast days should be said "after the sermon is finished." In public Masses people should be in attendance throughout and wait for the "most important part of the Mass, which is communion."[25] Luther was to attack the practice of private Masses, because for him a distortion of doctrine was involved at two points: The true Mass is not "said" but "preached." The word of God should be preached and the sermon should be an integral part of the liturgy. Secondly, communion is part of the Eucharist and cannot be separated from the consecration. Perhaps the shortest summary of Luther's position dates from 1533. Writing explicitly about the private Mass (*Dünkelmesse*) he says: "For Christ's ordinance and intention are to have the sacrament dispensed and to have Himself preached in order to strengthen faith. This ordinance they suspend and invert everything: They keep the sacrament for themselves alone and distribute it to no one; they remain silent and preach to no one; they strengthen the faith of no Christian but lead him from faith to the sacrifice and work of the Mass, which they apply or sell for money."[26]

These two points—which, as we noted, were also part of pre-Tridentine and Tridentine reform programs—are treated in the other two selections where Prierias deals with the relation of sacrament and sermon, and Hoen discusses the relation of consecration and communion.

Sylvester Mazzolini Prierias (*c.* 1456–1523) was twelve years the senior of Cajetan and like him an Italian Dominican. He held a chair at Padua, wrote against the Scotists, was an opponent of the Conciliabulum of Pisa, and an interpreter of Thomas, still finding time for more pastoral concerns. In 1503 he published the *Aurea Rosa,* an often reprinted collection of sermons on portions of Scripture officially designated for the whole Church year, accompanied by a series of important discourses on special problems. Owing to the influence of Cajetan, his superior in the Order, he was appointed *Magister sacri palatii* in December 1515. In this office he served as counselor to the pope in matters pertaining to faith and at the same time, by special decree, as General Inquisitor. Thus he participated first in the process against Reuchlin and then against Luther. As he himself indicates, he wrote his *Dialogue Against the Presumptuous Conclusions of Martin Luther About the Power of the Pope* within three days after reception of

Luther's theses. A series of ever sharper writings was exchanged until the battle lines changed and Luther became increasingly preoccupied with opponents closer to home and also—especially after *Exsurge Domine,* 1520—gave up hope for a reconciliation with the curia. Before he fell victim to the plague in 1523, Prierias was sent by Pope Leo X (1513–1521) on important missions and was drawn into the circle of confidants of the reform-minded Dutch Pope Hadrian VI (1522–1523).

Corneliszoon Hendrixzoon Hoen (†1524), a contemporary of Pope Hadrian, was probably born in Gouda, not more than twenty miles west of the latter's birthplace, Utrecht. We know exceedingly little about his life except that he went to school in Utrecht at the Hieronymus Gymnasium, then, as now, a center of humanistic learning, in many respects a product of the spirituality of the *Devotio Moderna.* In the early twenties this school became, under the rectorate of Hinne Rode, the focal point for a group of biblical humanists in close touch with a similar group in Delft to which, along with Georg Saganus and Willem de Volder (Gnapheus), Cornelisz Hoen was drawn while he was legal consultant attached to the Court of Holland, in The Hague.

On November 11, 1509, Jacob Hoeck (Jacobus Angularius), whom we met as Wessel Gansfort's epistolary opponent, departed. The responsibility for the library of the Canon at Naaldwijk and Pastor of Wassenaar fell to Martin Dorp, since 1504 Professor at Louvain University who, in turn, called upon Hoen to investigate its holdings. Here Hoen found among other writings of Wessel a treatise *On the Sacrament of the Eucharist,* which made a deep impression on him.[27] In the process of pondering Wessel's presentation and ordering his own reactions, the complexity of Wessel's doctrine of the Eucharist was lost. In his *Epistola,* published in 1525 by the Reformer of Zurich, Ulrich Zwingli, Hoen—perhaps as the spokesman for his group— rejects the doctrine of transubstantiation in favor of a spiritual eating of Christ through commemoration of the offering of Christ. In the words of consecration "This is My Body" (*Hoc est corpus meum*), the word *is* (*est*) is interpreted as a "trope" or figurative expression for *means* (*significat*).

Wessel had never denied the doctrine of transubstantiation, and in a completely traditional fashion distinguished between a sacramental and spiritual eating of the Body of Christ. What Wessel wanted to emphasize is indeed the spiritual communion with Christ in such a fashion that Christ "is also outside the Eucharist and without the species of bread and wine corporeally present when given to those that truly believe in him."[28]

Years later, after the rumors about the Leipzig (1519) Debate between Luther and Eck started to sweep the Low Countries, the group of biblical humanists consulted together and decided that the Utrecht Rector Hinne Rode should inform Luther of the discovery of Wessel's writings and to this purpose he traveled early in 1521 to Wittenberg with a selection of Wessel's works and, quite likely, the *Epistola* of Hoen. If we may believe Zwingli's indication in the title of his edition of the *Epistola*—"sent four years ago from the Netherlands to someone who was the highest authority in biblical exegesis, but spurned by him"—and if we are right in favoring the hypothesis that this was Luther[29] rather than Erasmus, Rode's mission was only a partial success. Wessel's eucharistic theology, radically interpreted by Hoen, found a more welcome reception in Switzerland. Upon his return to Utrecht, Rode was removed from his post, probably because of his contact with Luther (*propter Lutherum*). Forced to leave the Netherlands he went with his friend Saganus to Basel and in 1523 to Zurich, where the encounter with Zwingli must have taken place. We know from a letter by Zwingli to Johann Bugenhagen (†1558) how glad he was to get Hoen's letter. For some time he had realized that the phrase "This is My Body" should be interpreted figuratively, but he had not yet found the right key, namely, which word should be regarded as a trope: "And there I had the good fortune to make the precious discovery that 'is' is to be understood as 'signifies.'"[30] The next year, 1525, Zwingli published the *Epistola* without, however, giving his name to it. As for Hoen, he was arrested on the charge of "sacramentism" in February 1523, together with Gnapheus. After intervention of the vice-regent (Stadhouder), Margaretha of Parma, and protests by members of the Court of Holland, Hoen was released but forbidden to leave The Hague, where he died a year later.

Notes

1. ". . . in hac sacratissima nativitate, qua hec scribimus anno 1487 . . ." G. Biel, *Canonis Misse Expositio*, ed. H. A. Oberman and W. J. Courtenay, Wiesbaden, 1963, Lectio LXVIII G, vol. III, p. 124.

2. First published Basel 1500 or 1505. Biel mentioned by name fol. K 2ᵛ. We used the ed. Basel 1512. For a discussion of Biel's doctrine of the Eucharist see *Harvest,* esp. pp. 279 ff.

3. See *Luther und Luthertum in der ersten Entwicklung. Quellenmässig dargestellt von P. Heinrich Denifle,* 2d ed. Ed. A. M. Weiss, O.P., I, Schlussabteilung, Mainz, 1906, p. 870.

4. Fourth Lateran Council, 1215; classical formulation by Thomas Aquinas, *ST* III, q. 75, art. 4.

5. Cf. Biel, *Sermones de festivitatibus Christi,* Hagenau, 1510, 46 E; *Canonis Misse Expositio,* ed. *cit.,* I, pp. 264–268. Lectio XXVII K, L, N; Lectio CXXXV.

6. Bechofen, *Expositio* n 2ʳ; cf. o 5ʳ.

7. For further reading see B. J. Kidd, *The Later Medieval Doctrine of the Eucharistic Sacrifice,* 1st ed., London, 1898; 2d ed., London, 1958; C. W. Dugmore, *The Mass and the English Reformers,* London, 1958; F. Clark, S.J., *Eucharistic Sacrifice and the Reformation,* London, 1960, select bibliography, pp. 501 ff.

8. For data on Cajetan's life see J. F. Groner, O.P., *Kardinal Cajetan. Eine Gestalt aus der Reformationszeit,* Fribourg, 1951, esp. pp. 34–

56 and bibliography, pp. 66 ff.

9. *Acta Conciliorum et Epistolae Decretales,* X, col. 1621.

10. *Ibid.,* col. 1618.

11. *Ibid.,* col. 1576.

12. *Ibid.,* col. 1622.

13. ". . . ad Apostolicae Sedis cultum." *Ibid.*

14. Louis Bouyer, *The Spirit and Forms of Protestantism,* Westminster, Md., 1956, p. 164.

15. Francis Clark, *op. cit.,* pp. 365–368. Pages 369–375 give a short summary of our Cajetan selection, placing it in the context of the preceding and ensuing history of this issue.

16. B. J. Kidd, *op. cit.,* pp. 71–72, quoted by Clark, p. 366. Kidd has been led to this passage in Cajetan by the discussion in the *Apology* of Bishop John Jewel in 1562. In our time pursued by E. L. Mascall and C. W. Dugmore.

17. E. Iserloh, *Der Kampf um die Messe in den ersten Jahren der Auseinandersetzung mit Luther,* Münster i. W., 1952, p. 12. Cf. his *Die Eucharistie in der Darstellung des Johannes Eck,* Münster i. W., 1950, pp. 191–195, 226 f.

18. See especially Gabriel Biel, *Canonis Misse Expositio,* ed. *cit.,* I, Lectio XXVII L, p. 265.

19. *Ibid.,* Lect. XXVII K, p. 265.

20. *Ibid.,* Lect. XXVI H, p. 245.

21. *Ibid.,* Lect. XXVIII P, p. 205.

22. *Ibid.,* Lect. XXIX B, p. 290.

23. *Ibid.,* Lect. XXIX D, p. 292.

24. Iserloh, *Die Eucharistie in der*

Darstellung des Johannes Eck, p. 191.

25. Chapters XXIV and XXVI. Ch. XXVII presents the Catholic doctrine of the sacrifice of the Mass which could have been transcribed from the parts of Biel's *Expositio* summarized above. *Acta Reformationis Catholicae,* II, 1532–1542, ed. Georg Pfeilschifter, Regensburg, 1960, pp. 258–265.

26. *WA* 28. 235. 21 ff.

27. Reported in the *Vita Wesselli* by Dr. Albert Hardenberg; translated by Jared W. Scudder in the Miller-Scudder edition, *Wessel Gansfort,* II, pp. 334 ff. Hardenberg—and in his wake the later investigators—fails to distinguish between Wessel's thought and Hoen's interpretation. It is to Maarten van Rhijn, *Wessel Gans-*

fort, 's Gravenhage, 1917, p. 211, and *Studiën over Wessel Gansfort en zijn tijd,* Utrecht, 1933, pp. 40 f., that scholarship is indebted for unraveling the thought of these two fascinating theologians.

28. Gansfort, *Opera,* Groningen, 1614, fol. 696. For the translation of "credentibus *in* eum" as "to those that *truly* believe in him," see the glossary in *Harvest,* pp. 464 f.

29. See the Leiden church historian, A. Eekhof, in his facsimile edition: *De Avandmaalsbrief van Cornelius Hoen, 1525,* 's Gravenhage, 1917, p. xiv.

30. *CR* 91. 560. For this reference and further literature see Walter Köhler's edition of the *Epistola* of Hoen, from which the following translation was made: *CR* 91, *ZW* IV, 512–519.

CARDINAL CAJETAN, THOMAS DE VIO

The Celebration of the Mass

Question

Does the priest who celebrates the Mass for several persons fulfill his obligation to each one of them individually?

The question is whether or not a priest who has already agreed to say Mass for someone and then accepts a stipend from another person to celebrate a Mass for him also—whether or not such a priest fulfills his obligation to each of them by saying only one Mass.

Objections

The following considerations make it appear that the answer is negative.

(1) The effect of the Mass for him who has requested it and been promised it is limited. Now if this limited effect is divided among several persons, then each one receives less than he would if the Mass were said for him alone. Therefore, whatever is given to the second is taken away from the first so that neither gets his due. The premise that the effect of a Mass is limited is proved by the fact that many Masses are said for the same person.

(2) If it is true that a Mass actually promised to only one person but said for several can satisfy many or indeed all of these persons, then it was wrong for the Church ever to have instituted Masses for a limited number of people. Rather, the Church, the common mother of us all, ought to offer every Mass for all in order to obtain the common good of all without loss to any individual.

(3) If a priest can with one Mass fulfill his obligation to several persons, by the same token this one Mass could take the place of four Masses for which the priest had been paid. This, however, is obviously false because it has been condemned by the Church. If it were true it would mean that the saying of one Mass would give satisfaction equal to the thirty Masses of blessed Gregory.

Exposition

The position which affirms the question argues that the power of the Mass is infinite because it is the very power of Jesus Christ. This infinite power can be applied to any number of persons in such a way that what each individual receives is not diminished by the participation of others.

A.   The Mass as Sacrifice

Certain distinctions are necessary when discussing this question. First we note that the Mass has two parts, sacrifice and prayer, of which the sacrifice is the foremost part. Likewise, the effect of both these parts of the Mass is of several kinds, namely, merit, intercession, and satisfaction. Furthermore, there are two kinds of efficacy of the sacrament. First is that efficacy which depends only on the administration of the sacrament (*ex opere operato*). Second is the efficacy the priest and the participant bring with them to the sacrament (*ex opere operantis*). In order to furnish a complete and definitive answer to this question it is necessary to define all these terms.[1]

The celebration of the Mass has two aspects, namely, the sacrament and the sacrifice. The sacramental aspect of the Mass is irrelevant to the question at hand because as sacrament it is efficacious only for those who actually receive it. But the sacrificial aspect *is* relevant to the question. In the sacrificial sense the efficacy of the Mass is divided into that which depends on the sacrament alone and that which involves the preparation of the participants. And when the efficacy of the sacrament is viewed as that dependent only on its administration, the efficacy is subdivided into the efficacy in itself and efficacy as applied to the participant. The efficacy in itself is the immolation of Jesus Christ so that that which is offered up is Jesus Christ. Viewed quantitatively the sacrifice is infinite insofar as it is intercession, merit, and satisfaction. Thus the efficacy of the sacrament is infinite, just as is the passion of Christ and it is even more acceptable to God than all the sinners of the world.

The effect of Christ crucified is of infinite sufficiency but not of infinite efficacy. The efficacy, however, due to the limitless cause [the divine nature of Christ], is unlimited in scope and not directed to particular people. Thus the sacrifice in itself is of infinite sufficiency and unlimited efficacy, that is, it is not directed only to some particular people. But just as the efficacy of Christ's passion is applied to particular people through particular sacraments, so the efficacy of this sacrifice is applied through particular devotions. Devotion implies the application of the sacrifice; therefore, when one speaks of the effect of this sacrifice in itself and restricts the sacrifice to the administration of the rite, then it has no special effect on man at all. Only in its relation to God does the sacrifice have the value of thanksgiving, commemoration, and the like.

Now in this regard one can clearly see an error made by many. They think that this sacrifice when restricted to its administration has a certain merit or a certain satisfaction which applies to this person but not to that one. This has already been shown to be false, and is further confirmed by another consideration. When the sacrifice of the Mass is considered dependent on its administration alone, it has an infinite power, and there is no reason whatever to think that the Mass gives a certain limited amount of satisfaction.

If, however, we view the Mass in terms of its application to particular people, then the effect is finite. The amount of satisfaction depends on the devotion of those who offer it or those for whom it is offered. This is true because the application of the sacrifice involves two things: the directing to particular persons and the effect on those persons. The effect depends on the devotion. The intention (*intentio*) is the work of the priest, while the devotion is the work of both the priest and the recipients.

Thus, when saying the canon of the Mass, the priest applies the Mass to the believer with an act of intention by saying, "We offer up to Thee for Thy Holy Church, . . . for the Pope, etc." "Remember, O Lord, your manservants and your maidservants and all here present."

Thereupon the act of devotion is united to the intention. "Whose faith and devotion are known to Thee." This applies not only to those present but also to others, which suggests that the application of this sacrifice is realized not only through intention but also through devotion. To the degree that one has devotion for the sacrifice, satisfaction is applied to him out of the infinite power of the Mass.

The reason for this is that in sacrifice and oblations, the intensity of devotion is considered more important than the size of the offering. This is established by our Lord's comment regarding the widow's mite[2] and by the authority of Gregory's sermon. As Jesus was walking near the Sea of Galilee He said, "God does not value the size of the sacrifice in itself but rather in relation to the wealth of the giver."[3] And because that which is offered up in this sacrifice is infinite and can be neither used up nor diminished by the devotion of one lone person, the conclusion is that one sacrifice suffices for the devotion of many, yes, even an infinite number of persons. . . .

This is confirmed by the canon of the Mass in which the sacrifice is offered not only for the Church and the civil powers and all Christians, but also for those especially remembered and those who are present. But now it is clear that there is no limit to the number of those especially remembered and even less to those present. Nor do some share less in the effect of the Mass because of the participation of others. It is clear that the larger or smaller number is related to prayer, not to the sacrifice, because the priest says explicitly "for whom we offer Thee," or "who offers Thee" this sacrifice of praise. The fact that this is offered not only for intercession but also for satisfaction is made clear by the words "for the redemption of your souls." Now this redemption is a redemption from evil, as the Word itself signifies. The satisfaction is made by means of repayment, just as Christ repaid the ransom to the Father. This satisfaction can therefore be offered for an infinite number of persons to the loss of none. Every devout person receives according to his due.

We must beware, however, of concluding from this that one Mass satisfies just as much if it is said for one as for many. Such a conclusion does not follow, because we have not said that the effect of the sacrament is related to the intention but rather it is related to the devotion. I do not give satisfaction through this sacrifice in proportion to my intention, but I reap fruits in proportion to the amount of devotion I have. Therefore, if I, when I offer this sacrifice, have as much devotion as corresponds to one year's satisfaction and I intend to celebrate the Mass for the satisfaction of one man, then this one man will receive relief of punishment worth one year's satisfaction. If, however, I intend to apply this satisfaction for two equally, then each receives relief from punishment for a half year only, or if for three men, then for a third of a year only. And the same would be true in the case of St. Martin[4] if he were to have the same Mass celebrated; if it was celebrated for one, then one would receive all the fruits, if for more the fruits would be divided among all of them. And the same would be true for all others who have Masses celebrated.

For the satisfaction which accrues to each devout recipient is always finite. Therefore, if the satisfaction of one Mass is by intention applied to many, it is divided and each individual participant receives less. And thus we have shown the truth of that theological position which asserts that the effect of the sacrifice is finite and that, when applied to many, the share of each one is lessened. The way of sharing the effect of the sacrifice is not related to the number who participate but rather to the extent of the devotion the recipients have.

From this it is clear that, other things being equal, a Mass sponsored by many satisfies more than a Mass sponsored by a few, because it is offered up out of more devotion. Likewise, a Mass sponsored by several persons avails more for them than a Mass which is offered only out of the devotion of the priest who sponsored it, for in such a case the effect is not dependent on the devotion of the priest alone. On the basis of this teaching, which I take from Thomas, all the difficult issues regarding the value of the sacrifice are solved.[5] This position integrates all these factors: the infinite character of the sacrifice itself, the finite effects on the participant, the authority of the doctors, the liturgical practice of the Church in celebrating a Mass for one particular person, the fact that there is more effect when the Mass is intended for one than for several, and finally, the usage of the Church which includes both the participation of many in one Mass and also the celebration on feast days of Mass for many persons, and all this without fraud.

If, however, the sacrifice is considered in relation to the preparation the participants bring with them to the sacrament, the effect is dependent on the amount of devotion. But this is not the perspective from which we now view the sacrament, for the sponsor has not asked such preparation from the priest nor has the priest promised it to the sponsor. Insofar as the Mass is concerned, only the intention of the priest to apply the sacrifice is usually requested and given. Therefore I move on to the next issue.

B.   The Mass as Prayer

Moving on to the second part of the Mass, the prayer, it should be said that if the prayer is to be a religious act it should manifest praise to God, as St. Thomas says.[6] For by prayer the mind itself is offered to God, as Dionysius, Gregory, and St. Thomas say.[7] In itself prayer is part of the wider concept, sacrifice. "We will render the fruit of our lips."[8] "Through Him, then, let us continually offer up a sacrifice of praise to God, that is, the fruit of lips that acknowledge His name."[9] Prayer is not only a kind of sacrifice but as petition it has a connotation all its own which is to be distinguished from prayer as a meritorious act, an act of satisfaction, an act of intercession, an act of consolation. No one can fully merit (*meritum de condigno*)[10] anything for anyone other than himself. Spiritual consolation comes only to him who prays, and is derived from his concentration and meditation. Therefore, in this context prayer as a meritorious act or as an act of consolation is irrelevant. But the question before us is the effect of our prayers on others. Prayer as intercession on our own part is primarily dependent on the power of our own faith. As Christ said, "Whatever you ask in prayer, believe that you receive it and you will."[11] God's part depends on mercy. The faith which supports one request is not diminished by a second request. Therefore, prayer as intercession avails as well when made for many as for one, but it avails even more when it issues from greater trust in God's generosity and from greater love.

In determining the amount of satisfaction gained from prayer two factors must be considered. The first is the same as in any other sacrifice, the second is the extent to which the one who prays is subject to punishment as in other works of penance. First, since in any other sacrifice it is true that satisfaction depends on the amount of devotion on the part of those who bring the sacrifice (as is clear from above) or on the part of those for whom it is offered (as was shown before), the same holds true of the satisfaction for prayer as for the sacrifice of the Eucharist. The satisfaction depends not on how much is offered up but how much devotion is present. Therefore, we conclude that prayer, like sacrifice, can be made for many.

Second, if the priest who prays is subject to punishment, this is his personal issue, the prayer itself is not necessarily a work of penance and, therefore, the fact that one who prays is subject to punishment is no problem in this context. For the one who prays does not really ask for chastisement, as for example in fasting, but the intention of his prayer implies a sacrifice on the part of those who offer the prayer.

Now it is clear how the sacrifice of the Mass is related to intercession or merit. There is no need to doubt regarding the partial merit (*meritum de congruo*) which depends on God's condescension. We do all we can and God does His share.[12] The partial merits of sacrifices and prayers correspond to the devotion and faith of those who offer them up or those for whom they are offered. Therefore, the fact that a prayer is offered for many does no harm to each individual concerned. And, therefore, we may conclude with an affirmative answer to the question....

Answer to Objections

(1) From the foregoing the response to the first objection is clear. The effect of the Mass is finite insofar as the faith of the participant is concerned. This relates to intercession. It is also finite insofar as his devotion is concerned. This relates to satisfaction. Therefore these two are mentioned in the canon of the Mass, "Whose faith and devotion are known to Thee." And yet its potential is infinite to provide for everybody's finite satisfaction and intercession.

(2) The canon of the Mass does indeed prove that the Church has instituted Masses for individuals which are still always explicitly celebrated for all living and dead, as the canon of the Mass clearly

stipulates. Thus the provident and pious Mother Church desires first, that from her own devotion the sacrifice of the Mass should profit all, especially the civil powers, and second, that from private devotions profit might come to particular members. Thus without any deceit or harm the Church elicits the devotion of individuals themselves and others that in accordance with their devotion special fruit might be forthcoming. Moreover, there is another fruit which comes from specially arranged Masses; because it is natural that each individual desires his own good and neglects the common good, more devotion is elicited from those special Masses than from public Masses. One should add also that the effect on the priest himself should not be ignored. For with his own devotion he is also offering for people from whom he has received money or to whom he is particularly close.

(3) If those who offer a Mass and those for whom a Mass is offered had as much devotion in one Mass as in thirty, one would be as effective as thirty. But that this is not so is perfectly clear, since those who request the Mass invest more devotion in thirty Masses than in one. And this they do rightly because, other things being equal, one shows more praise to God in many Masses than in one. Therefore, he who promises to say thirty Masses is obliged to say them. This should suffice to answer the question.

Rome, December 1, 1510

Notes

1. For a discussion of the technical language used in connection with the Eucharist, see the article by I. Pohle, "Eucharist," in *The Catholic Encyclopedia,* New York, 1909, Vol. 5, pp. 572–590.
2. Luke 21:1–4.
3. This has not been found.
4. St. Martin was Pope from 649 to 655. He was taken prisoner by order of Emperor Constans II, taken to Constantinople, tortured, and then sent to death in exile. Many miracles were attributed to the power of this saint. His feast is celebrated on November 12.

   This is the crucial section to which we referred in the introduction. See also the answer to objection 3 below. It shows that late medieval Thomism here represented by Cajetan—though on grounds different from late medieval nominalism (namely on the

basis of the limited capacity for
devotion on the part of the celebrating priest rather than on the
basis of the limited objective efficacy of the Mass)—provides an
equally strong support for the
multiplication of private Masses.
Insofar as this is regarded today
as an abuse, it cannot be laid on
the doorstep of nominalistic theology alone. With more emphasis
on the devotion of the recipient
we find the same discussion with
an earlier representative of the pre-
Reformation revival of Thomism,
Henry of Gorcum (†1431). See
A. G. Weiler, *Heinrich van Gorcum,* Hilversum 1962, p. 154 f.
Cf. their common basis in Thomas
Aquinas, *ST* I., q. 79. art. 5 ad. 3.

5. For Thomas' position, see his
Commentary on the Sentences,
III. q. 79. art. 8.

6. Thomas, *op. cit.,* II.II. q. 83.

7. Cajetan refers to Dionysius and
Gregory without specifying more
exactly where this is to be found.
However, Thomas, in the previously mentioned question,
quotes them as evidence for his
position. See esp. art. 2 and 3.

8. Hosea 14:2.

9. Hebrews 13:15.

10. For a discussion of technical language describing merits, see Introduction, Chapter III.

11. Mark 11:24.

12. Cajetan here uses the well-known
phrase that man is required to do
what is in him. For a discussion
of this phrase, see *Harvest,* pp.
124–145.

SYLVESTER PRIERIAS

Word and Sacrament

Is it the more serious sin to listen inattentively to the Word of God or by inattention to permit the Body of Christ to fall to the ground?

Some say that the first is not a lesser sin than the second.[1]

To discuss this question let us note that there are three ways one thing can be preferred to another, namely, according to worthiness, according to necessity, or according to causality.

(1) I say, therefore, that the true Body of Christ is more worthy than His mystical body because nothing is greater than the Body and Blood of Christ. . . . As Thomas says, the humanity of Christ is greater than any conceivable creature, since it is united to the Word.[2] It might be objected that the true Body is a sign of the mystical body and that the sign is less than that which it signifies. Albert and Thomas answer that this is true only for those things whose sole function is to serve as signs, as, for example, the paschal lamb.[3]

(2) The true Body of Christ is of greater worthiness than the Word of God, as is clear from canon law. Further, this is proved by the fact that the Body is substance, while the preached Word is an accident. But in regard to necessity it is the other way around. The actual hearing of the Word of God is of greater necessity because faith and the knowledge of what is necessary to salvation come from hearing. It is the same in regard to causality because the true Word of God takes away those mortal sins of which one is not aware, as does the Eucharist, but beyond that it also takes away mortal sins of which one is aware. And further, it is efficacious in both good and evil persons.

(3) Thirdly I say that it is greater negligence to drop the Body of

Christ in respect to that which is neglected, as appears from the aforesaid. But negligence of the preached Word is greater in respect to
detrimental effect because neglect to hear the Word of God results in
ignorance of those things which ought to be done and believed as a
necessity for salvation. Therefore, in a sense it is the greater evil. According to Augustine, evil is evil because it does harm.[4] Therefore,
that which does the greater harm is the greater evil.

This makes it clear how wrong parish priests are when they insist
that people who have missed the sermon should hear the Mass in their
parish church; these priests milk and skin their flock rather than save
it. Nevertheless, those who on a feast day shun the Mass said by their
own priest in order to attend Mass elsewhere do sin unless there be
some good reason, such as to hear the Word of God or to be more
edified. . . .

But the objection to this is that since one has been commanded to
hear the Mass but not the Word of God, to hear the Mass is more
necessary. I deny this conclusion because it is easier to hear the Mass,
due to its numerous celebrations, than to hear the Word of God.
Therefore, the latter is more necessary.

Notwithstanding this, others say that one is commanded to hear
the Word of God not at specified times but rather when one has
urgent reason to hear it, or when one is ignorant of the things necessary for salvation. . . . But after all, one's own curates should not only
read the Mass but also preach, as canon law requires.[5]

Conclusions

(1) God loves Christ more than any creature, but nevertheless He
gave Him up to death for our salvation.

(2) The true Body of Christ is more worthy than the mystical body
and the Word of God.

(3) The Word of God, however, is more necessary than the Body
of Christ in the form of the sacrament because without the former
there would be no faith and for those who have come to maturity this
normally means no salvation.

(4) Except for sins of which one is unaware, the Body of Christ
does not take away mortal sin but only venial sin. It bears fruit only

in the good. The Word of God, however, provides the necessary disposition for the remittance of both mortal and venial sin and bears fruit in both good and evil men.

(5) The negligence of the Body of Christ is in an absolute sense greater. But when the resulting harm is taken into consideration, negligence of the Word of God is worse.

(6) Custom never sets aside divine or natural law but only human law and then only if it be reasonable or necessary.

(7) He who does not hear Mass in his own parish in order that he may hear the sermon of a preacher does rightly.

(8) Everyone ought to go often to preaching and ought to listen and meditate devoutly because this is the food of the soul. . . .

Notes

1. Early evidence, Caesarius of Arles, *Sermo* 75.2, ed. G. Morin, *S. Caesarii Opera omnia,* I, Maredsous, 1937, pp. 309–310. For references to canon law, Ulrich Surgant's *Manuale Curatorum,* and Gabriel Biel, see *Harvest,* p. 23.

2. Thomas Aquinas, *Sent.,* Bk. I, 44, art. 3.

3. Aquinas, *Summa Theologica,* III, 9, 60, art. 2.

4. Augustine, *Enchiridion,* Bk. I, ch. 12 in *PL,* vol. XXXVI, col. 236, 237.

5. Prierias quotes a number of authorities, e.g., *CIC,* vol. II, col. 192, cap. 15.

CORNELISZ HOEN

A Most Christian Letter[1]

Our Lord, Jesus Christ, promising many times to His own forgiveness
of sins and wishing to strengthen their souls at the Last Supper, added
a pledge[2] to the promise lest there be any uncertainty on their part;
in the same way that a bridegroom who desires to assure his bride,
lest she have any doubts, gives a ring to her saying, "Take this, I give
myself to you." And she, accepting the ring, believes him to be hers
and turns her heart from all other lovers, and, to please her husband,
concentrates only on him. Just so he who takes the Eucharist—the
pledge of the Bridegroom which is proof of the giving of Himself—
ought steadfastly to believe Christ now to be his, given for him, and
His blood shed for him. Wherefore he turns his heart away from all
whom he used to love and clings to Christ alone; and always seeking
after that which is pleasing to Christ, he is no longer solicitous of
himself but places all his care on Christ, whom he believes to be his
and who alone is abundantly sufficient for him in every respect. This
truly is what it is to eat Christ and to drink His blood, so that our
Savior may say, "He who eats My Flesh and drinks My Blood abides
in Me and I in him."[3]

But those who take the Eucharist without this faith seem rather to
eat the manna of the Jews than of Christ. But the Roman scholastics
have forgotten this faith, which is so vivifying, and they thought it
to be sufficient to persist in teaching another way, a dead faith, by
saying that after the consecration the bread has become the true Body
of Christ; about the way in which this occurs there are many subtle
theories but no scriptural proofs. It is clear, however, that this faith

which believes merely in historical facts,[4] the objective presence, cannot justify. But let us see whether this belief, assumed arbitrarily, cannot be condemned.

If this consecrated bread is adored and honored completely like God but is not God, how, I ask you, are we any different from those heathens who worshiped wood and stones? Indeed, they thought there was some sort of divinity in them which there was not, for they would not have wished to adore stones unless perhaps they had first arbitrarily assumed that these stones were gods.

But perhaps someone would say: "We have the Word of God which says, 'This is My Body.' "[5] That is true, you do have the Word of the Lord and likewise you have that quotation which encourages Roman tyranny: "Whatever you shall bind on earth is bound in heaven."[6] But if you really study this with some attention, you will find it does not at all provide a basis for tyranny. Wherefore let us confront these current ideas, lest by following blind guides we together with them fall into the pit.[7] For the Lord forbade us to believe them who said, "Here is Christ" or "There is Christ";[8] wherefore I should not have faith in those who say that Christ is in the bread: for just this reason, I could not excuse myself as having been deceived, since I have refused to listen to the warning voice of Christ. For now those perilous times have come of which He predicted that this would happen.

Nor indeed did the Apostles speak of the sacrament in this fashion; they *broke* bread, and they *called* it bread: no word about this Roman belief. Nor is this contradicted by St. Paul who, although he says, "The bread which we break, is it not a participation in the Body of Christ?"[9] does not say that the bread *is* the Body of Christ. It is therefore obvious that in this text "is" (*est*) should be interpreted as meaning "signifies" (*significat*); it is all the more clear from the comparisons St. Paul draws between our bread and the food offered to idols. Such food is, according to St. Paul, not changed in reality; notwithstanding this he can say: it "is," or "signifies," some sort of communion with the devil to whom the food is offered. Therefore St. Paul teaches us to abstain from food offered to idols,[10] so that we not use things without discretion. There were some in the time of Thomas Aquinas who said on this very issue that Christ was in the bread, but

only as a sign, that Christ was present not corporeally but only sacramentally. And although Thomas rejected this position as heretical,
the Romanists, who hang on his words as if they were an oracle, were
not able to explain away Christ's assertion, "If anyone says to you that
Christ is here do not believe him."[11] St. Paul seems to be speaking to
the same point when he says, "Your fathers ate the same spiritual
food in the desert as we."[12]

But let us first see on what foundation the Romanists build their
doctrine, a teaching so strange and stunning that nothing like it is
found in Scripture. We read that Christ became flesh (*incarnatus*) but
once only, and that in the womb of the Virgin Mary. And this incarnation was predicted by many prophetic oracles; it was demonstrated through Christ by His life, death, and His whole way of life,
and preached by the Apostles. But neither the prophets foretold nor
the Apostles preached that Christ would daily become bread (*im-
panatus*), so to speak, in the hands of any sacrificing priest. This
idea is founded only on this saying of Christ, "This is My Body, this
do in remembrance of Me."[13] If Christ, by these words intended that
which they say He did, certainly we do not doubt that just *one* word
should suffice. But I wonder why they do not also say that John the
Baptist was transubstantiated into Elijah, since Christ said of him,
"He *is* Elijah";[14] or that John was transubstantiated into Christ when
Christ said to him from the cross, "Woman, behold your son,"[15] or
that Christ was transubstantiated into a stone when He, referring to
Himself, said, "Upon this rock [*Petram*] I will build My Church";[16]
or that a rock was transubstantiated into Christ when Paul said, "The
rock [*Petra*] was Christ."[17] If we agree that this passage should be
exegeted by saying the rock (*Petra*) is Christ, that is, represents Christ,
should we not do the same for the proposition "This is My Body,"
especially when the next phrase is, "This do in remembrance of Me,"
since commemoration seems more appropriate for someone who is
absent, at least corporeally absent, than for someone who is present.
I know that long-established usage is the reason we find it abhorrent
to apply to this particular text the same kind of exegesis we use everywhere else without even a second thought; but I can find no reason
for the different exegesis of this "is." Many similar passages can be

quoted where Christ is the sacrifice,[18] the way,[19] the cornerstone;[20] Christ says, "I am the true vine,"[21] but we are not so rigid in exegesis as to say it means that Christ is biologically a vine. I cannot understand why this one passage always forces us into such an awkward position unless it be because of papal authority.

For a more thorough clarification of this issue let us consider the three kinds of spiritual bread: *Christ*, who is eaten by faith, as John says,[22] the *manna* which the fathers ate in the desert,[23] and the *Christian Eucharist,* which is the issue in dispute. Now let us see what the differences are among these three. The first two are very clearly discussed in the passage from St. John, previously quoted, where Christ says, "I am the bread of life. Your fathers ate manna in the desert and died. This is the bread which came down from heaven, he who eats this bread will live forever."[24] Here Christ clearly distinguishes between the bread the Jews received from heaven while they were in the desert and Himself as the bread which He was to give for the life of the world. For although this manna signified Christ, who was to come down from heaven for the life of the world, it was not Christ who is the living bread of life. This manna neither lived nor gave life and hence those who ate it died. But those who eat Christ do not die but live eternally. Thus we have the distinction between the first two.

Regarding the third kind of bread, St. Paul said that the spiritual food of the Israelites is the same as our eucharistic bread which we break in memory of Christ who came down for the life of the world, so that our eucharistic bread signifies that which has taken place, whereas the spiritual food of the Jews signified that which would take place.[25] Thus the Eucharist is neither a living bread nor a bread of life, because those who eat even this die. Just as the crossing of the Red Sea by the children of Israel signified the crossing through death to life eternal—although not all who crossed the sea attained to eternal life but only those who through faith died with the Christ to come— so our Baptism signifies our crossing from death to life—although not all baptized attain eternal life but only those who through faith have already died with the Christ now dead, and they will arise with Him through the same. Thus also the manna in the desert signified Christ, the bread of life, who preserved from eternal death. But not all who

ate the manna were preserved from this death. Only those were preserved from death who ate in faith the Christ to come, because although the manna signified Christ it was not Christ. According to
St. Paul the same is true for the Eucharist; whereby just as the manna
was not [substantially] what it signified—which Christ proves in the
Gospel of John, because those who ate it were not preserved from
eternal death—even so, by a similar logic, our Eucharist *is* not Christ,
although it signifies Him, because some who eat it are not preserved
from eternal death.

Therefore, St. Paul admonishes us[26] not to be lovers of evil, patting
ourselves on the back on account of our Baptism or because of our
Sacrament of the Bread with the claim that we are more privileged
than the Jews, or that we have the thing signified and they have only
the sign.[27] Such is not the case, said the Apostle, for your spiritual
food is just like that of your fathers, since just as they were not spared
when they sinned, so it will happen to you if you fall from the faith
active in true love; by this faith alone they, as we, receive the things
signified by the signs.

Therefore, it is written, "You do not allow your gift to be subject
to corruption."[28] But the consecrated bread is corrupted and consumed
by mice,[29] as experience proves; therefore the consecrated bread is not
Christ. But even if it were admitted that in the Lord's Supper Christ
by the word of his power transubstantiated the bread or so united
His Body with it that it could be said truly and simply: "Christ is that
which is bread" without any further explanation—yet nothing like
this will you find anywhere in Scripture to be performed by Christ or
His disciples who Christ had said, as you remember, would do
everything he did and indeed greater things—it would still not follow
that if Christ has done this a mere priest can do the same. Let us see
then by what words so much power is given to men.

According to the Romanists it is uncertain what is meant by these
words, "This do in remembrance of me": "This which I do, do," or
"This which you do, do in remembrance of Me." If we elect the first
alternative, uncertainty faces us again, since we do not know for sure
what He Himself did. There are some who say[30] that Christ first
consecrated the bread and only then said these words, "This is My

Body," with reference to the transubstantiated bread. But even if by the words "This is My Body" He *did* consecrate, who then would venture to eat and consume the Body of Christ without His mandate? Yet we would have no mandate to eat if "this do" is held to refer to the consecrating priest, not to the communicants. For the Gospel of St. John refers not to the eating by mouth but by faith.

If now one should say that the aforementioned words mean, "This which you do, do it to remember Me," that is, "Eat My Body," since no one among mortals can provide "this" body, what then are we supposed to do? Do we not await that moment when Christ comes and ministers or sends another who can give us "this," namely, that which we are commanded to take? And, I ask, if He gave this power to anyone else, by which words did He give it? The phrase, "This do in remembrance of Me," cannot mean two things nor can the singular "this" refer to more than one thing.

Some say that the celebration of the Apostles is an established fact and, since they could not celebrate unless there was someone who administered, the words, therefore, implicitly suggest that Christ delegated His power of administration and He gave it to the whole Church, which was empowered to set apart for this certain persons; it does so through the ordination of priests. But these assertions are fuzzy and extremely unclear. Even if all this is granted, I ask what bread does the priest consecrate by the aforesaid words? Only that bread, they say, which he designates as such by the word "this" in the formula of consecration. Therefore, the layman, who is not certain of the intention of the consecrating priest, is forced to assume that it is Christ; but that it is Christ he does not know for certain, nor can the layman ever be certain whether he receives the true sacrament or not. Certainly this religion is a profound mystery!

But let us leave these questions in order to examine the words of consecration, which are these, "Jesus took bread, blessed it, broke it, and gave it to His disciples saying, 'This is My Body.'"[31] Does the consecrating priest speak for himself or in the person of the Church or of Christ? If he speaks for himself, it seems more true to say that he produces [on the altar] his own body rather than that of the Lord. If it is said that he speaks these words in the person of Christ, it is not easily reconciled with the words, "He blessed, He broke, gave," which suggest one who remembers it having been done by Christ rather than one who speaks in the name of Christ. Nor did Christ say, "Do this in My name." He said, "This do in remembrance of Me." If it were said in the person of Christ, he ought to say, as in Baptism the minister says, "I baptize you in the name of the Father, Son, and Holy Spirit," "I bless, I break, I give, etc." Nor can the problem be correctly solved by saying that the priest first speaks for himself when he says, "He blessed it, He broke it and gave it to His disciples saying . . ." but after the word "saying" he suddenly begins to speak in the name of Christ; because this solution is forbidden by the words "which is shed for you" in the blessing of the cup. Wherefore there is no change from indirect to direct discourse in the blessing of the cup such as they claim to find in the blessing of the bread, unless one forces the meaning of the sentence against every accepted standard.

One can already see that everything our Romanists interject is here obscure and wavering and unable to stand unless upheld by human props. I think, therefore, that it is better to stick with that straight saying of Christ, "If anyone says to you, 'Here is Christ,' do not believe."[32]

There is still another reason for suspecting the Romanist faith, namely, since this transubstantiation would be an exceptional article of faith and should deserve some place of prominence, it is, nevertheless, not found in the Creed which they refer to as Apostolic. Nevertheless it is piously discussed in the decretals of the pope.[33] This absence from the Creed strengthens the suspicion that this is a papal or, rather, a satanic invention, which I believe no one will deny once he has quietly considered how much the whole religion of the popes is based on this one foundation. Christ, who is perceived by faith alone and worshiped by faith alone, taught that we should extend service of the flesh to our neighbor but that we should serve Him in the Spirit through faith; and in order to make this easier, He withdrew His bodily presence from us which He, speaking to His disciples, called an obstacle: "Unless I go away the Comforter will not come."[34] Satan, in order to pervert all things, has attempted to persuade us of the bodily presence of Christ not in the form of man, to be sure, but rather in the form of bread. And that bread which is perceived by eyes of the flesh, if we believed it to be God, requires a service of the flesh. It would be disgraceful indeed for God to be shut up in a humble cottage and to be left there without honoring Him. Hence come extravagant churches and sumptuous decorations of temples, hence torches and candles, hence sacred vestments woven of linen and gold, hence the bellowing of monks in the choir, anointings and purifications of priests, hence is part of the sacrament taken away from the layman.[35] In short, if the physical presence were eliminated the entire religion of the pope collapses. Who can doubt that it is to sink even lower once one sees that it is collapsed to such a large extent?

A human contrivance is its foundation, since if it were built upon a rock, it would stand invincible against all storms. Thus by these words, "This is My Body," the Savior did not want the bread to be transubstantiated but rather He wanted to give Himself through the bread, just as is our custom in certain places when a man who is going to sell some land gives the buyer a staff, straw, or stone and says, "By this token I give you the land." Likewise, the ownership of a house is transferred by handing over the keys. Just so the Lord gave himself to us by means of the bread, as if to say, "Take and eat. Do not regard the bread as unimportant; that which I give you signifies My Body which I give you by giving you this bread. When it has been given over and hung on the cross it will be for you; indeed, everything I have done or shall do is yours." These words are a great consolation and of exceeding sweetness if they are properly considered. And there was good reason why Christ said "is" instead of "signifies." This "is" makes more certain and immediate the meaning I have just explained, just as we refer more clearly to the first sign of rain by saying "this *is* rain" than by saying "this signifies rain." Scripture is full of similar examples. "The three branches are three days."[36] "The three baskets are three days."[37] "The seven good cows and the seven full ears are seven prosperous years."[38] Many others could be cited.

The Romanists, however, are unable to give a single biblical reference for their exegesis; nor can they show a place in Scripture where Christ is said to perform miracles contrary to the experience of the senses. He opened the eyes of the blind, raised the dead, and healed the lepers; but He did this so that it was clear to all that they were healed, alive, and with eyesight; people were not asked to believe such a thing contrary to sense experience. The miracles the pope and his entourage usually perform are rather to make of the worst wretch, pander, or robber a holy father and revered bishop whom we cannot see by experience to be any holier or wiser than before but whom we are supposed to believe to be holy and wise. Likewise, he performs such miracles as liberating souls from purgatory, of remitting part or even all of the punishment imposed for sins (perhaps for money), so that men are believed to be relieved from misery against all experience, since in time of pestilence or war those suffer no less whose punishment was remitted than those who have had no remission.

Let us distinguish, therefore, between the bread received by mouth and Christ, who is received by faith. But if anyone does not discern the Body of the Lord, thinking that he has eaten nothing more than what he took by mouth, he is answerable to the Body and Blood of the Lord, and he eats and drinks his own judgment, since, by his eating and drinking, he shows Christ to be present even while he separates himself from Christ by his own unfaith. May the Lord have mercy on us when we see how great is our abomination!

The children of Israel who had been freed from the yoke of Pharaoh and nourished by bread from heaven soon strayed from the path pointed out to them by Moses. They made for themselves a molten calf and worshiped it by sacrificing animals to it. They said, "There are your gods, O Israel, who brought you up out of the land of Egypt."[39] So we Christians just as quickly stray from the Word of Christ, our leader, who said, "If anyone says to you, 'Here is Christ,' do not believe him":[40] we elevate the bread and we say, "This is our God Who has redeemed us by His Blood."

Notes

1. The complete title given by Zwingli, in his edition of August–September 1525 reads: "A most Christian letter—sent four years ago from the Netherlands to some- one with whom stood the final judgment of Holy Scripture, but spurned by him.—This letter presents the Lord's Supper in a very different fashion than was hitherto

the case. At the end some additions have been made which are necessary for the Christian, especially in these dangerous times." *CR* 91, Leipzig, 1927, p. 509. For further literature see A. Eekhof, *De Avondmaalsbrief van Cornelis Hoen,* 's Gravenhage, 1917. For his relation to the sixteenth-century radical movements see George H. Williams, *The Radical Reformation,* Philadelphia, 1962, esp. pp. 35–37 ff., 347 ff.

2. The word "pledge" is used here to translate the Latin *pignus.* The word refers to the fact that the presence of Christ with men and His institution of the Church is viewed as only the beginning, a down payment, on the full achievement of the Kingdom of God. For the New Testament—especially Pauline—use of this concept see "Αρραβών" by Johannes Behm, *Kittel's Theologisches Wörterbuch zum Neuen Testament,* Stuttgart, Kohlhammer, 1933, vol. 1, p. 474.

3. John 6:57. Cf. the marriage imagery of Staupitz where not trust in fidelity but identification in love is the crucial point.

4. Note here the parallel with Faber's introduction to the *Quincuplex Psalterium.* For Hoen the Eucharist is carnal eating, "Jewish," and faith in "historical facts" when bread and Spirit are separated. For Faber biblical exegesis is "carnal," "Judaizing," and mere "chronicling" when letter and Spirit are separated. See page 298.

5. Luke 22:19; cf. I Corinthians 11:24.

6. Matthew 16:19.
7. Cf. Matthew 15:14.
8. Matthew 24:23.
9. I Corinthians 10:16.
10. I Corinthians 10:14–21.
11. Matthew 24:23. For Thomas' position see *ST* III 9.80, art. 3, ob. 2.
12. Cf. I Corinthians 10:1–6.
13. Luke 22:19.
14. Matthew 11:14.
15. John 19:26.
16. Matthew 16:18.
17. I Corinthians 10:4.
18. Cf. John 10:7, 9.
19. Cf. John 14:6.
20. Cf. Matthew 21:42.
21. John 15:1.
22. John 6:51.
23. John 6:49.
24. John 6:48–50.
25. Cf. I Corinthians 10:1–17.
26. I Corinthians 10:6.
27. This is the teaching of all schools in scholasticism; the Sacraments of the Old Testament are held to be effective on grounds of the faith of the recipient in the expected Messiah (*ex opere operantis*); the Sacraments of the New Testament function on grounds of the accomplished messianic task of Christ (*ex opere operato*).
28. Psalms 16:10.
29. This is an allusion to the scholastic thesis—again common to all schools—that also the mouse who takes the consecrated bread receives the Body and Blood of Christ. Luther, in contrast to Zwingli, accepted this formulation. Hence it expresses—in the sharpest possible fashion—that the presence of Christ is the condition for faith, rather than that the

presence of faith is the condition for Christ.

30. Erasmus in his annotation to I Corinthians 11, *Opera,* vol. VI, Leiden, 1705, col. 716E.
31. I Corinthians 11:24.
32. Matthew 24:23.
33. Cf. *De Summa Trinitate et Fide* c. 1, X, (1, 1), ed. Friedberg II, 5.
34. John 16:7.
35. This is the oldest polemic of a kind that would lead to "puritan" Church decoration.
36. Genesis 40:12, etc.
37. Genesis 40:18.
38. Genesis 41:26.
39. Exodus 32:4.
40. Matthew 24:23. The *CR* edition assigns one more sentence to Hoen before it prints Zwingli's addition. Since this last sentence is not organically related to the main text and since we are inclined to believe that it refers back to Luther's 1520 writing "On the Babylonian Captivity of the Church" (*WA* 6. 510—as its first editor Eekhof saw), it is here transferred to the notes: "Though this is abhorrible, one should also, I believe, beware of giving credence to those who claim that 'the Body of Christ is in the bread as fire pervades the iron,' unless we want to close our ears to Christ's word: 'So if they say to you, "Lo, he is in the inner rooms," do not believe it.'" [Matthew 24: 26.] If this clause belongs to the original text of Hoen, it is as such sufficient explanation why Luther would spurn it, since it is this image which reflects Luther's doctrine of consubstantiation: the fire does not replace the substance of the iron but is intimately united with it by pervading it.

Chapter Six

Exegesis

Biblical Exegesis: The Literal
and the Spiritual Sense of Scripture

Since early in the history of the Christian Church, the Old Testament has posed the chief exegetical problem to the biblical interpreters. The New Testament seemed clear and straightforward by comparison. The Gospels contain the history of Jesus Christ, while the other writings principally contain the interpretation of this history and its application to the life of the Church. But how can one apply the Old Testament to Christ, how can one make good the claim of the Church that the Books of Moses are her books? The apostolic writings were themselves a constant reminder of the place and function of the Old Testament at the very beginnings of the Church, before the formation of the New Testament canon, when "the Scriptures" meant only one thing, namely, what later came to be looked upon as the Old Testament.

Jesus, Peter, and Paul had appealed to "the Scriptures" as prophecy of the events now fulfilled or in the process of being fulfilled. The apologetes such as Justin Martyr (*c.* 165) used the Old Testament to prove that Christianity was not an innovation but was older than any of the other respected traditions. After 135, in his famous *Dialogue with Trypho,* a Jewish teacher, Justin argued that every move and word of Christ had been predicted in the Old Testament. At the other end of the spectrum the gnostics or gnosticizing Christians, embarrassed by the humanizing descriptions of God in the Old Testament as one who gets angry, laughs, and changes his mind, were intent on showing behind the outer crust of the mere letter of the text the hidden meaning discernible only by those with true *gnosis* (knowledge, understanding). Their apologetic stance against Hellenistic philosophies required an immutable and immovable God rather than the "movable" God of the Jewish Scriptures.

The most radical position of all was taken by Marcion (†c. 160), the founder of a large Church which was not absorbed into Manichaeism until the end of the third century. In his *Antithesis* he rejected the Old Testament completely: the God of the Old Testament forms for him an absolute antithesis to the God of the New Testament. The God of the Law has nothing to do with the God of Jesus Christ, the God of Love. Hence he rejected the allegorical[1] method of interpreting the Old Testament that had served the apologetic enterprise of the Church so well against both the Jewish and the philosophical traditions.

Although Marcion's concern is indicative of digestive disorders in the very system of the Church, occasioned by its efforts to absorb the Jewish tradition, his solution was not determinative for the future. In the rabbinic exegesis of "the Scriptures" and in the Greek philosophical investigation of Homer, the allegorical method had been employed; furthermore, St. Paul had used the term in Galatians 4:24: "These things contain an allegory." In the Alexandrian school of Clement (†c. 215) and Origen (†254) this method was further developed, probably under the influence of Philo (†50).[2] For Philo, as for Clement and Origen, the use of allegory to search for the meaning hidden in the text did not imply the rejection of the letter. Actually Origen admitted a literal, moral, and spiritual sense in correspondence with his understanding of man as body, soul, and spirit. Insofar, however, as the spirit is infinitely higher than the body, the allegorical sense is clearly superior to the letter in which it is contained.

The school of Antioch, on the other hand, did not reject the allegorical method but used it very sparingly. And in the case of one of its most articulate representatives, St. John Chrysostom (†407), it is clear that he not only prefers the historical-literal sense but actually rejects allegory. The discussion of the relation of letter and spirit, of word and intention, became a significant factor in the Christological debates which dealt with the relation of the human and the divine nature of Christ. The question whether one finds the *spirit* through the letter (Alexandria's search for the spiritual sense) or, rather, finds the spirit through *the letter* (Antioch's emphasis on the literal sense) is clearly related to the Christological debates of the fourth and fifth centuries. Antioch, interested in the historical reality of Jesus, the Christ, would emphasize that God was in *Christ*. Alexandria, concerned with preserving the unity between God, the creator and ruler of the cosmos, with the Incarnate God, stressed rather that *God* was in Christ.

For a time the problem of the Old Testament did not seem acute, and the exegetical issue was subordinated to the Christological problem. In 451, at the fourth ecumenical Council of Chalcedon, the Christological extremes on both sides were condemned; it was not until 553, at the fifth ecumenical Council of Constantinople, that the two exegetical extremes, Origenistic speculation and Antiochian literalism, were stamped as heretical.

St. Augustine, the founding father of the Western exegetical tradition, in his conversion to Christianity experienced the exegetical problem as central. In his *Confessions,* Book IV, 3–5, he describes how much he owed in this respect to his bishop, Ambrosius of Milan. For a considerable period Augustine had been attracted by Manichaeism, which had been keen to show—with the same literal approach as Marcion's—how the use of the Old Testament necessarily led to absurdities. The sermons of Ambrose clarified for Augustine how, through the use of allegory, the Old Testament yielded its innermost secrets. This does not imply a disregard for the letter: To ward off uncontrollable allegorical speculation he states that "it is most shameful to interpret a particular text allegorically if not clearly supported elsewhere by nonallegorical, literal interpretation." Thus the concerns of Origen and Chrysostom had been reconciled; the schools of Alexandria and Antioch had found a common heir. This aspect of St. Augustine's thought would provide a basis for later developments.[3]

Yet Augustine's hermeneutics, his rules for the exegesis of Holy Scripture, were part of his total view of the nature of theology that would not satisfy the scientific requirements of twelfth- and thirteenth-century theologians. For him there is no objective standard by which to separate the literal sense—or the clear places in Scripture—

from the allegorical sense—or the obscure places. This difference is not contained in the text and therefore not scientifically (uncommittedly!) discernible, but largely dependent on the relation of the reader to God.

In his chief hermeneutical work, *On Christian Doctrine,* Augustine says that the way to differentiate between the two senses is to find out whether the text furthers one's love and faith; if so, it is to be taken literally; if not, it is apparently allegory: "Whatever there is in the Word of God that cannot, when taken literally, be referred either to purity of life or soundness of doctrine is to be classified as figurative."[4] If constant meditation is required to yield love for God and the neighbor, a text is obscure and allegorical; if not, the text can be taken literally.[5] The allegorical sense differs, therefore, from the literal sense insofar as it is not immediately accessible or "fruitful." Not the meaning but the mode of understanding is different.

Allegory has the great advantage of humiliating human pride; it exercises the mind in true piety; and above all it separates the readers into two groups, the truly pious who persevere in their ardent search, and the unworthy and indifferent investigators.[6] Languages, history, biology, astronomy, and dialectics are great tools: "But when the student of Scripture, thus prepared, starts his investigation, let him constantly meditate upon the saying of the Apostle: 'Knowledge puffs up, but love builds up.'[7] For so he will feel that whatever may be the riches he brings with him out of Egypt, yet unless he has kept the Passover, he cannot be safe. Only when he is meek and humble, carrying the easy yoke of Christ and laden with his light burden, does the knowledge of the Scripture not puff him up."[8]

In a bold effort to summarize St. Augustine's hermeneutics in one sentence, one can say: God the author of Scripture speaks through Scripture to two kinds of audience in two modes with the one purpose: to foster faith and love.

When, due to the scientific revolution of the twelfth century, Scripture became the *object* of study rather than the *subject* through which God speaks to the student, the difference between the two modes of speaking was investigated in terms of the texts themselves rather than in their relation to the recipients. The literal sense of Scripture was increasingly analyzed as one would study any other literary document. St. Thomas Aquinas is the culmination of a development furthered by Hugh (†1141) and Andrew of St. Victor (early twelfth century) which would pay increasing attention to the literal sense of Holy Scripture and seek to find objective standards to define its nature. Here we stand at the cradle of our modern standards for "sound" biblical exegesis. Andrew had little hesitancy in availing himself of "the treasures of Egypt" and liberally drew on the resources of contemporary Jewish exegetes.

Thomas provides for the theoretical clarification which solved the problem—especially urgent with respect to the Old Testament—of how to allow for a scholarly investigation and yet interpret the relevant text in the light of Christian faith. In his *Summa Theologica* he concluded his discussion of the nature of theology with a section on the question "whether in Holy Scripture a word may have several senses." He answers: "The author of Scripture is God in whose power it is to signify his meaning not only by words, as man can do, but also by things themselves. So, whereas in every branch of scholarship things (*res*) are signified by words (*verba*), this science (theology) has an additional property, the things (*res*) signified by words have themselves also a signification (*res*). Therefore, that first signification (*verba-res*), whereby words signify things, belongs to the first sense, the historical or literal sense. That signification whereby things signified by words have again themselves a further signification (*res-res*) is called the spiritual sense, which is based on the literal and presupposes it."[9] In accordance with preceding tradition this second signification—that the realities intended by the literal sense refer again to other realities—is the allegorical sense when "things of the Old Law signify things of the New Law"; the tropological or moral sense when things apply to individual Christians on their way to perfection; and the analogical sense when things apply to the eschatological mysteries or to the Church triumphant. This fourfold sense, probably introduced by John Cassiodorus (†550), does not differ in principle from the twofold sense (literal, spiritual), but serves as a classification and specification of the spiritual sense. St. Thomas made quite clear that this multiple sense could not lead to confusion, "since all the senses are founded on one—the literal—from which alone any argument can be drawn, and not from those intended in allegory." The central importance of the literal sense is cleary enunciated.

Through the mediation of Nicholas of Lyra[10] (†1349) a particular interpretation of the Thomistic definition came to determine biblical studies, even in those schools where St. Thomas was not the accepted authority. Usually referred to as the "Postillator," because of his monumental commentaries on the Old and New Testaments (*Postilla Litteralis* and *Moralis*), Lyra has been called the best-equipped biblical scholar of the Middle Ages. He argues for the crucial significance of the literal sense: "Through the usually practiced exegesis, the literal sense has almost been smothered." He does not reject the allegorical exegesis but announces: "With the help of God I plan to concentrate on the literal sense and to insert only a few short spiritual interpretations." To establish the literal sense he employs both the Christian and the rabbinic tradition. He quotes St. Thomas in arguing that the first signification, the simple or historical literal sense, is the conscious intention of the human author. However, it may have been the intention of an author in the Old Testament to prophesy about the coming Christ. Thus Lyra can say in his comment upon Isaiah 11:1: "Here the prophet turns again to a description of the mystery of Christ, his main intention." As Lyra says once explicitly, this view entails a double literal sense, of which one applies to the time of the prophet or the Old Testament and the other to the time of Christ or the New Testament.

Notwithstanding his criticism of the Franciscan Lyra, the Dominican Archbishop Paul of Burgos (†1435) accepts in his *Additiones* to Lyra's *Postilla* the theory of the double literal sense. Here and in his later works he is concerned to show that a literal interpretation of the Old Testament and faith in Christ can be reconciled. The result of this whole development is the acknowledgment of a historical literal sense and a prophetical literal sense. Again, this allowed for the combination of an Old Testament literal sense and a New Testament literal sense and thus could satisfy at once the claims of scholarship and of faith.

This is the context in which we have to read the selections from Faber Stapulensis, Jacques Lefèvre d'Étaples, the Prefaces to his edition of the Psalms (1509) and to his Commentary on the Epistles of St. Paul (1512). Pursuing St. Augustine's emphasis on God as the one and only author of Scripture who speaks through His word to further love and faith, Faber identifies, at least for the Book of Psalms, the spiritual with the literal sense, rejects the twofold literal sense, and posits—what we may call in the light of the foregoing—the prophetical literal sense or the New Testament literal sense as the only valid sense of the Psalms: The intention of the prophet is identical to the intention of the Holy Spirit, Who speaks through him.

When we compare Faber's interpretation with the tradition which has preceded him, his innovation seems only a difference in degree. Lyra had granted that a comparatively small number of Psalms literally refer to Christ, this being the intention of the historical author. Paul of Burgos added to this number. As a recent analysis of the Psalms commentary of the Spanish Augustinian Jacobus Pérez of Valencia (†1480) has established,[11] Pérez applied this rule to all Psalms without exception. A closer investigation may well show that Faber is actually dependent on Pérez. Yet Pérez allowed for a "precise literal sense" which is usually judged by him to be useless or even false, but is sometimes regarded as appropriately understood in its Old Testament setting. Faber has gone a step further by claiming that this "precise" or "historical literal sense" is the letter which kills the spirit.[12]

In his polemics Faber directs himself explicitly only against the "rabbinic" tradition; it is clear from his concern for the spiritual health of the monks in the monasteries which he visited that he wants to present an antidote against a literal, "objective," unconcerned reading of Holy Scripture. In a contemporary source—the counterattack by Noel Beda—we see that readers of Faber take his critique of "Jewish" exegesis to be directed against scholasticism and its methods. Faber follows Lyra in anchoring the "New Testament sense" in the intention of the human author rather than—as Thomas had taught— in the intention of God as the divine and original author; the five examples he gives of a wrong non-Christological exegesis of the Psalms do not apply to Lyra's *Postilla*. Yet he opposes Lyra's twofold literal sense as a dangerous inconsistency, or at least as an incomplete break with the preceding tradition. In the more florid Preface of 1512

Faber makes the same point again when he emphasizes that "Paul is only an instrument." We should study Paul as the spokesman inspired by God, not as the historical figure Paul.

Yet to regard "literal exegesis" as Faber's only target would be to misunderstand him. His position can best be regarded as a two-front war. The true literal sense is not only the spiritual sense, but, vice versa, the true spiritual sense is the literal one. When the text itself requires allegory because it contains a type or figure of speech, it is permitted, but in all other cases allegory is the wrong "spiritual sense." Faber's interest in the actual text appears in his concern to establish the true original text and in his excuse for St. Augustine's allegories, that they are due to the faulty texts available to him. At the same time it is clear that for Faber the spiritual, that is, the literal sense, is not available through simple grammatical exegesis. The unbeliever cannot discover the real meaning because he approaches the text without the most necessary exegetical tool of all, that selfsame spirit which created Scripture.

The difference between Faber's two Prefaces of 1508–1509 and 1512 is that in the first the issue of the twofold literal sense is pre-eminent, sparked by the lack of "spiritual food" which certain monks got out of studying the "literal" sense. In the second Preface there is a change of emphasis from the *exegetical* issue to the problem of *justification*. The barren or sterile reading of St. Paul is mentioned, but Faber's main concern is the contrast of the works of man with the grace of God. He continues the theme of the two ways of reading Scripture, but relates this more explicitly to two ways of man's relation to God. This interdependence of the themes of exegesis and justification would be a chief characteristic of Luther's first Bible commentary (1513–1516).[13]

There is one more aspect of Faber's view of the literal sense that we should not pass over in silence. It is intimately interwoven with the problem earlier discussed of the relation between Scripture and Tradition. This can perhaps best be illustrated by a comparison between Faber Stapulensis and another Frenchman who had marked the pre-eminence of the University of Paris a century before, Jean Gerson (†1429). Notwithstanding first appearances, their positions on this matter are vastly different. Gerson is as much interested as Faber in the literal sense of Scripture and is convinced, again as Faber, that mere grammatical analysis will not yield the true literal sense. Nevertheless, Gerson fights quite a different battle which leads him in a very different, even radically opposite, direction.

Faber deplores the influence of "rabbinic" exegesis upon the Christian interpretation of the Scriptures, for he feels that the uninspired "rabbinic" reading of Scripture reveals nothing more than "the letter which kills," the naked letter, *litera sola.* To discover the true meaning of Scripture, its true literal sense, he turns to "our first leaders, the Apostles, the Evangelists and the Prophets." Though he grants that he is not a prophet himself, he draws upon these men who saw God with their own eyes and heard Him speak with their own ears. Thus he is helped to discern the true literal sense for the most part "by the joint witness of the Scriptures."

Gerson, on the other hand, directs his defense of the true literal sense against the Hussites, who—as he reports—have been able to find supporters in England, Scotland, Prague, and Germany: "Yes, O horror, even in France. . . . They disseminate heresies and oppose the truth which they acknowledge or should acknowledge, since they call themselves Catholics; they say that their doctrines are based on Scripture and Scripture's literal sense, which they call 'Scripture alone.' "[14]

Gerson does not oppose *litera sola* but *scriptura sola,* not the isolated and naked letter but the isolated and naked Scripture. With Faber he turns to "the first leaders" to discover the true literal sense, but he does not find this by means of "the joint witness of Scripture" but by means of the Tradition of the Church: "The literal sense of Scripture was first revealed by Christ and the Apostles, illustrated by miracles, confirmed by the blood of martyrs; the holy doctors further developed the truths implied in this literal sense by their alert and learned warfare against the heretics; finally these truths were officially defined by the holy councils."[15] In short, "the literal sense of Scripture is not to be defined in terms of the insights of any given individual but in terms of the decisions of the Church, inspired and governed by the Holy Spirit."[16]

It is noteworthy that Luther in his first commentary on Scripture, on the Psalms (1513–1516), takes up the battle cries of both Gerson and Faber by opposing at once "the arbitrary exegesis of the heretics" and the threat of "the letter which kills." In his exposition of Psalm 1:2, "in His law does he [the righteous] meditate day and night," Luther points to the Judaizers who continue to kill the prophets of God, as the Jews of the Old Covenant had before, by smothering the Word of God, that is, its living sense intended by the Holy Spirit. Secondly, there are those who meditate on the law but not on the law of God; the canon lawyers, the arbitrary exegetes, meditate on human laws and human traditions such as the decretals of the popes. Ultimately, however, these Judaizers and heretics all fall into one and the same category: their meditation is not in "the law but the law is in them" and thus they prove their own opinions by the authority of Scripture.[17] Luther pursues in this early stage the battle of both Gerson and Faber, without, however, admitting a two-front war. In his later works the two fronts come to coincide completely and to delineate the common basis for his doctrine of the authority of Scripture and his doctrine of justification in which a sharp contrast is drawn between the Gospel and the law.

For the purpose of this introduction it will be enough to indicate that we find in Luther a parallel to Faber insofar as the young Reformer is equally interested in defending the "living sense" of Scripture against the Judaizers. Gerson opposed heretical arbitrary interpretation and had some harsh things to say about the canon lawyers, as did Luther, but for Gerson papal legislation accepted by the Church contains the literal sense of Scripture, just as do the decrees of councils. There can be little doubt that Gerson would have numbered Luther among "the Hussites" who teach naked Scripture, *scriptura sola*. Whereas for Luther the appropriate context for the true literal sense is *Scripture* itself ("Meditation is continuous beating on the rock of Scripture [as Moses did] until the waters of Wisdom pour forth"[18]), for Gerson the context of the literal sense is to be found in the Tradition of the *Church* just as much as the context of Scripture is for Faber the Holy Spirit.[19]

In 1522 Faber published his Commentaries on the four Gospels. By this time Luther's Reformation was no longer a German affair. Some of Luther's writings were available in Paris, and while the Sorbonne pondered Luther's case his stand in Leipzig and Worms had earned for him the name of a modern Hercules in humanist circles. Faber had read Luther's ninety-five theses and the *Babylonian Captivity of the Church* with approval,[20] and Faber openly pleaded for reform: "Let this be in all things the only zeal, comfort, desire: to know the Gospel, to follow the Gospel, to promote the Gospel everywhere. Let all firmly hold to what our Fathers and the primitive Church, red with the blood of martyrs, felt: to know nothing but the Gospel, since to know that is to know everything." An admirer of Zwingli, familiar with Farel and the young Calvin, Faber never identified himself openly with the cause of the Reformation. He died in the same year as Erasmus, 1536.

His edition of the Psalms had been an important aid to Luther in the years 1513–1516. Luther insisted, as did Faber, on the historical prophetical sense of the Psalms, and criticized Lyra time and again in his first Psalm-commentary for having allowed himself to be mis-led by "rabbinic" literal exegesis. Yet over these same years Luther came increasingly to appreciate Lyra's historical emphasis; his early praise of Faber was to disappear, and this French savant was not to be mentioned in any of the lists of those whom Luther names as influential guides, or "Forerunners."

Another line parallel to the one from Lyra through Burgos, Pérez, Faber, to Luther can be traced running via Gerson in the direction of the Counter Reformation. The introduction to Prierias' *Aurea Rosa* of 1503 is an elaborate hermeneutical treatise, "The Rules for the Exegesis of Holy Scripture." Here the identification of literal and spiritual sense, which we met with in Faber, is rejected as untenable. In line with—and actually quoting—Thomas, Lyra, and Burgos, Prierias argues that there is one literal sense which is subject to human investigation, and another literal sense—and here a Gersonian emphasis comes through—which is derived from the teaching authority of the Church. In case the doctors of the Church should not agree in their exegesis, there is not merely a twofold but a manifold literal sense in Scripture, although it never concerns truths necessary for salvation and authoritatively taught by the Church.

In his first attack on Luther in 1518, Prierias spells out what such a view of Scripture implies for the relationship between Scripture and

Tradition: "Whoever does not rely on the teaching of the Roman Church and the Roman Pontiff as the infallible rule of faith, from which also Holy Scripture draws its power and authority, is a heretic."[21]

During the sixteenth-century confessional debates, the problem of the relation between Scripture and Tradition of the Church assumed a place of pre-eminence. The first stirrings of biblical criticism in the eighteenth century increasingly focused again the attention of biblical scholars on the question of the interdependence of the literal and spiritual sense of the Bible. Whatever the emphases may have been in different periods of history, the intimate bond between these two issues is undeniable and actually plays an important part in the ecumenical dialogue in the mid-twentieth century. The discussion of the so-called *sensus plenior* and the distinction between *Historie* and *Geschichte,* so central in the work of Rudolf Bultmann, are sufficient proof of the ongoing concern with the problem of exegesis of Holy Scripture.[22]

In the same year that Prierias published his *Aurea Rosa,* Desiderius Erasmus of Rotterdam brought out his *Enchiridion Militis Christiani,* "Manual (or Dagger) for the Christian Soldier." Here we find exactly the same observation Faber would make five years later: "I believe that there is no other reason for the disappearance of monastic devotion, piety, and fervor everywhere than this, that they stick as long as they live to the letter and do not search for the spiritual understanding of Scripture."[23]

A year later, in the summer of 1504, Erasmus discovered in a Premonstratensian monastery just outside Louvain a manuscript of the *Annotations* on the New Testament by Lorenzo Valla (†1457), a collection of notes on the Gospels, the Epistles, and the Book of Revelation. Valla's treatise on pure Latin, *Elegantiae,* had been for the young Erasmus *the* example of true love for the good letters. In March 1505 Erasmus had the *Annotations* printed in Paris, together with an explanatory letter. This publication was more daring than the *Manual,* since Erasmus was very well aware that Lorenzo Valla, who had denied the authenticity of the Donation of Constantine (a cornerstone of the temporal claims of the medieval papacy), was a suspect character. Even more important than the effect of this publication on the outside world was the effect on Erasmus' own future course. The great historian Johan Huizinga suggests that the discovery of the *Annotations* probably "led Erasmus, who was formerly more inspired with the resolution to edit Jerome and to comment on Paul [he was to do both at a later date], to turn to the task of taking up the New Testament as a whole, in order to restore it to its purity."[24]

During his second stay in England from 1505 to 1506 he first made a new translation of the New Testament, later adding a critical Greek text with notes. In the beginning of 1516, the *Novum Instrumentum* appeared, which contained a new Greek text together with a Latin translation, vastly different from, though as it turned out not much better than, the Vulgate text. In comparison Valla's and Faber's work seems highly conservative. In that very year Erasmus' New Testament reached Wittenberg, where it was eagerly put to use by Luther who had just then turned from the Psalms to St. Paul's Epistle to the Romans.

This did not help to enhance Erasmus' name in Louvain, Paris, or Cambridge. In his famous letter of May 30, 1519, Erasmus wrote to Luther from Louvain: "I could never find words to express what commotions your books have brought here. They cannot even now eradicate from their mind the most false suspicion that your works were composed by my aid and that I am the standard-bearer of this 'party' (sect), as they call it. They thought that they had found a handle wherewith to crush good learning—which they mortally detest as threatening to dim the majesty of theology, a thing they value far above Christ . . ." Nor did Erasmus' open attack on Luther in his *Diatribe on the Freedom of the Will* (1524) bring him the coveted aureole of orthodoxy.

It is quite clear that Erasmus was not merely averse to Luther's sharp pen. Ten years after his Louvain letter to Luther he put down on paper his reaction to the burning in Paris of the leader of the Reformation movement, Louis Berquin: "If he did not deserve this lot I regret it," he writes on May 9, 1529, "if he did deserve it, I regret it doubly." His main concern at this point, as it was ten years before, is that Berquin, who had been an admirer of Erasmus and had translated some of the latter's writings in French, had compromised the cause of humanism: "His fall plays into the hands of Beda, who will now with increased arrogance oppose the lovers of languages and the good letters."

Indeed this same Noel Beda (†1534), author of *Annotations* directed against Faber and Erasmus (1526), was instrumental in arranging the Sorbonne censure of parts of Erasmus' work. As Adrian VI before, Pope Paul III (1534–1549) invited Erasmus in 1535 to Rome "to defend the Catholic religion both in word and writing before and during the Council." But this council, finally convened at Trent (1545–1563), condemned several of Erasmus' writings, and the Index of 1559 condemned all Erasmus' exegetical work, his commentaries, translations, and annotations.

Although there is a different texture to the mystical antidogmatism of Faber and the cultured antidogmatism of Erasmus, both died suspect of heresy; neither had joined arms either with the Reformation or the Counter Reformation, but both expected that their textual criticism would revivify a practical spirit of piety able to help the Church of their day conform to the primitive Church of Apostles and Martyrs.

Although the discussion about the relative merits of Faber and Erasmus continues to our day and their exact place in the sixteenth-century crossfire is yet to be established,[25] they determined, together with Lyra and Burgos in the preceding period, the exegetical context of the theological debates in the age of the Reformation.

Notes

1. We use here the term in its general sense of nonliteral interpretation. In a more precise usage, it came to stand for one of three spiritual senses, together with the tropological (moral) and anagogical (eschatological) sense. See further below.

2. See the important chapter "The Allegorical Method" in Harry Austryn Wolfson, *The Philosophy of the Church Fathers*, vol. I, 2d

ed., Cambridge, Mass., 1964, pp. 24–72; further bibliography there. Cf. Robert M. Grant, *The Letter and the Spirit*, London, 1957, pp. 121 ff.

3. For the following see Beryl Smalley, *The Study of the Bible in the Middle Ages*, 2d ed., Oxford, 1952. In French: C. Spicq, O.P., *Esquisse d'une histoire de l' exégèse latine au moyen âge*, Paris, 1944, and Henri de Lubac,

S.J., *Exégèse Médiévale: Les quatre sens de l'Écriture,* especially II, 2, Paris, 1964. In German: Gerhard Ebeling, *Evangelische Evangelienauslegung,* 2d ed., Darmstadt, 1962; "Die Anfänge von Luthers Hermeneutik," *ZTK* 48 (1951), pp. 172–230; article "Hermeneutik," in *Die Religion in Geschichte und Gegenwart,* 3rd ed., III, Tübingen, 1959, col. 242–259. Further bibliography there.

4. Augustine, *De Doctrina Christiana,* III. 10.14, in *PL,* vol. XXXIV, col. 71.

5. *Ibid.,* III. 15. *PL, ibid.*

6. Jean Pépin shows that Augustine in this high evaluation of allegory draws upon Clement and Origen as well as on Greco-Roman pagan theology: "Saint Augustin et la function protrêptique de l'allégorie," in *Recherches Augustiniennes,* I (1958), pp. 243–286.

7. I Corinthians 8:1.

8. *De Doctrina Christiana,* II, 61; *PL* XXXIV, col. 64.

9. *ST* I, q.1 art. 10 c.a.

10. See the second part of Herman Hailperin's important study *Rashi and the Christian Scholars,* Pittsburgh, 1963, pp. 137–246.

11. Wilfrid Werbeck, *Jacobus Pérez von Valencia: Untersuchungen zu seinem Psalmenkommentar,* Tübingen, 1959, esp. pp. 123 ff.

12. In principle Pérez agrees; cf. Werbeck, p. 137, note 1.

13. It has been argued that Faber, a few years before Luther, made "Luther's discovery." Cf. the careful evaluation by W. F. Dankbaar, *Nederlands Theologische Tijdschrift,* 8 (1954), pp. 327–345.

14. ". . . quam solam scripturam dicunt . . ." "De sensu litterali sacrae scripturae et de causis errantium," in Gerson, *Opera Omnia,* ed. L. E. Du Pin, vol. I, Antwerpiae, 1706, col. 2 A.

15. *Ibid.,* 3 C.

16. *Ibid.,* 3 A. When Gerson argues in another treatise that the literal sense is to be drawn from "Scripture in its context" (ex circumstantiis scripturae), the Church is to be regarded as the most crucial part of this context. Cf. "Declaratio compendiosa quae veritates sunt credendae de necessitate salutis," in *Opera Omnia,* vol. I, col. 24 B. See also the excellent monograph by G. H. M. Posthumus Meyjes: *Jean Gerson: Zijn Kerkpolitek en Ecclesiologie,* 's Gravenhage, 1963, esp. p. 264. Vol. X in the series *Kerkhistorische Studien.*

17. *WA* 55.II.1.13, 14–14, 22. This section dates from Fall 1516.

18. Exodus 17:6; *WA* 55.II.1.15, 10 f.

19. Whereas we know that Zwingli had a copy of Faber's *Quincuplex Psalterium* in his library, we have been unable to ascertain this as regards Calvin. Calvin's doctrine of the "internal testimony of the Spirit" as required for the fruitful reading of Scripture has, however, Faberian overtones. See *Institutes,* ed. cit., I. vii.4; cf. parallel places and secondary literature in the edition by John T. McNeill, *Calvin: Institutes of the Christian Religion,* I, Philadelphia, 1960, p. 70.

20. See further, Augustin Renaudet, *Humanisme et Renaissance,* Genève, 1958, pp. 201–216; *Préré-*

forme et Humanisme à Paris, 2d ed., Paris, 1953, esp. pp. 628–638.

21. Decalogus . . ., in praesumptuosas Martini Lutheri Conclusiones, de Potestate Papae," Fundamentum tertium, in *Vollständige Reformations—Acta und Documenta,* by Valentin Ernst Löschern, vol. II, Leipzig, 1722, p. 15.

22. "The *sensus plenior* is that additional, deeper meaning intended by God, but not clearly intended by the human author . . ." R. E. Brown, *The sensus plenior of Sacred Scripture,* Baltimore, 1955, p. 92. *History* is here the collection of external data, and *Geschichte* is the existential interpretation of the meaning of historical events.

23. Erasmus, *Opera Omnia,* ed. J. Clericus, vol. V, Leiden, 1704, col. 9.

24. *Erasmus and the Age of the Reformation,* Harper Torchbooks, New York, 1957, p. 57. See further, M. Phillips, *Erasmus and the Northern Renaissance,* New York, 1949; E. H. Harbison, *The Christian Scholar in the Age of the Reformation,* New York, 1956.

25. Cf. L. Febvre, *Au coeur religieux du XVIᵉ siècle,* Paris, 1957; Louis Bouyer's critique of Renaudet in *Autour d'Érasme,* Paris, 1955, esp. pp. 123 ff. We note the interesting comparison between Erasmus and Faber. Luther's letter to Georg Spalatin, dated Wittenberg, January 18, 1518: "In closing I shall say nothing on Erasmus' *Defense,* but I am very sorry that such a conflict should have broken out between these great princes of learning. Erasmus is certainly by far the superior of the two, and he is a greater linguist. However, he is also more violent, though he makes a great effort to preserve friendship." *W A Br* I, 134; we follow the translation of Gottfried G. Krodel, ed. *Luther's Works,* vol. 48, Philadelphia, 1963, p. 55. The *Defense* mentioned is Erasmus' sharp 1517 rebuttal of Faber's *Apologia.* See Allen, *op. cit.,* III, 163, 220.

JACOBUS FABER STAPULENSIS[1]

Introduction to Commentary on the Psalms

Paris, 1508

Whereas almost all studies are apt to yield nothing but pleasure and gain, only study of divine matters serves not merely pleasure and gain but promises the highest felicity. "Blessed are those," the Psalmist said,[2] "who study your testimonies." What is better for us to pursue? To what should we dedicate ourselves more completely? Indeed for a long time I pursued human concerns and paid only "lip service," as the expression goes, to theological studies (which are exalted and ought not to be approached casually). But even after a haphazard sampling of divine things I saw so much light shine forth that, by comparison, the human disciplines seemed like darkness. They breathed a fragrance of such sweetness that nothing like it can be found on earth, nor could I believe that there is any other earthly paradise whose odor could lead souls toward immortality.

I have frequently visited monasteries, but I have become convinced that those who do not love this sweetness certainly have not the slightest notion of the true food of the soul. For our spirits live "by every Word that proceeds from the mouth of God,"[3] and what are these words but Holy Scripture itself? Those who do not love this sweetness are dead in spirit. And from the moment that these pious studies are no longer pursued, monasteries decay, devotion dies out, the flame of religion is extinguished, spiritual things are traded for earthly goods, heaven is given up and earth is accepted—the most disastrous transaction conceivable.[4]

I often asked the few monks who tried to find nourishment in Sacred Scriptures what sweetness they experienced and savored. Most of them answered that as often as they fell into—I do not know what —literal sense, especially when they tried to understand the divine Psalms, they became utterly sad and downcast from their reading.

Then I began to consider seriously that perhaps this had not been the true literal sense but rather, as quacks like to do with herbs, one thing is substituted for the other, a pseudo sense for the true literal sense. Therefore I went immediately for advice to our first leaders, I mean the Apostles, the Gospel writers, and the prophets, who first entrusted the seed to the furrows of our souls and opened the door of understanding of the letter of Sacred Scripture, and I seemed to see another sense of Scripture: the intention of the prophet and of the Holy Spirit speaking in him. This I call "literal" sense but a literal sense which coincides with the Spirit. No other letter has the Spirit conveyed to the prophets or to those who have open eyes (not that I should want to deny the other sense, the allegorical, tropological, and anagogical, especially where the content of the text demands it).

To those who do not have open eyes but nevertheless *think* they have, another letter takes its place, which, as the Apostle says,[5] kills and opposes the Spirit. This letter is pursued today by the Jews, in whom even now this prophecy is being fulfilled. Their eyes are darkened so that they cannot see and their whole perspective is completely warped. This kind of sense they call literal, not the literal sense of their prophets, to be sure, but rather of certain of their rabbis. These interpret the divine hymns of David for the most part as applying to David himself, to his anxieties during the persecution by Saul and the other wars he fought.[6] They do not regard him in these Psalms as a prophet but rather as a chronicler of what he has seen and done, as if he were writing his own history. But David himself says regarding himself, "The Spirit of the Lord spoke through me, his word is upon my tongue."[7] And divine Scripture calls him *the* man in all of Israel to whom it was given to sing about the Christ of the God of Jacob and the true Messiah. And where else is this granted to him than in the Psalms?

And so I came to believe that there is a twofold literal sense. The one is the distorted sense of those who have no open eyes and interpret divine things according to the flesh and in human categories.[8] The proper sense is grasped by those who can see and receive insight. The one is the invention of human understanding, the other is a gift of God's Spirit—the false sense depresses, the other bears it up on high. Hence there seems to be good reason for the complaint of those monks that as often as they fell for "literal" exposition they came away from it somber and upset. All their religious devotion had suddenly collapsed and had completely disappeared, as if ice water had been thrown on a burning fire. For just as the healthy body is aware of what is harmful to it, so also the spirit is aware of what threatens it. Therefore it is not without good reason that I feel this kind of letter should be avoided and that one should aspire to that sense which is animated by the Spirit, as colors are by light.

With this goal in mind, I have tried to write a short exposition of the Psalms with the assistance of Christ, Who is the key to the understanding of David and about Whom David spoke, commissioned by the Holy Spirit, in the book of Psalms. In order that it might be more obvious how great the difference is between the proper and improper sense, I offer a few examples which demonstrate this. Let us first take Psalm 2: "Why do the nations conspire and the peoples plot in vain? The kings of the earth set themselves up and the rulers take counsel together against the Lord and his Anointed."[9] For the rabbinic interpreters, the literal meaning of the text is that the inhabitants of Palestine revolted against David, the Anointed One of the Lord. But Paul and the other Apostles take the literal sense to refer to the Anointed of the Lord, the true Messiah and true Son of God (which is both true and appropriate).

For the rabbinic interpreters, the literal meaning of Psalm 18 is that David expresses thanks to God for being liberated from the hands of Saul and his other enemies. Paul has taken the literal sense to mean the Anointed One of the Lord. The rabbis understand Psalm 19 to deal with the first giving of the law. Paul takes it to be not the first but the second giving of the law when through the blessed Apostles and their successors it was promulgated to all nations. Furthermore, the rabbis, in a literal interpretation of Psalms 1 and 21, refer them to the persecution of the Israelites in the time of Artaxerxes.[10] Matthew, John, and Paul, full of God, took the Psalms to refer, in a literal sense,

to those things which happened to the Anointed of the Lord, the King
of Glory, in His passion.

But it would be tedious to go through each Psalm to show that what
the rabbis contrive to be the literal sense is not the literal sense at all,
but rather a fiction and a lie. Isaiah appropriately prophesied these
things when he said:

> For they are a rebellious people,
> lying sons,
> sons who will not hear
> the instruction of the Lord;
> who say to the seers, "See not,"
> and to the prophets,
> "Prophesy not to us what is right,
> speak to us smooth things,
> prophesy illusions,
> level the way, turn away from the path,
> let us hear no more of the Holy One of Israel."[11]

Certainly those who see such "smooth things" see errors and stray
from the true way, which is the Anointed One, and "turn away from
the path" so that they cannot see "the Holy One of Israel," which is
Christ Jesus, the most highly blessed forever.

How, therefore, can we rely on the interpretation of those whom
God has stricken with blindness and terror, and not fear that when
a blind man offers us guidance we will fall into a ditch together? It
is impossible for us to believe this one to be the literal sense which
they call the literal sense, that which makes David a historian rather
than a prophet. Instead, let us call that the literal sense which is in
accord with the Spirit and is pointed out by the Spirit. "We know,"
says Paul, the spokesman of God, "that the law is spiritual,"[12] and if
it *is* spiritual, how could the literal sense, if it is really to be the sense
of the law, not be spiritual? Therefore the literal sense and the spiritual
sense coincide. This true sense is not what is called the allegorical or
tropological sense, but rather the sense the Holy Spirit intends as He
speaks through the prophet. It has been our total purpose to draw out
of this sense all that the Holy Spirit has put into it.

Now, if anyone would hold against me that I have not done this
as worthily as I should, I would be most ready to grant it. For who can

interpret in a fitting manner a prophet who is not himself a prophet nor has received the spirit of a prophet? I cannot say that of myself nor do I claim what is described by Homer:

> We are not led by man's divinations,
> but with my own eyes I have seen,
> and with my own ears I have heard,
> that God revealed all those things by
> bringing them to light.[13]

But those by whose "divinations" I am led and whom I follow were able to say this [that they saw with their own eyes and heard with their own ears], and above all the joint witness of their Scriptures has been our abiding guide.

But perhaps there will be others who will stamp this enterprise of ours as redundant, since I am writing after Didymus, Origen, Arnobius,[14] and Cassiodorus commented on the Psalms. We shall answer that these Fathers treated everything most clearly, but that what they have done elaborately we shall treat succinctly. They worked with several senses; we have been intent on one primarily, namely, that sense which is the intention of both the Holy Spirit and the prophet. They had only one text of the Psalms available, so that Augustine, for example, worked with the Old Psalter[15] which is less reliable than the others. Therefore he was often forced to make excurses without relation to the text. Cassiodorus followed the Roman Psalter, and others have worked with the text that was available to them. We have consulted various text traditions, so that from these we could truly establish the original sense.[16]

Introduction to the Commentaries on Paul's Letters

O most wise Father,[17] accustomed to delight in things given by Providence, it is not hidden from you that when the farmer plows the field, however great his competence may be and whatever the extent of labor he invests, if plants grow and he brings in his rich harvest, the gift is God's. Nor is there anyone among the faithful who would for a moment doubt or deny this. If, therefore, the earth which is marked by the hoofs of cattle is made fruitful by divine favor, all the more is the rational earth of the human mind subject to divine inroads—the mind which is marked by the footsteps of the divine. But if anyone should examine the land which is not cultivated, which does not feel the heavenly rain, he would find it unfit for human use, full of thorns, briars, and brambles, without any useful plants.

In the same way those human minds which do not feel the divine ray, if they bring forth anything at all it usually does more harm than good, and does not provide any real nourishment for the mind. The fruits of minds deprived of divine favor are only brambles, thorns, and stones. And when these people take up the pen to write about either human or divine things, their works are full of such fruits. I except only those who proceed to their writing moved not by themselves but by God, and it is that movement which reaches up to the Highest and most Lucid.

The human mind in itself is sterile; if it believes itself able to function by itself it is presumptuous; anything it brings forth will be sterile, ponderous, obscure, and detrimental to the mind, rather than being its true sustenance furthering the life of the soul. Therefore, if the visible earth gives forth fruit which fulfills the needs of the human body, this is the clearest indication of the gift from above. But how much more does this apply when the human mind produces a fruit which sustains life and salvation of the soul.

Therefore, one ought not give his attention to the mind itself, to the human agent (or whoever might finally be commissioned by God as His instrument), but one ought to attend above all to the heavenly gift and to the Divine Giver Himself. And therefore you, most humane Father, and all you who are about to read the Epistles of God's spokesman, Paul, gathered in this volume, I would pray and beseech not to pay attention so much to Paul himself as to the grace of Paul and the Giver of this grace. This applies all the more to expository sections of mine which might be read: If the reader would find traces of food for the spiritual life of the soul, he should not concentrate on the human authors themselves, but he should realize that this power to bear fruit is a gift from above, and should recognize the true author and follow Him with all his might in purity and piety. This is the only way to reach Him Who accomplishes all in all things.

If, however, the readers find no sustenance for the mind, if the pasture of the human mind does not feel the dew of the Holy Spirit, then [that is a sign that] no rain came down from the Holy Spirit but rather the human mind produced its own fruits, useless sprouts; as the divine Word has said: "Cursed is the earth in your labor, it shall bring forth thorns and thistles for you."[18] The gifts which arise out of the "second birth"[19] are not our work but result from the blessing of God. In the gift of spiritual food the readers should see the divine blessing as the active agent, but in the spiritual dryness the curse of the first birth. The result of this curse is as much to be avoided as the result of the benediction is to be sought after.

Whatever is to be sought, the human author should not be given credit (which is worth saying), because it should be very clear that "he who plants is nothing, nor he who waters, but He Who gives the increase, that is God, is all."[20] So much the less shall those be entitled to praise who concern themselves with that which has *already* been planted and watered and has *already* received the increase from God.

However, there is a great gift in all these things and in the concern
for all these things; those who grasp this prepare themselves to receive
grace. For what else does the Giver of all gifts want than to grant
grace to those who are ready, just as He lets His light shine for all
eyes able to behold it.[21]

Those who understand these Epistles and the comments thereupon
to be gifts of God shall profit from them. They owe such profit not to
themselves but to grace. But those who attend to the worldly agent—
yes, even to St. Paul himself who is more than worldly—as if these
Epistles were his work and not the work of a higher energy working in
a divine fashion in him, and come with their own understanding, they
will receive little fruit from it. Full of their own carnal ideas and
interpreting by much forcing of the text, they get lost in trifles and
before long their mind will begin to be diseased. It is no little gift
when it is given to someone to see that such is the state of affairs.

Let Christ, the author of divine gifts, be present to give grace to all,
to preserve and increase it in order that no one should presume to
interpret by his own sense. For Paul is only an instrument. He himself says, "You desire proof that it is Christ speaking in me."[22] For
his is the doctrine of Christ, not of anyone else. Let those who wish
to be His disciples "with joy draw water from the wells of salvation"[23]
contained in the divine Word. This is the doctrine which is formulated in Hosea, "I desire the knowledge of God rather than burnt
offerings."[24]

But if Paul is only the instrument of this divine knowledge, what
can those who come after him accomplish? Indeed, is not everything
they can say very slender and tenuous, and is not the extension of an
instrument less and inferior to the original instrument? Yet it is a
great thing to be, in this way, an extension—yes, even less than an
extension—of the instrument; it far surpasses human power. To those,
therefore, who approach this reading piously, not Paul nor anyone
else but Christ and His exceedingly good Spirit will be present so
that the readers might grow in piety. Those who approach in presumption and pride are rejected, not just by Paul or by anyone else,
but by Him Who "resists the proud and gives grace to the humble."[25]
Sweet is the manna from heaven that is formed from the dew and
sweet is the honey from heaven that is gathered from the flowers; but

sweeter than all these things is the gift of God to those whom He Himself grants this taste. But no more: the devout readers have been sufficiently warned by us.[26]

Notes

1. The two following introductions —to the Psalter and to the Letters of St. Paul—are translated from *Quincuplex Psalterium,* Paris, 1509; *Sancti Pauli Epistolae XIV,* Paris, 1512. Part of Faber's third introduction—to the Gospels—can be found in *Renaissance Reader,* ed. J. B. Ross and M. M. McLaughlin, New York, 1953, pp. 84 ff. For references to this study of the Gospels we used the *Commentarii initiatorii in quatuor Evangelia,* Basel, 1523.

2. Psalms 119:2.

3. Deuteronomy 8:3; Matthew 4:4; Luke 4:4.

4. See Charles Trinkaus' important analysis: "Humanist Treatises on the Status of the Religious: Petrarch, Salutati, Valla," *Studies in the Renaissance,* XI (1964), 8–45. For his insistence upon a spiritual —nonliteral—reading of Scripture as basic to piety Faber may be dependent upon the mentality of the *Devotio Moderna* on which he was raised; in the first pages of the *Imitation of Christ* by Thomas à Kempis, it is stated: "The whole of Holy Scripture has to be read in the Spirit by which it was written. We had better look at Scripture for what is edifying than for precision of language." Bk. I, ch. 5.

5. "The letter kills, but the Spirit gives life." II Corinthians 3:6.

6. Faber must have had in mind Nicholas of Lyra (†1340). Influenced by Rabbi Solomon ben Isaac (Rashi, †1105), Lyra programmatically opposed current allegoristic interpretations of the Bible. In his *Postilla* on the Psalms, he often applies the text "literally" to David and David's historical circumstances, where Faber applies it to Christ.

7. II Samuel 23:2.

8. The Latin text reads here *passibiliter.* To read Scripture "in human categories" means that the reader of the false literal sense makes Scripture the object (passive) of his reading, whereas the true sense is found when Scripture is the subject and the reader the object. The true reader of Scripture "does not act but is acted upon"; his own human insights give way to the influx of the Holy Spirit.

9. Psalms 2:1–2. The five examples of rabbinic interpretation which Faber is going to give he could have taken from Lyra's *Postilla.* The Latin word used, *Hebraei,* can mean Jews, but stands here for the rabbinic tradition and more generally for all those who are versed in Hebrew.

10. Artaxerxes I (465–424 B.C.).
11. Isaiah 30:9–12.
12. Romans 7:14.
13. Iliad, Bk. 24, 220–223.
14. For modern readers perhaps an unexpected name in this illustrious company. Faber must have had in mind Arnobius Junior—not the apologete Arnobius († c. 330)—who wrote strongly allegorizing commentaries on the Psalms and the Gospels. Erasmus published the editio princeps of Arnobius' *Commentaries* in Basel in 1522. This Semi-Pelagian opponent of St. Augustine died soon after 455.
15. In his *Quincuplex Psalterium,* Faber brings in five (quinque) parallel columns five texts of the Psalter, that is, of the psalms as used in the liturgy of the Church. In the fourth column is printed the *Psalterium Vetus,* or Old Psalter. It is old in the sense of "pre-Jerome." Jerome (†420) made three improved translations. The first was 383, introduced into the Roman liturgy by Pope Damasus (366–384) and hence carries the name Roman Psalter, or *Psalterium Romanum.* Today it is used only in St. Peter's Church in Rome. It relies completely on the Septuagint. This text appears in the second column of Faber. In the first column we find the *Psalterium Gallicum* (c. 392), thus called because it was introduced in France by Gregory of Tours (†594). Much better than the Romanum, which Jerome admitted to have been a hasty job, the Gallicum presupposes Origen's tex-

tual criticism. It became the Vulgate, or official medieval text. Faber brings in the third column the *Psalterium Hebraicum,* Jerome's translation from the Hebrew (c. 400). The fifth column brings the *Psalterium Conciliatum* which, as Faber says, "adds and changes a few things in the Vulgate text." This text is indeed basically the Gallicum with emendations on grounds of the Hebraicum as well as Faber's own knowledge of Hebrew.
16. In the closing paragraph, Faber gives a short introduction to the five columns and their background history, very much like our note 15. He defends his Conciliatum text with reference to Origen's highly lauded Hexapla (six columns). The last sentence reads: "We should pray Christ, the Lord, who is the beginning and the purpose of the whole Book of Psalms, that this work may not only be acceptable to Him, but also help many to reach happiness."
    In the year of Christ 1508.
17. Bishop Guillaume Briçonnet, the protector of Faber, to whom this work—as well as the *Quincuplex Psalterium*—is dedicated. Briçonnet was first Bishop of Lodève, then formed a circle of reform-humanists around Faber at Meaux when appointed bishop there on the last day of 1515.
18. Genesis 3:17, 18.
19. Cf. "I say to you, unless one is born anew, he cannot see the Kingdom of God." John 3:3.
20. I Corinthians 3:7.

21. Cf. Aquinas, *Summa contra Gentiles,* III, 159.
22. II Corinthians 13:3.
23. Isaiah 12:3.
24. Hosea 6:6.
25. James 4:6.
26. In the closing section, Faber gives a short introduction to the history of the Pauline letters and their interpretation. He furthermore explains his own procedures in establishing the text and defends himself against the charge that it would show lack of respect for St. Jerome to draw on the Greek original. Whatever the critique may be, Faber concludes, "I want this edition to be of no other use to you, than that you everywhere encounter the one and only benefactor."

DESIDERIUS ERASMUS

Laurentius Valla's
Annotations to the New Testament

To the most splendid and illustrious Christopher Fisher, Papal Protonotary and Doctor of Canon Law:[1]

During the past summer as I was hunting through a certain very old library[2] (in no forest is there more pleasant hunting), there fell into my nets by chance a booty by no means ordinary—the annotations of Laurentius to the New Testament. Immediately I wished to recommend this strongly to all who are devoted to learning, for I would be reckoned selfish indeed to devour alone and in silence that which I had stumbled upon in the hunt. But I was somewhat frightened away both by the long-standing unpopularity of the name of Laurentius and by this specific work, which is most unpopular. But as soon as you had considered the book, you not only confirmed my opinion, with your authoritative evaluation, but you also began to urge and press me that I should not, because of the criticisms of a few, defraud the author of his due glory and at the same time deprive so many thousands of students of such an advantage. You maintained, without hesitation, that this work would be useful and indeed pleasing to sound and open minds, while the others in their sickness should be completely disregarded.

Subsequently you offered yourself as Valla's patron and defender so that he might become known in public, indeed at your risk alone. I think, most illustrious Christopher, that your Valla, although he had always a bold disregard for unpopularity, would be somewhat more confidently given to battle supported both by the protection of so great and so invincible a champion as you, and fortified by my Preface as

308

by the shield of Ajax. In this Preface I shall now discuss the rationale and usefulness of this work on the basis of your opinion of it. But first we must remove from a few the general unpopularity of the name of Laurentius.

First, therefore, if we ourselves grant the fairness which we demand of others to men to whom we ought not to wish ill but to whom we should even be grateful, then indeed the name of Laurentius should be considered not hateful but pleasing and venerable among all who love the good letters. For indeed he has been one who has taken on himself the most taxing tasks involved in the restoration of the good letters. For such an acute man could not fail to see that a long-standing illness could not be remedied except by painful medicines, cauteries, and surgeries, and with great pain to many.

Moreover, he knew that not only those whom he had touched at some sore spot would cry out, but also those who pretend to fear contamination; and he knew that mortal ears are so spoiled that even among good men it is scarcely possible to find one who hears the truth gladly. Yet aroused by a sort of holy passion, he refused no task nor unpopularity for himself so long as he might pass on his benefit to a limited group which could appreciate his work (although *all* should have been grateful). But indeed, because of our sinful nature, this perversion occurs, so that servility makes friends and truth produces hatred.

They claim, now, that he is a raging bull and that he harms many. However, is it to be regarded as harming when one's evil is restricted to dissent on literary issues and when, in the enthusiasm of teaching, one mostly praises and adds only a few corrective criticisms? If, according to Fabius, nothing is more efficacious in teaching than to demonstrate in works of art not only what ought to be imitated but also what ought to be avoided,[3] how much more necessary is it to unlearn certain things! Laurentius dared to attack authors about a certain word—a crime hardly worthy of the name! As if Aristotle had not attacked everybody about almost everything! As if Brutus had not despised the style of Cicero in its entirety, and Caligula that of Vergil and Livy, Fabius and Aulus Gellius that of Seneca, Jerome that of Augustine and Rufinus, and finally Philelphus that of Quintilian.

This dissent and debate in the field of scholarship ought not to be labeled a vice but should rather be strongly desired. For Hesiod wrote that these disagreements are of greatest service as long as it be added that they should not be developed into mad rages and get out of hand.[4] To my mind the friend who applauds would be no more pleasing than the enemy who rebukes, so long as the shoemaker does not sew beyond the shoe. For just as the one who praises nearly always does harm, so also the one who rebukes is always of benefit to us. Indeed if his rebukes are to the point I come away better informed, while if his rebukes are unjustified I wake up sharper and more stimulated, I will respond more attentively and cautiously, I will be more spirited in the defense of truth. To this extent the desire for glory is less of a spur than the fear of disgrace.

Now as to the charge that he condemned some in every respect, what, I ask you, was more necessary than to destroy the authority of the uneducated (to separate the lion from the ass), lest the mob of unlearned follow the worst instead of the best? For if in these matters one man seems to shine out overmuch, the fault is not his but should be assigned to these distorters. Finally, it would have been much wiser to lay the fault on another than, because of a single blot, to cut one's self off from so many advantages. For there are certain necessary evils which the wise have been accustomed to employ for their own purposes. Such depraved and contaminated writings required a Zoïlus[5] and a scourge of barbarians rather than a Vergil, that is, they needed a sharp critic and a certain sort of faultfinding—if need be, even an insolent critic who would dare to break wind against the thunder,[6] as the old comedy has it, who would apply a bad wedge to a bad knot.

Indeed the sting (as some prefer to call it) of one Laurentius has contributed considerably more to the good letters than the inept sincerity of so many persons who marvel at everything and everybody without discrimination, praising each other and mutually scratching each other on the back, as the saying goes. But if anyone were to examine how badly these Goths have disorganized all disciplines, with what great pride they teach stupidity, how with obtuse stubbornness they both defend their own ignorance and despise the erudition of others, perhaps the modest rancor and pious anger of Valla would, instead of an insolent rebuke, seem a necessity. Indeed, the favor of the learned is deserved for this reason, that, although in itself an unpleasant task, nevertheless it was undertaken by Laurentius to help us.

And see, I beseech you, how at this point we are unequal to the task, indeed how useless to ourselves. Pogius,[7] who is so raving and ignorant that even without his obscenity he would be unworthy of our attention, is, however, so foul that even had he been the most learned of men he would still have been rejected by respectable men—this man, I say, is at many places welcomed just like an upright man without any stigma of unpopularity, and his work has even been translated into other languages. Laurentius, on the other hand, who is not obscene and is a hundred times more learned, suffers from the unpopularity of his sharp tongue and is avoided like a goring bull by those who have never read his writings. There are those—and they are really absurd—who have learned nothing at all about Valla except that he is sharp-tongued, but in this particular way they imitate him; or, rather, they outdo him—they attack an unknown man. In a word, learned men prefer to remain barbarians because Laurentius is sharp-tongued. Should we not follow here the beautiful rule of Epictetus, and grasp each man with that handle by which he can be most comfortably held? This is certainly the way that Vergil handled Ennius, Cyprian handled Tertullian, and Jerome among others, Origen, and Augustine Tyconius. Why should we seize hold of Laurentius by this single handle, his sharpness, when there are so many handles by which he can be more usefully grasped? Why do we not rather weigh this slight fault against his many virtues? Indeed, why do we ungratefully debase necessary freedom by calling it slander?

But enough of this subject—we must now proceed to examine the actual content of his work. I suppose there will be some who, having scarcely read the title and knowing nothing about the work itself, will, as in the tragedy, exclaim "O heaven, O earth!" As Aristophanes so appropriately warns in his Plutus,[8] "Do not complain and shout before you are hit." I suppose the most horrible clamor will come from those who could benefit most from the work, namely the theologians. They will say that it is an intolerable insolence that the grammarian, having molested all other disciplines, does not restrain his impudent pen from Sacred Scripture. But now, if we bring to mind Nicholas of Lyra, a man surely not ignorant but well-informed, who dares to tutor Jerome and to tear apart many things hallowed by the consent of so many centuries on the basis of Jewish books (from which, I grant, our Vulgate edition stems, although I do not know if they were not intentionally corrupted); what, then, is the crime of Laurentius, if he, having collated some old and corrected Greek texts, has annotated in the New Testament those passages which doubtlessly stem from these very sources?

Furthermore, he commented upon those passages where there are variants or which are inappropriately rendered due to careless translation and are, thus, more clearly stated in the original. And finally he annotated those passages which have apparently been corrupted by us! Will they say that Valla the grammarian does not have the same right as Nicholas the theologian? In order not to answer right away by asserting that great men count Laurentius not only among the philosophers but also among the theologians, I ask: When Lyra examines a word, does he not play the role of a grammarian more than that of a theologian? Indeed the whole task of translating Scripture is the task of the grammarian. Nor is it absurd if in certain of these matters Jethro is wiser than Moses.[9]

Nor do I assume that theology, the very queen of all disciplines, will think it beneath her dignity if her handmaiden, grammar, offers her help and the required service. For even if grammar is somewhat lower in dignity than other disciplines, there is no other more necessary. She busies herself with very small questions, without which no one progresses to the large. She argues about trifles which lead to serious matters. If they answer that theology is too important to be limited by grammatical rules and that this whole affair of exegeting depends on the inspiration of the Holy Spirit, then this is indeed a new honor for the theologian that he alone is allowed to speak like a barbarian!

Let them explain Jerome's intention when he wrote to Desiderius: "It is one thing," he said,[10] "to be a prophet, but to be an exegete is something else. In the case of the prophet the Spirit predicts things that are to come; the exegete, on the other hand, employs his erudition and command of vocabulary to translate what he himself understands." Why does Jerome bother to give instruction about the way to translate Scripture if this ability is a matter of divine inspiration? Finally, why is Paul said to be more eloquent in Hebrew than in

Greek? If it could be that the interpreters of the Old Testament erred here and there, especially in regard to questions that do not touch upon the faith, why could not the same hold true for the New Testament? Jerome did not really translate the New Testament but, rather, corrected an old translation and not completely at that, because —as he himself testifies—he passed by certain words which are now the principal object of Laurentius' examination. Indeed, shall we now attribute our errors to the Holy Spirit? The scholars might have translated correctly, but what they have translated correctly can still be misinterpreted. Jerome made corrections, but what he had corrected is corrupted again. Save only that today there is perhaps less audacity on the part of the semilearned, or greater expertise on the part of linguists, yet the corruption of texts is easier, due to the art of printing that immediately reproduces one error in a thousand copies.

But they say it is not permissible to change anything in Scripture, where even the jots hold a mystery.[11] This very fact shows how much more wrong it is to corrupt Scripture and how carefully the learned should be in correcting Scripture which has been adulterated through ignorance. Such correction should be done with the caution and temperance one owes to all books, especially to those which are sacred. Indeed, they say that it was improper for Laurentius to assume for himself the same role which Jerome had by mandate of Pope Damasus.[12] But the two projects were not at all alike. Jerome substituted a new edition for the old one; Laurentius presents his annotations as his own individual commentary and does not ask you to alter anything in your own Bible, although the variant readings in our copies are sufficient evidence that these texts are not without error.

Furthermore, just as the reliability of our versions of the Old Testament should be established on the basis of the Hebrew manuscripts, so also the accuracy of the New Testament must be measured by the Greek textual witnesses, as Augustine says in canon law.[13] In regard to this issue I think that no one is so hard as not to pity or so grave as not to laugh at that most absurd comment made by some unknown dreamer who affirms that Jerome claims in his letter to Desiderius that the Latin text is better than the Greek, and the Greek better than the Hebrew. This dreamer did not understand that Jerome was establishing his own position by stating a completely untenable proposition

which he introduces with a phrase that makes all the clearer that he
held the opposite to be the fact.[14] If Jerome really thought the Latin
text was best, what sort of madness would have led him to alter the
Old Testament according to the Hebrew and to correct the New
Testament according to the Greek? If, in fact, our translations are
better, why were the Church authorities so concerned with establishing, at the Council of Vienne, for example, that teachers of three
languages should be trained?[15] On the other hand, in this last case I
am astonished that this Council should have dropped the Greek language requirement.

I believe that this is enough advice to the learned. But others claim
that the ancient exegetes, trained in the three languages, have provided
an explanation for every passage that needed it. First, I would prefer
to see the original with my own eyes rather than through someone
else's, and further, the ancient exegetes, granted that they have said
a great deal, left much for later interpreters to explain. Is it not true
that in order to understand their interpretations, at least an average
knowledge of languages is required? And finally, when you come
upon old texts in various languages that are corrupt (as indeed they
are), what will you do?

Therefore, most learned Christopher, what you so often are wont
to say is very true—they have neither sense nor ground to stand on who
venture to write about the Holy Scriptures or more generally about
original sources without an average training to read either kind. For
it happens that all their straining and struggling to present themselves
as very learned only makes them look very foolish in the eyes of those
who know their languages, and all their uproar proves to be an empty
balloon as soon as one Greek word enters into the discussion. And if
there are those who have time to learn Greek thoroughly, they will
find Valla to be of great assistance. He has examined the entire New
Testament with remarkable keenness and, incidentally, includes annotations from the Psalms—the edition which we are accustomed to
is based on the Greek, not on the Hebrew text. Indeed, scholars will
owe much to Laurentius, and Laurentius will owe much to you. For
you provided a public hearing for him; your judgment will make him
more attractive to good minds; your patronage will leave him better
equipped to face abuse. Farewell.

Paris, 1505

Notes

1. The letter is addressed to Christopher Fisher (†1511), English humanist in the service of the papal court.

2. The Premonstratensian monastery of Parc, near Louvain, Belgium, in the summer of 1504. Erasmus' edition of Valla's *Annotationes* was printed by Josse Baden, Paris, in March 1505. The footnotes to this section are largely dependent upon the work of P. S. Allen, *Opus Epistolarum Desiderii Erasmi Roterodami,* Tom. I, 1484–1514, Oxford, 1906, pp. 406–412.

3. Marcus Fabius Quintilianus, *Institutio Oratoria,* Bk. II, ch. 5, and Bk. X, ch. 2, Loeb Classical Library ed., translated by H. E. Butler, London, 1921, vol. I, p. 251, and vol. IV, pp. 75–91.

4. *Works and Days,* Hesiod, line 19, translated by Hugh G. Evelyn-White, London, 1914, p. 3.

5. Zoïlus was a bitter attacker of Isocrates, Plato, and Homer.

6. Aristophanes, *The Clouds,* line 293; Loeb Classical Library ed., translated by Benjamin B. Rogers, London, 1924, vol. I, pp. 290, 291.

7. Pogius is the popular author of *Facetiae*: Poggio Bracciolini. His "jests" are less than puritan.

8. Aristophanes, *The Plutus,* line 477; Loeb Classical Library ed.,

translated by Benjamin B. Rogers, London, 1924, vol. III, pp. 404, 405.

9. Jethro was the father-in-law of Moses. Cf. Exodus 3:1, 2:16 ff.

10. *Praefatio in Pentateuchum, PL,* vol. XXVIII, col. 182. Desiderius is Jerome's friend, to whom he dedicated his translation of the Pentateuch.

11. Cf. Matthew 5:18. For examples of rabbinical discussion of the theological meaning of the "jot" see Strack-Billerbeck, *Kommentar zum Neuen Testament,* vol. I, pp. 247–249.

12. Pope Damasus I (366–384) asked Jerome to revise the Vulgate.

13. This passage is quoted from Jerome's Epistle 71, 5. In Gratian's *Decretum,* I, dist. 9, it is erroneously attributed to Augustine.

14. See note 10.

15. The reference is to the *Constitutions* of Clement V; promulgated after the Council of Vienne, 1311–1312, Bk. 5, tit. 1, cap. 1, in which for the better conversion of the infidels it was ruled that two teachers for each of the three languages, Hebrew, Arabic, and Chaldean, should be appointed in each of the four universities, Paris, Oxford, Bologna, and Salamanca. Also in *CIC,* vol. 2, col. 1179.

Bibliography

Primary Sources

1. Collections

Acta Conciliorum et Epistolae Decretales, X, A.D. 1438–1549.
Acta Reformationis Catholicae, II, 1532–1542, ed. Georg Pfeilschifter, Regensburg, 1960.
Collectio Judiciorum de Novis Erroribus, ed. Charles du Plessis d'Argentré, I, Paris, 1724.
Enchiridion Symbolorum, 32d ed., ed. H. Denzinger—A. Schönmetzer, Freiburg i. Br., 1963.
Documents of the Christian Church, 2d ed., ed. Henry Bettenson, London, 1963.

2. General

Anselm of Canterbury, *Opera* in *PL,* vol. CLVIII, modern edition by F. S. Schmitt, O.S.B., vols. I–IV, Edinburgh, 1938–1951; vol. I, 2d ed., 1946.
Antoninus of Florence, *Prima Pars totius summe maioris,* Lyon, 1516.
Aristophanes, *The Clouds,* Loeb Classical Library, transl. Benjamin B. Rogers, London, 1924.
Aristophanes, *The Plutus,* Loeb Classical Library, transl. Benjamin B. Rogers, London, 1924.
Aristotle, *Nicomachean Ethics, Opera,* ed. Academia Regia Borusica, Berolini, 1831–1870.
Augustine, *Opera,* in *PL,* vols. XXXII–XLIII, and in *CSEL,* vols XXV, XXVII–XXVIII, XXXIII–XXXIV, XXXVI, XL–XLIV.
Bechofen, Johannes, *Quadruplex missalis expositio,* Basel, 1505.
Beda, *Expositio in Joannis Evangelium,* in *PL,* vol. XCII.
Biel, Gabriel, *Canonis Misse Expositio,* 4 vols., ed. H. A. Oberman et W. J. Courtenay, Wiesbaden, 1963– .
——— *Defensorium obedientie apostolice,* Hagenau, 1510.

319

Caesarius of Arles, *S. Caesarii Opera Omnia*, I, ed. G. Morin, Maredsous, 1937.

Calvin, John, *Institutes of the Christian Religion*, ed. John T. McNeill, transl. Ford L. Battles, Library of Christian Classics, XX, XXI, Philadelphia, 1960.

Chrysostom, *Homiliae in Joannem*, Homilia X in *PG*, vol. LIX, col. 76.

Contarini, Gasparo, *Epistola de Justificatione*, ed. F. Hünermann, *Corpus Catholicorum*, VII, Münster i. W., 1923.

Erasmus, Desiderius, *Opera Omnia*, ed. J. Clericus, Leiden, 1704–

———— *Ecclesiastes sive de ratione concionandi*, Basel, 1535.

———— *Opus Epistolarum Desiderii Erasmi Roterodami*, ed. P. S. Allen, Oxford, 1906–1958.

———— *Spongia adversus adspergines Hutteni*, ed. *cit.*, X, 1796, pp. 1631–1672.

Fisher, St. John, *Assertionis Lutheranae confutatio iuxta verum ac originalem archetypum, nunc diligentissime recognita. Aeditio ultima, varijs annotationibus in margine locupletata*, Cologniae, 1525.

Gansfort, Wessel, *Wessel Gansfort*, Jared W. Scudder and Edward W. Miller, New York, 1917.

Gerson, Jean, *Opera Omnia*, ed. L. E. Du Pin, Antwerpiae, 1706.

Gregory the Great, *Moralium Libri sive expositio in librum B. Job*, in *PL*, vol. LXXV.

Hoen, Cornelisz, *Avondmaalsbrief*, 1525 ("Epistola christiana admodum"). In facsimile uitg. en van inleiding voorzien door A. Eekhof, 's Gravenhage, 1917.

Hus, Jan, *Documenta Magistri Joannis Hus*, ed. F. Palacký, Prague, 1869.

———— "Super IV Sententiarum," *Opera Omnia*, II, ed. W. Flajšhans et M. Komínková, Prague, 1905.

Jerome, *Commentarius in Evangelium secundum Mattheam*, in *PL*, vol. XXVI.

———— *Praefatio in Pentateuchum*, in *PL*, vol. XXVIII.

Löschern, Valentin Ernst, *Vollständige Reformations—Acta und Documenta*, Leipzig, 1722.

Lombard, Peter, *Libri quattuor Sententiarum*, in *PL*, vol. CXCII.

Luther, Martin, *Luther's Works*, Vol. 31, *Career of the Reformer*, 1, ed. Harold J. Grimm, transl. L. J. Satre, Philadelphia, 1957.

———— *Luther's Works*, Vol. 48, ed. G. G. Krodel, Philadelphia, 1963.

———— *Luther: Lectures on Romans*, ed. Wilhelm Pauck, The Library of Christian Classics, XV, Philadelphia, 1961.

———— *Vorlesungen über I Mose; WA* 42–44.

Melanchthon, Philip, *Melanchthon: Selected Writings*, eds. Elmer E. Flack, L. J. Satre, Minneapolis, 1962.

Menot, Michel, *Sermons choisis de Michel Menot*, ed. Joseph Nève, Paris, 1924.

Nicholas of Lyra, *Biblia cum Glossa ordinaria Nicolai de Lyra postilla, moralitatibus eisdem Pauli Burgensis additionibus, Matthiae Thoring* (= Doering) *replicis*, 6 vols., Basel, 1498–1502.

Occam, William of, *Dialogus*, ed. M. Goldast, in *Monarchiae S. Romani Imperii sive Tractatuum de iurisdictione imperiali, regia, et pontifica seu sacerdotali,* II, Frankfurt a. M., 1668, pp. 354–957.

Origen, *Homiliae in Lucam* in *PG,* vol. XIII.

Pelagius, *Pelagius's Expositions of Thirteen Epistles of St. Paul,* ed. A. Souter, *Text and Studies,* IX, 1–3, Cambridge, England, 1922–1932.

Pseudo-Ambrose, *Commentary on I Tim.* in *PL,* vol. XVII.

Pseudo-Augustine, *Liber de Vera et Falsa Poenitentia,* in *PL,* vol. XL.

Quintilianus, Marcus Fabius, *Institutio Oratoria,* Loeb Classical Library, transl. H. E. Butler, London, 1921.

Rosenplüt, Hans, "Priameln," in *Lyrik des späten Mittelalters,* ed. Hermann Maschek, Leipzig, 1939, p. 248.

Surgant, Iohannis Ulricus, *Manuale curatorum predicandi prebens modum,* Basiliis, 1503.

Thomas Aquinas, *Opera Omnia iusso impensaque Leonis XIII. P.M. edita,* Romae, 1882–1948.

Thomas à Kempis, *De imitatione Christi, Opera Omnia,* ed. M. J. Pohl, Freiburg i. Br., 1904. English translation, *The Imitation of Christ,* transl. Leo Sherley-Price, Penguin Books, Harmondsworth, Middlesex, 1952.

Wyclif, John, *Johannis Wycliffe, De civili dominio,* I, ed. R. L. Poole, London, 1900; II, ed. J. Loserth, London, 1904.

———— *Johannis Wycliffe, De dominio divino,* ed. R. L. Poole, London, 1890.

———— *De Ecclesia,* ed. J. Loserth, London, 1886.

Zwingli, Ulrich, *Opera,* ed. M. Schulero et I. Schulthessio, VII, Turici, 1830.

———— *Opera,* in *CR,* Vols. 88–90, 1905– .

3. Sources of selections translated

John Brevicoxa
  "Tractatus de Fide et Ecclesia, Romano Pontifice et Concilio Generali," in *Johannis de Gerson, Opera Omnia,* ed. L. E. Du Pin, Antwerpiae, 1706, I, col. 805–904.

M. Wesseli Gansfortii
  Opera, Groningae, 1614, fol. 871 ff. First English translation by Jared W. Scudder and Edward W. Miller, *Wessel Gansfort,* Vol. I, New York, 1917, pp. 276 ff.

Robert Holcot ·
  Super Libros Sapientiae, Hagenau, 1494, *Lectiones* 35 B, 52 B, and 14 B.

Thomas Bradwardine
  De Causa Dei contra Pelagium, London, 1619, Bk. I, ch. 47.

Gabriel Biel
  Sermones de festivitatibus Christi, Hagenau, 1510, "De Circumcisione Domini," Sermo II, in ordine 14.

Johann von Staupitz
  Libellus de executione eterne praedestinationis, Nuremberg, 1517.
Jan Hus
  Tractatus de Ecclesia, ed. S. Harrison Thomson, Cambridge, 1956. Selections
  taken from ch. 2 through 5, and ch. 7.
Pope Pius II
  "Execrabilis," in *Bullarum Diplomatum et Privilegiorum Sanctorum Ro-
  manorum Pontificum,* Augustae Taurinorum, V, 1860, pp. 149 ff.
Thomas Cajetan (Thomas de Vio)
  Opuscula Omnia, Vol. II, Lyons, 1580 (first edition 1509), col. 110 f.
Silvester Prierias
  "Quaestiones impertinentes," casus secundus, in *Aurea Rosa,* Venetiis, 1582
  (first edition 1503), fol. 339 f.
Cornelisz Hoen
  "Epistola christiana admodum," in *CR,* Vol. 91, Leipzig, 1927, pp. 509 ff.
Jacobus Faber Stapulensis (Jacques Lefèvre d'Étaples)
  Quincuplex Psalterium, Paris, 1509, fol. 1 ff. *Sancti Pauli Epistolae XIV,*
  Paris, 1512, fol. 1 ff.
Desiderius Erasmus
  Epistola, in *Opus Epistolarum Desiderii Erasmi Roterodami,* ed. P. S. Allen,
  Oxford, 1906, Tom. I, pp. 406 ff.

Secondary Sources

1. Collections and encyclopedias

Die Religion in Geschichte und Gegenwart, 3rd ed., Tübingen, 1957–1965.
Mémoires de la Société de l'Histoire de Paris et de l'Île de France, IX.
Jewish Encyclopedia, New York, London, 1905.

2. General

Bainton, Roland H., *Bernadino Ochino,* Firenze, 1940.
Brandi, Karl, *Deutsche Reformation und Gegenreformation,* I, Leipzig, 1927.

Benz, Ernst, "Creator Spiritus, Die Geistlehre des Joachim von Fiore," *Eranos–Jahrbuch 1956*, XXV (1957), 285–355.

———— *Ecclesia Spiritualis*, Stuttgart, 1964 (first edition 1934).

Bloomfield, Morton W., "Joachim of Flora: A Critical Survey of his Canon, Teachings, Sources, Biography and Influence," *Traditio*, XIII (1957), 249–311.

———— *Piers Plowman as a Fourteenth Century Apocalypse*, New Brunswick, 1961.

Bouyer, Louis, *Autour d'Érasme*, Paris, 1955.

———— *The Spirit and Forms of Protestantism*, Westminster, Md., 1956.

Brown, R. E., *The sensus plenior of Sacred Scripture*, Baltimore, 1955.

Clark, Francis, S.J., *Eucharistic Sacrifice and the Reformation*, London, 1960.

Cohn, Norman, *The Pursuit of the Millennium*, Harper Torchbook, New York, 1961.

Collingwood, R. G., *The Idea of History*, 4th ed., New York, 1961.

Congar, Yves, "Ecclesia ab Abel," in *Abhandlungen über Theologie und Kirche, Festschrift für Karl Adam*, ed. Marcel Reding, Düsseldorf, 1952, pp. 79–108.

Connolly, James, *John Gerson: Reformer and Mystic*, Louvain, 1928.

Constable, Giles, "Seminar III. Reformatio," *Ecumenical Dialogue at Harvard*, ed. Samuel H. Miller and G. Ernest Wright, Cambridge, Mass., 1964, pp. 330–343.

Cross, Frank Moore, Jr., *The Ancient Library of Qumran and Modern Biblical Studies*, revised edition, New York, 1961.

Dankbaar, W. F., "Op de grens der Reformatie; De rechtvaardigingsleer van Jacques Lefèvre d'Étaples," *Nederlands Theologisch Tijdschrift*, 8 (1954), pp. 327–345.

Denifle, Heinrich S., O.P., *Luther und Luthertum in der ersten Entwicklung. Quellenmässig dargestellt*, I (Schluss-abteilung), 2d ed., ed. Albert M. Weiss, O.P., Mainz, 1906.

Dettloff, W., *Die Lehre von der Acceptatio Divina bei Joh. Duns Scotus*, Werl, 1954.

Dohna, Lothar Graf zu, *Reformatio Sigismundi, Beiträge zum Verständnis einer Reformschrift des fünfzehnten Jahrhunderts*, Göttingen, 1960.

Douglass, Jane Dempsey, *Preaching Justification in the Later Middle Ages*, Leiden, 1966.

Dugmore, C. W., *The Mass and the English Reformers*, London, 1958.

Ebeling, Gerhard, "Die Anfänge von Luthers Hermeneutik," *ZTK*, 48 (1951), pp. 172–230.

———— "Hermeneutik," *Religion in Geschichte und Gegenwart*, III, Tübingen, 1959, cols. 242–262.

———— *Evangelische Evangelienauslegung*, 2d ed., Darmstadt, 1962.

Ehses, St. v., "Der Reformentwurf des Kardinals Nikolaus Cusanus," ed. St. v. Ehses, *Historisches Jahrbuch*, 32 (1911), pp. 281–297.

Febvre, L. *Au coeur religieux du XVIᵉ siècle*, Paris, 1957.

Feret, Pierre, *La Faculté de théologie de Paris et ses docteurs les plus célèbres.* Moyen âge, IV, Paris, 1897.

Fraenkel, Peter, *Testimonia Patrum; the Function of the Patristic Argument in the Theology of Philip Melanchthon,* Genève, 1961.

Gelder, Enno van, *The Two Reformations,* 's Gravenhage, 1962.

Grant, Robert M., *The Letter and the Spirit,* London, 1957.

Groner, J. F., O.P., *Kardinal Cajetan. Eine Gestalt aus der Reformationszeit,* Fribourg, 1951.

Headley, John M., *Luther's View of Church History,* New Haven, 1963.

Hagen, Karl, *Deutschlands literarische und religiöse Verhältnisse im Reformationszeitalter,* I, Erlangen, 1841.

Hailperin, Herman, *Rashi and the Christian Scholars,* Pittsburgh, 1963.

Harbison, E. H., *The Christian Scholar in the Age of Reformation,* New York, 1956.

Hardenberg, Albert R., *Vita Wesselli Groningensis.* In *Opera,* fol. I–II.

Harnack, Adolf v., *Lehrbuch der Dogmengeschichte,* 5th ed., III, *Die Entwicklung des kirchlichen Dogmas,* Tübingen, 1932.

Haubst, R., "Reformentwurf Pius des Zweiten," ed. R. Haubst, *Römische Quartalschrift,* 49 (1954), pp. 188–242.

Hauffen, A., "Huss eine Gans—Luther ein Schwan," *Festschrift Joh. v. Kelle,* II, Prag, 1908, pp. 1–28.

Hauréau, M., *Histoire littéraire du Maine,* III, Paris, 1871.

Holborn, Hajo, *On the Eve of the Reformation. "Letters of Obscure Men,"* Harper Torchbook, New York, 1964.

Huck, Johannis, *Joachim von Floris und die joachitische Literatur,* Freiburg i. Br., 1938.

Huizinga, Johan, *Erasmus and the Age of Reformation,* Harper Torchbooks, New York, 1957.

Hyma, Albert, *The Christian Renaissance: A History of the Devotio Moderna,* New York, 1925.

Imbart de La Tour, Pierre, *Les Origines de la Réforme,* 2d ed., II, Melun, 1944.

Iserloh, E., *Die Eucharistie in der Darstellung des Johannes Eck: Ein Beitrag zur vortridentinischen Kontroverstheologie über das Messopfer,* Münster i. W., 1950.

———— *Der Kampf um die Messe in den ersten Jahren der Auseinandersetzung mit Luther,* Münster i. W., 1952.

Jacob, Ernest F., *Essays in the Conciliar Epoch,* Manchester, 1953.

———— *The Fifteenth Century, 1399–1485,* Oxford, 1961.

Janssen, Johannes, *Geschichte des deutschen Volkes,* I, *Die allgemeinen Zustände des deutschen Volkes beim Ausgang des Mittelalters,* Freiburg i. Br., 1878; 19th ed. revised by L. v. Pastor, Freiburg i. Br., 1892.

Jedin, Hubert, *Geschichte des Konzils von Trient,* I, 2d ed., Freiburg i. Br., 1951.

———— *A History of the Council of Trent,* transl. D. E. Graf, St. Louis, 1957– .

Kaminsky, Howard, "The Free Spirit in the Hussite Revolution," in *Millennial Dreams in Action*, ed. Sylvia L. Thrupp, Comparative Studies in Society and History, Supplement II, The Hague, 1962, pp. 166–186.

Kantorowicz, Ernst H., *Frederick the Second, 1194–1250*, 2d ed., New York, 1957.

Kidd, B. J., *The Later Medieval Doctrine of the Eucharistic Sacrifice*, 1st ed., London, 1898; 2d ed., London, 1958.

Ladner, Gerhart B., *The Idea of Reform, Its Impact on Christian Thought and Action in the Age of the Fathers*, Cambridge, Mass., 1959.

————— " 'Reformatio,' " *Ecumenical Dialogue at Harvard*, ed. Samuel H. Miller and G. Ernest Wright, Cambridge, Mass., 1964, pp. 172–190.

Landgraff, Arthur, *Dogmengeschichte der Frühscholastik*, I, 1, *Die Gnadenlehre*, Regensburg, 1952.

Léonard, Émile G., *Histoire générale du Protestantisme*, I, *La Réformation*, Paris, 1961.

Letter, P. de, *De ratione meriti secundum sanctum Thomam*, Rome, 1939.

Loofs, Friedrich, *Leitfaden zum Studium der Dogmengeschichte*, II, 5th ed., ed. Kurt Aland, Halle-Saale, 1953.

Lortz, Joseph, *Die Reformation in Deutschland*, 2d ed., I, Freiburg i. Br., 1941.

Loserth, J., *Hus und Wyclif, Zur Genesis der Hussitischen Lehre*, Prag, 1884; English translation by M. J. Evans, London, 1884.

Lubac, Henri de, S.J., *Exegèse médiévale: Les quatre sens de l'Écriture*, I, Paris, 1959.

Massner, Joachim, *Kirchliche Überlieferung und Autorität im Flaciuskreis*, Berlin, 1964.

Mundy, John H., and Kennerly M. Woody, *The Council of Constance: The Unification of the Church*, New York, 1961.

Oberman, Heiko A., *Archbishop Thomas Bradwardine, A Fourteenth Century Augustinian; A Study of his Theology in its Historical Context*, Utrecht, 1958.

————— "*De Praedestinatione et Praescientia*: An Anonymous 14th-century Treatise on Predestination and Justification," in *Nederlandsch Archief voor Kerkgeschiedenis*, n.s. 43 (1960), pp. 195–220.

————— Daniel J. Callahan, and Daniel J. O'Hanlon, S.J., eds., *Christianity Divided: Protestant and Roman Catholic Theological Issues*, New York, 1961.

————— " 'Facientibus quod in se est Deus non denegat gratiam': Robert Holcot, O.P., and the Beginnings of Luther's Theology," *HTR*, LV (1962), 317–342.

————— *The Harvest of Medieval Theology*, Cambridge, Mass., 1963.

————— "Quo vadis? Tradition from Irenaeus to Humani Generis," *Scottish Journal of Theology*, 16 (1963), pp. 225–255.

———— "Das tridentinische Rechtfertigungsdekret im Lichte spätmittelalter-licher Theologie," in *ZTK*, 61 (1964), pp. 251–282.

Oediger, Friedrich W., *Über die Bildung der Geistlichen im späten Mittelalter*, Leiden, 1953.

Pastor, Ludwig von, *Geschichte der Päpste seit dem Ausgang des Mittelalters*, II, Freiburg i. Br., 1886.

Pelikan, Jaroslav, "Luther's Attitude Toward John Huss," *Concordia Theological Monthly*, 19 (1948), pp. 747–763.

———— *Luther the Expositor*, St. Louis, 1959.

———— *Obedient Rebels*, New York, 1964.

Pépin, Jean, "Saint Augustine et la function protrêptique de l'allégorie," *Recherches Augustiniennes*, I (1958), pp. 243–286.

Peuckert, W. E., *Die grosse Wende. Das apokalyptische Saeculum und Luther*, Hamburg, 1948.

Phillips, M., *Erasmus and the Northern Renaissance*, New York, 1949.

Picotti, G. B., "La pubblicazione e i primi effecti della Execrabilis di Pio II," *Arch. della soc. Romana di storia patria*, 37 (1914), pp. 5–56.

Plinval, G. de, *Essai sur le style et la langue de Pélage*, Fribourg en Suisse, 1947.

Pohle, I., "Eucharist," *The Catholic Encyclopedia*, New York, 1909, Vol. 5, pp. 572–590.

Polman, Pontien, *L'Élément historique dans la controverse réligieuse du XVIᵉ siècle*, Gembloux, 1932.

Preuss, Hans, *Die Vorstellungen vom Antichrist im späteren Mittelalter, bei Luther und in der konfessionellen Polemik*, Leipzig, 1906.

Renaudet, Augustin, *Préréforme et humanisme à Paris pendant les premières guerres d'Italie (1494–1517)*, 2d ed., Paris, 1953.

———— *Humanisme et Renaissance: Dante, Pétrarque, Standonck, Érasme, Lefèvre d'Étaples, Marguerite de Navarre, Rabelais, Guichardin, Giordano Bruno*. Genève, 1958.

Rhijn, Maarten van, *Wessel Gansfort*, 's Gravenhage, 1917.

———— *Studiën over Wessel Gansfort en zijn tijd*, Utrecht, 1933.

Rice, Eugene F., Jr., "The Humanist Idea of Christian Antiquity: Lefèvre d'Étaples and his Circle," *Studies in the Renaissance*, IX (1962), 126–160.

Ritschl, Albrecht, *Geschichte des Pietismus*, I, Bonn, 1880.

———— *Die Christliche Lehre von der Rechtfertigung und Versöhnung*, 4th ed., I, *Die Geschichte der Lehre*, Bonn, 1903.

Rückert, Hanns, "Das evangelische Geschichtsbewusstsein und das Mittelalter," in *Mittelalterliches Erbe—Evangelische Verantwortung*, ed. Evangelische Stift, Tübingen, 1962, pp. 13–23.

Schmidt, Martin A., "Who Reforms the Church?" *Ecumenical Dialogue at Harvard*, ed. Samuel H. Miller and G. Ernest Wright, Cambridge, Mass., 1964, pp. 191–206.

Seeberg, Reinhold, *Lehrbuch der Dogmengeschichte*, III, *Die Dogmengeschichte des Mittelalters*, 5th ed. Basel, 1935 (reprint of 4th ed., 1930).

Smalley, Beryl, *The Study of the Bible in the Middle Ages*, 2d ed., Oxford, 1952.

Spicq, P. C., O.P., *Esquisse d'une histoire de l'exégèse latine au moyen âge*, Paris, 1944.

Spinka, Matthew, *Advocates of Reform: From Wyclif to Erasmus*, The Library of Christian Classics, XIV, Philadelphia, 1953.

Spitz, Lewis W., *The Reformation, Material or Spiritual?* Boston, 1962.

———— *The Religious Renaissance of the German Humanists*, Cambridge, Mass., 1963.

Tierney, Brian, *Foundations of the Conciliar Theory: The Contribution of the Medieval Canonists from Gratian to the Great Schism*, Cambridge, 1955.

Trapp, Damasus, O.S.A., "Harvest of Medieval Theology," *Augustinianum*, V (1965), 147–151.

Trinkaus, Charles, "Humanist Treatises on the Status of the Religious: Petrarch, Salutati, Valla," *Studies in the Renaissance*, XI (1964), 8–45.

Ullman, Karl H., *Reformatoren vor der Reformation vornehmlich in Deutschland und den Niederlanden, I, Das Bedürfniss der Reformation in Beziehung auf den Gesammtgeist der Kirche und einzelne kirchliche Zustände*, Hamburg, 1841; II, *Die positiven Grundlagen der Reformation auf dem populären und wissenschaftlichen Gebiete*, Hamburg, 1842.

Ullman, Walter, *The Origins of the Great Schism*, London, 1948.

Vandenbroucke, F., "Nouveaux milieux, nouveaux problemes du XIIe au XVIe siècles," in J. Leclercq *et al.*, *La Spiritualité du moyen âge*, Paris, 1961, pp. 275–644.

Vasella, Oskar, *Reform und Reformation in der Schweiz: Zur Würdigung der Anfänge der Glaubenskrise*, Münster i. W., 1958.

Vignaux, Paul, *Justification et prédestination au XIVe siècle: Duns Scot, Pierre d'Auriole, Guillaume d'Occam, Grégoire de Rimini*, Paris, 1934.

Vooght, Paul de, *Hussiana*, Louvain, 1960.

———— *L'Hérésie de Jean Huss*, Louvain, 1960.

Werbeck, Wilfrid, *Jacobus Pérez von Valencia: Untersuchungen zu seinem Psalmenkommentar*, Tübingen, 1959.

Williams, George H., *The Radical Reformation*, Philadelphia, 1962.

Wolf, Ernst, *Staupitz und Luther: Ein Beitrag zur Theologie des Johannes von Staupitz und deren Bedeutung für Luthers theologischen Werdegang*, Leipzig, 1927.

Wolfson, Harry A., *Philo, Foundations of Religious Philosophy in Judaism, Christianity, and Islam*, 3rd ed., Cambridge, Mass., 1962.

———— *The Philosophy of the Church Fathers*, 2d ed., Cambridge, Mass., 1964.

Wunderlich, Paul, *Die Beurteilung der Vorreformation in der deutschen Geschichtsschreibung seit Ranke*, Erlangen, 1930.

Zeeden, Ernst W., *Martin Luther und die Reformation im Urteil des deutschen Luthertums*, 2 vols., Freiburg i. Br., 1950–1952.

Zöpffel, Benrath, "Pius II," *Realencyklopädie für protestantische Theologie und Kirche*, Vol. 15, col. 422–435.

INDEX OF NAMES

Numbers in italics refer to notes

329